05-1730 $24.95

356.16
Halberstadt
War stories of the Green Berets

D1055309

6TR
2007

5/09

WAR STORIES OF THE GREEN BERETS

By Hans Halberstadt

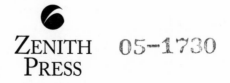

ZENITH PRESS

First published in 2004 by Zenith Press, an imprint of MBI Publishing
Company, Galtier Plaza, Suite 200, 380 Jackson Street, St. Paul, MN
55101-3885 USA

Zenith Press titles are also available at discounts in bulk quantity for
industrial or sales-promotional use. For details write to Special Sales
Manager at Motorbooks International Wholesalers & Distributors,
Galtier Plaza, Suite 200, 380 Jackson Street, St. Paul, MN 55101-3885
USA.

ISBN 0-7603-1974-X

Printed in the United States

To the memory of Staff Sergeant Paul "P. J."
Johnson, 1st Battalion, 505th Parachute Infantry
Regiment, 82nd Airborne Division; killed in action,
October 20, 2003, Fallujah, Iraq.

Contents

Foreword 6

Preface to the Second Edition 8

Acknowledgments 11

SNAKES, SNATCH, AND MAGNET ASS .13
Dennis Mack

Becoming a Green Beret 40

GREEN BERETS GONE WILD 42
Russell Mann

Special Forces Medics 62

PARTY TIME WITH MARTHA RAYE 64
John Padgett

John Wayne and Rambo 80

THE BOY CAPTAIN 81
Kenn Kubasik

Montagnards 99

SLOGGING THROUGH DONG XOAI .100
Roy Jacobson

Green Beret Weapons 112

EXTRACTING WATER BUFFALO 113
Charles Berg

Special Forces: A Short History 118

The Legend of the Green Beret 121

DUMB STUNTS 123
Gerry Schumacher

THE LATE, GREAT WALT SHUMATE 138
Doy McPhail

MONTAGNARD MUTINY 140
Vernon Gillespie

MEN, WUSSIES, AND BUMMERS 145
Otis Hedges "Bane" Ashley III

RIDING THE SHIT-CAN EXPRESS TO THE HANOI HILTON 163
Stephen Leopold

HAPPY NEW YEAR, SPECIAL FORCES STYLE 176
  Anonymous

LBJ 180
  Andy Dulina

The Special Forces A-Team 183

HOOD, RIDING, RED, LITTLE 184
  Jim Morris and Green Beret magazine

CHRISTMAS WITH THE CONG 186
  Dan Pitzer

PIGEONS AND TIGERS 188
  Clay Scott

Medals 191

STYLE POINTS 193
  Mike Witcosky

MARTHA RAYE—GREEN BERET 203
  Jack Abraham

"ALOHA," AND MORE FUN WITH MARTHA RAYE 205
  Clyde Sincere

The Agency 216

MORE WALT SHUMATE, EVEN MORE MARTHA RAYE 217
  Conrad "Ben" Baker, CISO

SHELL-SHOCK 222
  Jon Caviani

The Airborne Mystique 242

BRIMFROST 1989 243
  Gerry Schumacher

THE GREEN BERET COOKING ACADEMY 251
  J. R.

AFGHANI T AND A 258
  John Anderson

THE BATTLE OF DEBECKA PASS 277
  Frank Antenori

AFTERWORD: IRAQ AND THE HUNT FOR WMDS 301
  Gerry Schumacher

INDEX 317

FOREWORD

Aaron Bank and other great men who designed the framework for today's U.S. Army Special Forces (SF) planted a seed that has permeated the genealogy of Green Berets ever since. Occasionally old-timers are heard to lament, "The new breed is different. The training's not tough enough. They're too young. They're too old. It's too easy. They don't have the right mix." From time to time I have expressed some of those fears myself. Someone should have said to me, "Oh, ye of little faith." Getting a fresh look at SF today, I find the reality is they are as good as any who preceded them.

Today's Special Forces soldiers are everything we had hoped they would be. Sure, there are occasions when someone slips through the cracks, someone drops a ball, or some vogue training concept temporarily sends chills through us old guys. Then the genes they inherited overcome popular trends. Like a sophisticated honing system the Special Forces community always makes the adjustment, calculates the direction, and locks on to the basic operational tenants of its forefathers. It is no wonder that they are the most respected, most revered, most loved, most intelligent, and the most creative men ever to bear arms for the United States of America.

Some mockingly refer to Special Forces as *just* "teachers." And yes, we *are* teachers. Others have tried to denigrate us by laughing at our inclination for living "native," which we do. Many don't seem to understand why we place so much importance on cultures, customs, traditions, languages, religions, agriculture, politics, and economies. They have often scoffed that such training has no application in military operations. Still others have insinuated that our reserved use of force is an indicator of weakness. Nothing could be further from the truth. Woe to the foe that mistakes kindness for weakness in today's Special Forces soldier.

So misled are the poor souls who see victory only in terms of lethal capabilities. No doubt, a Special Forces A-team's application of brute force would stagger the imagination of our most competent adversary. The team members' individual strength, skills, survival instincts, and most important, ability to persevere is without equal. But it is their inherent ingenuity and passion for the human race that is their true strength.

To SF soldiers, victory is defined by a productive and free society. The route to checkmating a ruthless, tyrannical government is not in reigning destruction on the populace. Rather, it is our A-teams around the globe, leading by example, that give hope to people who had none. It is the SF soldiers who toil with indigenous peoples, eat with their families, sleep among them, care for their health, assist in the birth of their children, share in their grief, and rejoice in their successes that make for permanent change in this world.

We believe the peoples of the world are basically good. The Concept of Operation for every SF mission always considers "how might we achieve a lasting, positive result with the fewest casualties on each side. For that matter, how can we do it without firing a shot." As a practical matter, the peaceful path sometimes fails and Special Forces teams will unleash a fury known only to the occasional enemy survivor of such an encounter.

As we face more and more enemies without a name, without an identifiable country, without an organized army, enemies that hail from what we've come to call *non-nation states,* we will need Special Forces more than ever before. It is the indigenous people of any given country—because of hatred against Americans or indifference toward us—who allow the enemy to survive. Since their inception, Special Forces A-teams have been neutralizing hatred and indifference wherever they have left their imprimatur.

SF has long been adept at an art that many military forces find difficult to grasp and most shun—nation building. Our country can't afford not to have this asset in our arsenal. We must preserve it, expand it, trust in SF soldiers' judgment, and listen, *really listen,* to their assessments. For it is from their experiences that we will be able to develop meaningful strategies for world peace.

Colonel Gerald L. Schumacher (ret.)
United States Army Special Forces

PREFACE TO THE SECOND EDITION

A lot has changed in the 10 years since the first edition of this book was published. The Army's Special Forces (SF), along with special operations forces (SOF) from all the American armed forces, are now a key component of real world operations in a way that wasn't true a decade ago. During that 10 years, huge amounts of money have been invested in SpecOps, invested in more people wearing green berets, more people supporting them in the background, new communications systems, specialized aircraft and the people to fly them, exotic weapons, and even better training.

At the same time, Army Special Forces has been called to action even more than in the past. During this last decade, all the special forces—their skill sets, missions, and organizational capabilities—have been worked into battle plans in much larger roles than ever before. There was a time when conventional force commanders, traditionally hostile to unconventional warriors, tasked SOF units with tactical missions on the edges of the big picture, assigning them roles that were not really important. Now, conventional commanders ask for SF units early and often, work them into the plan, and depend on them for critical tasks. The stories that follow describe some examples of such integration.

That attitude began to shift in the 1970s, matured as a result of lessons learned on the ground in Grenada and Panama, and was refined in the first Gulf War. Today, SOF units often work side by side with conventional units, combining the virtues and values of each community in highly successful operations in Afghanistan and Iraq. This is a sort of golden age for the U.S. Army's Special Forces. History is being written and rewritten on hostile battlefields far from home, and it is an extremely positive and successful history.

But, for somebody like me who has, at this writing, been watching the Army's unconventional warriors in their green berets for more than 40 years, there are some interesting constants to the story. The missions are still largely the exact ones defined during the Kennedy administration of the early 1960s, with the sole addition of the counter-terror role. The A-team is now called an A Detachment, or, formally, Operational Detachment Alpha (ODA), but it is still a group of just 12 men, with the same roles and responsibilities as an A-team had in 1962. That team can still be split in two, as was done back then, and the two halves sent off to work miracles in two places.

In an era of smart bombs, satellite communications, and multi-million-dollar tanks that can, in darkness, hit targets miles away on the first shot, this curious little band of brothers remains essentially unchanged in its fundamentals—a few men, working together, doing big things in dangerous places. Forty years ago, I was thrilled to see SF soldiers turn primitive Montagnard tribesmen into effective combatants in the highlands of Vietnam. All these years later, today's SF soldiers have been doing almost exactly the same thing with tribesmen in Afghanistan and Iraq, the same old Unconventional Warfare mission that was so central to the foundation of SF.

Today's SF soldier resembles his warrior ancestors in some remarkable ways. It is still, as in the past, a profession dominated by people with large egos, tremendous self-confidence, and, almost always, extensive experience. As before, the line between the few commissioned officers in the community and the predominant old sergeants is much more blurred than in conventional units, and SF officers often come up through the SF enlisted ranks. As always, the essence of SF is the experience and maturity of its core group, its sergeants, and especially its team sergeants. You'll hear the voices of some of them in the stories that follow.

The SF community (generally referred to in-house as "the Community") is a bit aloof with outsiders, especially civilians. Part of that is because of tradition and the real risk of security issues, part is because of a high level of maturity that (compared, say, to Navy SEALs) discourages the "hey, look at me—I'm a living legend!" behavior, and finally, it is partly because these guys are real busy. Special operators of all kinds are spending a lot of time "down-range," quietly executing the same kinds of missions they've been doing since the beginning of Special Forces so long ago.

The stories that follow are entertaining and instructive. They are eye-witness accounts of events that are the foundations of history. Some are amusing, some aren't funny at all, but each is a little insight into the people and the missions that make this community a special place in a special time.

ACKNOWLEDGMENTS

The idea for this book was entirely the fault of several members of the late, great 3rd Battalion, 12th Special Forces Group (Airborne), who, back in the mid-1980s, tolerated having me underfoot for a year and a half. I suppose the most guilty of these is Colonel Gerry Schumacher, then commander of the battalion, who—in the grand tradition of Special Forces—met me at a saloon to negotiate the terms and conditions whereby I would be authorized to report on the antics of his unit. This may have been the bravest thing Gerry ever did, because another tradition in Special Forces is to escape and evade people in my line of work. A lot of his contemporaries— superiors and subordinates both—thought this idea was just a few french fries short of a Happy Meal. Thanks, Gerry.

Special thanks to Steve Sherman and Radix Publishing for linking me up with some of the folks here. Steve is making a terrific contribution to the maintenance of Special Forces history by developing a database of who was where, when, in Southeast Asia.

I'd also like to salute the whole rat pack at MBI Publishing Company for having the vision to authorize this book and to encourage its randy, rowdy style. This is an unusual book for all of us.

Thanks to all of the following interrogation subjects and other sources—all the guys I told, "Your secrets are safe with me!"

Colonel Jack Abraham (ret.)
John Anderson
Frank Antenori
Steven Bronson
Lieutenant Colonel Otis Hedges Ashley III (ret.)
Sergeant Major John Caviani (ret.)
Fred Fuller
Vernon Gillespie
Don Green
Harold Jacobson

Roy Jacobson
Lieutenant Colonel Kenn Kubasik (ret.)
Staff Sergeant Dennis Mack
Master Sergeant Russell Mann (ret.)
Sergeant Major Doy McPhail (ret.)
Jimmy Monaghan
Captain Jim Morris (ret.)
Cliff Newman
Captain John Padgett (ret.)
J.R.
Colonel Gerry Schumacher
Clay Scott (ret.)
Steve Sherman
Clyde Sincere
Howard Sochurek
Colonel Larry Trapp (ret.)
Mike Witcosky
Anonymous

SNAKES, SNATCH, AND MAGNET ASS
DENNIS MACK

*Dennis Mack was a sergeant in the Command and Control
(C&C) program run by the Central Intelligence Agency (CIA;
often referred to by Special Forces operators as "the Agency").
It was a sometimes odd arrangement where things didn't always
happen by the book. Dennis emerged from his adventures without
much damage, mental, or physical. He works for a utility company,
lives in the country, and still serves in the Special Forces as a
member of 3rd Battalion, 12th Special Forces Group.*

Snake Tales

When I first got to C&C, I didn't really know what to think. I'd
heard a lot of stories about guys going on missions and nobody
coming back. Well, about 40 of us rookies showed up at FOB-2 at
Kontum, and nobody knew anything about what was going on.
They sat us in a briefing room, showed us the targets, and
explained what everybody was doing: mining the Ho Chi Minh
Trail, snatching prisoners, and so forth. I started getting nervous. It
was what we had trained for, but I don't think any of us ever really
thought we would actually have to do it.

I was assigned to a guy who was supposed to train me. I can't
remember his name now, but he had a big red nose and bright red
hair, and he worked for the CIA. He started talking to me, and I had
to get up and walk around. I was sick to my stomach. I thought, I'm
not John Wayne. I started to leave, and he walked up behind me
and said, "We're going on an operation in two days."

He took me to his hooch and started showing me what to take on the operation, how to load my rucksack, how to set up my web gear. Then he got some of the Yards [an affectionate nickname for the tribal people of the highlands, shortened from the French term for these peoples, *Montagnards*, which translates as *mountaineers*] together, and we went into the bush to practice patrolling. We practiced hand and arm signals and immediate action drills. It all went so fast that I really couldn't keep up. Before I knew it, I was on the helicopter; it landed, and we were out in the jungle on the operation.

Nobody said a word. Communication was with hand and arm signals. It went like that for three or four days, nobody saying anything. Then, while we were patrolling along, he suddenly stopped. He said to me, "I smell a snake!"

With that nose of his, I figured he could probably smell anything but that this was all bullshit. So I sat down and took a break in place. All the Yards were looking around, and then he pointed at a log and said, "There it is!"

I looked, and sure enough, there was a huge snake's head poking out from under the log. I thought, Now, that is a snake! It was the biggest snake I had ever seen.

Well, he dumped everything out of his rucksack, and the Yards took it all and spread it out among their own. He ran over to the snake and started pulling it out from under the log, by the head! All the Yards jumped on it, and they managed to get it out. The jaws seemed to dislocate and opened incredibly wide; it was hissing loudly. I wanted nothing to do with this! The team leader put a stick in the snake's mouth and tied it shut with his cravat [a neck scarf worn to absorb perspiration]. Then he stuffed this big snake into his little canvas rucksack and tied it shut. I asked him, "What are you going to do with that thing?"

"Take it back to the FOB," he said. "It is worth big money."

I'll bet this thing weighed 30 or 40 pounds, and he carried that snake for another two or three days. Well, it was a recon mission, and we never saw anybody or anything associated with the enemy at all. Finally, we got to the pickup area, and he said, "Tomorrow they'll come and get us."

We set up security, and it started to get dark. He took off his rucksack and put it beside a tree and lay down beside it. I was 5 or 6 feet away. I woke up in the middle of the night and was thinking, I can't wait to get out of here. I couldn't sleep, waiting for that helicopter to show up. Then I heard that hissssss again, and thought, Oh, no! I could hear the snake moving through the bamboo, but I couldn't see a thing. It was black out! I got out my K-bar knife and was waiting for that damn snake to attack me. I sat there for the rest of the night, that knife in my hand, waiting for that snake to get me. But I was ready for it. If it did grab me, we were going to have it out, right now.

The next morning, when the team leader woke up, I poked him and whispered, "Your snake's loose. I heard him moving around last night."

He didn't believe me at first; but he checked, and I was right. Then he whispered, "That's okay—they don't go far. We'll find him."

So he and the Yards took off, with me minding the radio. Sure enough, they were back in about an hour, and they had that damn snake. Well, the helicopters came and got us, and pretty soon we were back at Kontum. The team leader got about 50 bucks for the snake—a lot of money back then. They kept it in a cage at the club for a long time. It was a big snake!

Laying on a Recon Mission

The team sergeant was God. If a captain or lieutenant went along, he was just along for the ride. The Yards were serious about it, and if someone tried to give me any crap, they'd have to deal with the team. They knew that one guy could talk on the radio; one guy could get them out. I carried the code book and the radio—nobody else.

I trained the team. It was essential to have a well-trained team. The sad part was that I was always getting a different American to accompany the team on each mission. They were always quitting, or if they were good, they would get a team of their own.

When it was time for a mission, I got called into the S-2 shop, and they'd show me on a map exactly what they were going to have me do. After the briefing, I went into the files and pulled all the information on the area and studied it. I got out my map and marked all the areas where there had been mines planted, read about any contact with the enemy that had been reported in the area, and essentially memorized the whole operation and every detail within those five grid squares. Then the team and I would practice whatever we were supposed to do on the mission—a prisoner snatch, for example—for a day or two.

On the day of the insertion we assembled early in the morning at the air head. I inspected everybody to make sure they all had everything they were supposed to have. Then I had them walk around the pad while I watched them. Sure enough, once in a while I'd find somebody limping. One time I found that my tail gunner had shot himself in the leg with his .45 pistol and was afraid to say anything about it. When we took a look at his leg, I found that the bullet had gone into his thigh and had come out by the knee—and he was going to go on the operation. He was upset when I didn't let him go! The Yards were tough like that.

Everybody test-fired their weapons, and then we climbed on the helicopters. The ride to the insertion point often took all day, from early in the morning until just about dark. We'd refuel a couple of times before crossing over into Cambodia and then into where we were supposed to go.

Insertion was a critical time. The helicopters only had enough fuel for a few minutes on station. If we started taking fire in the LZ [landing zone], they would usually come back and get us out of there.

As soon as we hit the LZ, the team set up security—a perimeter defense—and we were all perfectly silent. We waited and listened. If there were any NVA in the area moving toward us, we would be able to hear them crashing through the brush.

While we were listening, I had to check the map to make sure that we'd been inserted in the right place (once we got dropped off miles from where we were supposed to be, and the helicopters were already on their way home). It was very hard to verify the location from the air; it really had to be done on the ground. When I realized what had happened, I called them on the radio and said, "You get back in here now!" When the time came for us to get extracted, the slicks would have gone to the intended landing zone—and we wouldn't be there. They'd figure we got wiped out. I think that's what happened to some of the teams that disappeared during the war. They weren't wiped out, they just were put in the wrong place and nobody ever heard from them again. So I made sure that the recon plane didn't get out of radio range until I was absolutely sure we were in the right place.

Once I was sure we were in the right place and hadn't been noticed, I gave the hand and arm signal for the route I wanted us to travel. It would always be the worst, most unlikely way—up a steep hill, through heavy brush, anything to make it difficult to be followed—and we'd take off. We moved until we reached a RON [remain overnight position] site and set up for the night, just as it got to the point where you could barely see.

My technique for occupying the RON was to find the site, indicate it to the team, and then move past it for a ways. We stopped again, pretended to occupy this site, then went back to the original site by a different route. Other than the one time I got lazy, this worked perfectly.

That time, which I thought was my last time in the field, I did two things I never did before: occupied the RON too early and didn't RON on the side of a hill. We got hit really bad. It was embarrassing.

Live and Let Live

I went on eight or ten operations into Cambodia to mine the Ho Chi Minh Trail. The way we did these missions was that the intel shop would tell us where they wanted the thing placed, then they'd fly us in on the helicopters, drop us off a few klicks [kilometers] from the trail, and we would move up to the location.

Once we got close, the team spread out, on line, and then moved up to the trail itself. We set up on the trail like an ambush—point man on one end, tail gunner on the other. My job, as the team sergeant and engineer, was to set up the mine.

On one of these missions, we set up in the usual way, and I started digging with my K-bar knife. The dirt on the trail was extremely hard packed from the passage of all the trucks, and digging was quite difficult and slow. I had just gotten a pretty good-sized hole dug and was just about to put in the mine when one of the guys on the team signaled that someone was coming. I moved back into the brush, out of sight, with my CAR-15 at the ready.

The sentry ambled up the trail, with his AK-47 slung over his shoulder, behind his back. He got to the hole, looked down at the dirt, and kept looking at the hole and the fresh dirt. Then he started exploring and walked off the trail, into the brush—right toward me. I was 15 or 20 feet off the trail, and he just walked right up to me! He never unslung his rifle, which was still behind his back, but I had my CAR-15 pointed right at him, right at his face. He looked at the rifle—and he looked at me—and he didn't know what to do!

Well, I smiled at him, thinking, You are in big trouble now, buddy. He smiled back. Then he backed up, got back on the road, and kept on walking! I let him go. I really didn't want to shoot him; I really couldn't shoot him! If I had shot him, his buddies would have known where we were, so I thought, The heck with it. He never went for his weapon. I watched him back up to the road, and I figured that he would try for his weapon when he got to the road—but he didn't! He started walking, and I just let him go.

I went back out, finished putting the mine in, put the dirt back over it, wet it down with water from my canteen, and we pulled back to a RON site not too far away.

That night, about dusk, we heard the trucks fire up, and a little while later you could hear them pull out. I thought, I don't believe it! Then, a little while later we heard the mine go off! He didn't tell anybody; live and let live!

Russians

There was a black guy who was cooperating with the NVA from somewhere in Cambodia. He was calling in American artillery on American ground units. He sounded like he knew what he was talking about, scared and excited on the radio. Although he didn't have the right code words for authentication, a lot of batteries would execute the fire mission anyway.

We were sent in to get this guy. They figured out his location with radio direction finders and thought they knew where he was. It was a really stupid mission. The chance of actually seeing this guy was maybe one in a million. And the only way to actually take him out, if we did find him, was with a sniper. So I got elected to be the sniper, and the only sniper rifle we had was an M1 with a sniper scope. I spent a whole day trying to zero that weapon, and then that's what I carried on the operation.

We got on the ground and moved for two or three days without seeing the enemy at all. Then, on the third or fourth day, I saw tracks. They were fairly old, but I figured there was somebody in here. We were within 500 meters of the coordinates where the guy was transmitting from, according to the briefing.

It was getting dark and time to pick a RON position. Ordinarily I always picked a site on the slope of a hill because the enemy is just like anybody else—lazy. He'll go up the hill, down the hill, or around the hill, but he won't go crashing along a slope when there's an easier way to travel.

The op had been going perfectly, but I screwed up and decided that we'd sleep on level ground. I picked a site on a little finger of land above a river. The slope was far too steep for anyone to come up, so the only way we'd bump into NVA would be if they came up this narrow finger of the hill. We put the Claymores [command-detonated devices that spray steel balls across a wide sector, a bit

19

like firing twenty 12-gauge shotguns all at once] out, and I started writing my message for the recon plane.

While I was preparing the message, I got the feeling that something was wrong. The team was kind of scurrying around, uneasy about something, not talking. I looked up, and there were two Europeans in green uniforms, with caps and AK-47s, just standing there, maybe 50 meters away—really close! I thought, what the hell is this? I could see the point man wanted to kill them, right now, but the interpreter was holding him back. I found out later the interpreter thought we were supposed to meet these guys here. The interpreter had to make a decision, and fast, so he said, in English, "Halt! Who are you?"

One of the two guys held his AK over his head and said, in Vietnamese, "Company, ASSAULT!" When he said that, I set off the Claymores! The Claymores just shredded these guys—boots and everything flying through the air. The jungle just erupted.

Their first assault went right through us. They outnumbered us maybe 20 to 1, but they got to the edge of the slope and they hesitated. That's when we got a lot of them. I shot two or three in the back, right there. They assaulted through us again, then pulled back. I thought, Oh, no—what are we gonna do now? I was scared!

I told the interpreter to get the team out of the position and down the hill; they jumped up and ran. I watched them go over the crest of the hill, then stood up to follow. But the NVA had moved up some sort of automatic weapon, and when I got up it opened up on me. One bullet went through my pant leg; then it went through my rifle magazine, hit the bolt, and froze the weapon. Another went into the radio. I got off one round and the rifle jammed. I threw it down and got out a grenade.

The only thing that saved me was that when they jumped up, their officer said, in Vietnamese, "Whoever kills that American, I will kill! I want him!" When he said that, I threw the grenade and went over the hill, with two of them right on my ass. We were all rolling down the hill, and when we got to the bottom, the interpreter and point man were there. They shot both of the NVA. I grabbed the AK and spare magazine from one of them, and we took off down the trail.

They had a lot of captured American M79 grenade launchers, and once we got to the river those rounds were just raining on us. We were running as fast as we could, and the grenades were keeping up with us. They were firing at us from above and could see us pretty clearly, but we got away and kept going all night.

I gathered the team together and told each of them, one at a time, "You will not fire your weapon! If you fire at them and they see us, they will surround us immediately. If they fire at us, do not fire back." They came within 10 or 15 meters of us that night. They were searching everywhere, with flashlights, and they were serious!

The recon plane came by, but the radio was out and I couldn't contact him. I thought, boy, we are in big trouble now! So we were headed toward Thailand, away from Vietnam, because there were so many NVA along the border that there was no way we were going to walk back through them all. I had five Yards and one other American. He was wounded pretty bad, shot in both hands. He was in pain all the time and wanted me to give him morphine, but I wouldn't do it. We couldn't carry him, and we weren't going to leave him, so he had to keep going. Everybody was wounded at least once, but there were so many grenades going off and M79 rounds exploding, it was hard to notice when you got hit unless it was pretty bad.

On the second day the interpreter came to me, and he had tears in his eyes. He said, "Are you going to make it?" So I got out my signaling mirror and took a look at myself. There was blood all over my face, little pieces of metal in one eye, and a little piece of metal sticking out of my neck. I thought, I don't look too good!

Our assigned AO [area of operations] was a five grid-square [5 kilometers by 5 kilometers] area on the map. Within a day or so we were well out of it. We could hear the recon plane come over, but without the radio there was no way to talk to him. I still had a small PRC-38 [the small radio pilots carried as part of their survival equipment]. But it only had a range of about 2 miles, and that meant the plane just about had to be overhead.

We came to a clearing, and I decided to stay put there for a few days in the hopes that we'd get lucky and somebody might come by and we could try signaling to them. We were there for two days when I heard a couple of A1-Es [Douglas Skyraider attack planes] somewhere nearby doing a bomb run. I waited, hoping they would come our way. Sure enough, they did. I pulled out that antenna and started transmitting. They were overhead right away, and I just stood there waving. I figured they'd strafe me, but they came by and buzzed us, over and over, then went high and orbited.

They stayed overhead for two or three hours, and then we could hear those old blades coming. The gunships came in first and orbited the clearing a couple of times, looking us over carefully. All I could do was to wave to them, but finally the slicks [troop-carrier helicopters] came in, and we piled on.

It was a bad operation. We must have been really close to the base camp when we were discovered. I still think about it, about all the things I could have done. There was nothing gallant about the whole thing; it was just run and hide!

"You Get to Blow a Bridge!"

I came off a mission and was just getting off the helicopter when Captain Gail and Colonel Smith (I think it was) grabbed me. They said, "Dennis, have we got something for you! You will love this mission, but you will have to go right away!" They knew I was an engineer, and they said, "You get to blow a bridge!"

I said, "Wow, really?" That's something you train for as an engineer, but hardly anybody ever gets to do it.

They took us to the briefing room, and it turned out that they not only didn't know what the bridge looked like, they don't even know where it was. "We ain't never seen it, but we know it is there!"

"How are we supposed to find it if you don't even know where it is?" I asked them.

Well, they could tell from aerial photographs that one branch of the trail crossed this river somewhere under the jungle canopy. They couldn't actually see where, but they knew that the trucks had to get across this river, and it was too deep to ford. So there had to be a bridge there somewhere. They thought it might be a pontoon bridge that they floated out there at night.

We only had two hours to plan the mission; then it was time to go. We collected all the C4 explosive we could carry, put it in the rucksacks, and off we went. The helicopters arrived, and we all piled aboard and headed for the insertion point. Since we didn't know exactly where the bridge was, we had the helos put us into the general area, and we started looking for the thing.

We spent five or six days searching for that damn bridge. We walked along the river, then moved away from it, over and over. We moved up to the water, looked upstream and down—no bridge! We could hear the trucks moving at night, but we just couldn't figure out where they were crossing.

After about six days of this, I told Specialist 5 John Kendenberg, "Enough is enough. We are going to get out on the Ho Chi Minh Trail, and we are going to walk down it until it crosses the river. That's where the bridge has to be."

John said, "Do you really think we ought to do that?"

Well, I was tired, and dirty, and annoyed. "That's what we are gonna do!"

"Well, okay," he said. So we put the point man out front, we got on the trail, and off we went. The recon plane came over, right on schedule, and we got off the road to make contact with him.

"Hey, be careful!" the recon pilot said on the radio. "I just saw a patrol walking down the trail!"

I called him back and said, "That's us." He didn't believe me that we were just walking down the Ho Chi Minh Trail, so I said, "Okay, take a look again," and we all went out in the middle of the road where he could see us.

"Holy crap!" he said. "Are you guys crazy?"

"No," I said, "but we are going to find that bridge! Come back in a couple of hours. I have a feeling that it is going to be something that we are not going to be able to blow up with what we have with us." So he left.

We kept walking, and sure enough, we finally came to the water. The point man signaled that he saw someone moving on our side of the water. Apparently the NVA bridge guards ran across the river from the side we were on. We carefully moved up to the water, on line. On the far side of the river was a bunker and inside were four guys. They watched us and we watched them, nobody shooting.

But there was no bridge! The bunkers on our side of the river were empty, and we figured that the guards weren't sure who we were and moved across until they could figure us out. I brought the team up on line, everybody's weapons aimed at the guys in the bunker. I gave LAWs [light antitank weapons, small rocket launchers designed for bunker-busting and light armor targets; notoriously unreliable weapons] to two of the Yards and told them that if the guys in the bunker fired, to hit them with the LAWs.

John and I walked out into the water. There was a bridge, all right, but it was completely submerged. The NVA had placed four culverts in the water, then piled rocks on top of them to form a roadway. The water covered the road for a foot or so and flowed through the culverts. No wonder the planes couldn't see anything.

Well, John and I couldn't figure out how we were going to blow this thing up. We stood there, talking, with the NVA guards watching us, and the Yards watching them. So we went back to the shore, got the rucksacks together, and put all the C4 in three of them. We decided that we could use another ruck filled with rocks as an anchor, light the fuses, and drop the charges into one of the culverts. So we set the fuses for about a two-minute delay, called the recon plane to watch for the explosion so somebody would at least know where the bridge was, and got ready to light the fuses. It was really stupid, in a way. We would hardly be able to put a dent in this thing with our charges, but we figured we had to do something as long as we had come this far. So we placed the charges, lit the fuses, collected the Yards, and started jogging back up the Ho Chi Minh Trail.

The recon plane called, "I see you," as we were running along the trail. We didn't get very far before the charges went off. It was raining rocks and mud and water. No sooner did the junk stop falling from the sky than we had the fast-movers overhead. They saw the explosion, and now they knew where the bridge was. They started bombing. I thought they were going to kill us all! "Stop! Stop! We gotta get out of here!" I was yelling on the radio. They really pasted this thing.

I always wondered what those guys in the bunker must have been thinking. They just looked out at us, like, What the hell is this all about? I think they must have thought we were North Vietnamese. We certainly weren't wearing American uniforms.

After we got away, I was curious about those LAWs and decided to fire them, to see how they worked. Neither one fired. I thought, of all the missions I have carried these things, if I knew they didn't work I wouldn't have bothered with them! I was pissed. So that was my bridge assignment with John Kendenberg.

Eavesdropping on the Enemy

One mission they gave my team involved attaching a tape recorder to the NVA commo wire along the Ho Chi Minh Trail. They gave us a big, heavy box (it must have weighed at least 70 pounds) and explained that it would record anything the NVA were talking about. There were two wires with clips attached that I was supposed to clamp to their wire. There was about 30 pounds of explosive in the machine too; it was designed to explode if anybody tampered with it.

I was given a short class on the machine. It was supposed to be buried near the wire, armed with a key. There was a little meter on it that showed if it was recording properly. When somebody was talking on the wire and the machine was hooked up correctly, the

25

needle moved. "Don't leave until you see the needle move!" the guy told me. The machine came with its own rucksack, and it was so heavy that I had to have other members of the team carry my gear.

Well, they gave me the coordinates where they said there were 30 or 40 pairs of commo wire running along the trail; they wanted me to go tap into one. I thought, This is ridiculous. But I decided to give it a try.

The other American they assigned to go on the mission was a reservist. The guy had six kids at home, but he had volunteered to go to Vietnam, and they sent him to me. I thought, This guy does not belong here, but I spent about a week working on the team signals and SOPs [standard operating procedures] with him, checking him out. I thought I had him down pat—had him throw a few grenades in the grenade pit and test fire his rifle. He was good to go.

We were inserted and moved up to the trail. You could see the commo wires running along it, but the North Vietnamese were walking up and down the trail, constantly. So we moved up, on line, where we could observe the trail and still be at a safe distance from it, hidden in the jungle. Finally, when there didn't seem to be anybody nearby, I moved up to the trail to attach the box.

There were wires from ground level to about 10 feet up, running through the trees. I started digging a hole for the box, buried it part way, then clipped the leads to one of the pairs of commo wires. I attached the leads to the box, and right away the needle started moving! I thought "All right!", put some leaves over it, and left.

We waited in the brush for 24 hours, then moved back up to retrieve the recorder. The needle was still moving! There were so many NVA walking up and down the trail that I decided not to undo the clips but to just disconnect the box and take it with me. I disarmed it, took it out of the hole, and moved back to the team. After I got the recorder back in its rucksack we started to move away from the trail—the point man first, then the interpreter, then me. The other American was toward the end. We started moving down a steep hill, and about the time I got to the bottom, I heard firing up at the top. There was a firefight going on! The rest of the team came running down the hill, and the reservist ran up to me and said, "Holy shit, they saw the wires! As soon as you left, a guy came up and tugged on the wires—so we shot him! And they started shooting back!" And then he said, "Oh, no! Did you hear a grenade go off? I think I forgot to pull the pin! I hope they don't throw it back!"

Well, we ran off and got away. When we got back I explained exactly what had happened. I waited for a couple of days, then went to the S-2 [intelligence] shop and asked them what was on the tape.

The S-2 said, "You ain't gonna believe this, but there wasn't anything on the tape—you hooked onto an electric wire! They were using that wire to run a light bulb or something; all we got was a hum."

Ghost Helicopter in the Jungle

We were on a mission to mine one of the branches of the Ho Chi Minh Trail in Laos. There was only one place in the area where we could get off the helicopter without rappelling, and that was in the middle of a stream. This was my primary insertion point. We had to jump out into the water because there was no other place to go. We got off the helicopters without any problems and were good to go. Once we got off the helicopters we waited and listened to hear if anybody was moving toward us. There was no sound, so we moved off, up to the top of a little hill nearby.

The insertion was late, and it was getting dark, so—even though we were pretty close to the landing zone—we started looking for a RON position. I chose a spot and sent the team out to place the Claymores. The team took the mines out 50 meters and set them up. Then the interpreter came back, and he had a number written on his hand. He showed me the number and indicated that it came from a helicopter. My first thought was that we had blundered onto an NVA helicopter landing pad, and I thought, boy, did we goof this up!

27

So the interpreter and I went back out, and sure enough, there was a helicopter in the jungle. The guns were still mounted on it, and the inside was clean as a whistle! The rotor was intact, and nothing seemed to be damaged. Just inside the door was a leather medical kit bag like a doctor would carry, but it was all decayed. Inside were medical instruments. Hanging from the machine gun was an albumen can. The rubber tube was gone, but there was a skeleton on the ground underneath, with the remains of the needle. Some of the clothing was still there, along with a wallet.

On the other side, in a little ditch, were several other skeletons, all lined up with carbines pointed down toward the river we had come from. I couldn't figure it out. There were no bullet holes in the helicopter, no signs of any kind of fighting that I could find. It was really weird!

Well, the recon plane came by not long after that. I wanted to have him relay a message about the helicopter, but I didn't want to send it in the "clear" [in uncoded, plain language]. Well, I kind of screwed up and didn't encode the whole message, but got the message off to the plane. He retransmitted it to a relay station somewhere, and I could hear the pilot telling the relay station operator the helicopter identification numbers. Then I heard the retrans operator ask the pilot, "What did they do, find a helicopter?"

Well, when I heard that I thought we were in real danger; the NVA were probably listening, and now this guy has just given away the game. I told the team, "That's it. Pick up the Claymores; we're getting out of here!"

We got down to the stream and started moving, and we kept moving downstream until midnight or one in the morning. The streams were the fastest way to move. The jungle was too thick; you made too much noise. But if you got in a stream you could move pretty quickly, without making any noise. The only problem was that the enemy was there, too, to get water. So you had to be careful. Even so it was faster than walking through the jungle. If I had to get someplace in a hurry, I used the streams, just like a highway.

We slept until daylight, then got back in the stream and took off in the direction of the Ho Chi Minh Trail to complete the mining operation. While we were en route, the recon plane came back over, and the pilot radioed, "Go back to the helicopter. The intel guys want to know more about it."

I told him, "I am not going back!"

I tried to ignore the order, and we kept moving toward the place where we were supposed to put out the mines. About three days after we left the helicopter, the recon plane came over with the word that if we didn't go back to the helicopter, they were not going to pick us up. We were about 500 meters from the trail at that point, and about to set the mines, but I was mad. So I got the interpreter, and I told him that we were going to follow the stream back—and we were going to get back there in one day. So we hustled and got back there that night.

When the recon plane came by, I told him to make sure the helicopters were on the ground at the site the next morning, and we'd have the bodies for them. So we took our ponchos and collected all the bones in the ponchos. When the med-evac chopper arrived the next morning, they kicked some body bags off, and I threw them back on, along with our big bag of bones. They were furious; they wanted them all kept separate. But I did sort out the wallets, and we climbed on the helicopter and handed the wallets to the medic. He just sat there, dumbfounded, looking at that big bag of bones.

Later the S-2 told me that there had been a doctor on the helicopter and four Vietnamese, along with the crew. They had been en route to a village in Laos to help with an epidemic, and apparently the helicopter had pooped out on them. After they sorted out the bones, they found that the doctor and the pilot were missing, and they figured that they tried to walk out.

Standing Guard for the NVA

People who didn't adapt didn't survive. You couldn't just do things the way they taught at Bragg or you would die. There were a million things you had to adapt to. For instance, when we set up a

29

RON position, we put everybody within touching distance and not one person stayed awake. I made sure everybody was asleep. Then, if something was wrong, you'd sense it and wake up, and you could warn the people near you by touch. When that happened you could feel a kind of electric tension! When the danger passed you could just doze off again.

Our procedure for selecting and setting up at a RON site was to find a place on a slope, preferably in the brush, where nobody would naturally go. We put out Claymore mines. The guys went out about 50 meters past the end of the Claymore wires, just so they knew the terrain, then came back in.

One night (now, this was crazy) we set up late, well after dark, and the guys didn't go out as far as they should have. Sometime in the middle of the night, much later, I woke up. It sounded like a herd of buffalo was moving through our RON site! You could hear them coming, crashing through the brush!

You could hear the NVA move right into our position, and then you could tell that they were sitting down! I was cussing to myself, thinking, I know there's a trail within 50 meters, and these idiots of mine didn't see it! We were all basically just holding our breath.

Then the brush moved a little, and the interpreter came up to me and whispered in my ear, "*Chung-si* [Vietnamese for *sergeant*], one of the North Vietnamese told me that I have guard duty next!"

I still hadn't actually seen any of them, but I thought, Boy, this is bad! I figured we had to do something, but I didn't know what. We couldn't set off the Claymores. I thought maybe we would just abandon the Claymores, and if they were still there when it started to get light, we would just try to move away from them. Then, just before dawn, the brush started moving again. They got up and moved out. That was close!

Boy Robin

Sergeant Mike Tremell was on ST [Spike Team, a heavy team of two or three Americans and eight or more Yards, sent out with the expectation of contact with the enemy] Colorado, and I had ST New York. Tremell was teamed with Sergeant Sherman Batman (his real last name), the highest ranking team leader we had. Naturally, since Tremell had red hair, we all called him "Boy Robin." When Batman left the team, Tremell was put in charge of the team.

Mike Tremell was also known as Magnet Ass. He never went on an operation where somebody didn't get shot—killed or wounded—so the guys didn't want to go out with him anymore. So he got put in the recon planes and would talk to the teams when the plane flew over. His first day out, the recon plane got shot down. Tremell got the pilot out, and they had to walk for a couple of days in the jungle to get out. So then the recon pilots said, "We don't want him to fly with us anymore."

After that they had him run the club. But one day while he and another guy were doing PT [physical training], they took sniper fire! Now, FOB-2 [a forward operating base set up to support the units in the field] had never taken a round of fire, ever! After that everybody said, "Keep this guy in the compound! He is bad luck!"

Well, on Tremell's first operation with the team, he got them in big trouble. Most of the team got killed off, and he had one guy with him who had never been in combat before.

My team was on ready reserve at the time, so when the call came from Tremell, they tossed us on the helicopters and shot us out there. It was getting dark, and we had to rappel in on top of his team to reinforce and maybe save them. Well, while we were riding in, I was listening on the radio, and I could hear Tremell. He said, "It's getting dark here, and it looks like we aren't going to make it. But we will fight to the last man! They will not take us alive!"

He kept this up for maybe half an hour. It was really dramatic. Then the helicopter gunships got out there and worked over the area outside the perimeter. The slicks came in and picked up what was left of the team on McGuire rigs [harnesses that allowed the team to be quickly extracted by attaching themselves to a rope hung from a helicopter] and brought them out. Finally they showed up at the FOB, and I said to him, "Tremell, what was all that crap on the radio?"

31

He said, "You know what? I always wanted to do that! Wasn't that impressive? If I hadn't made it out, wouldn't you have been impressed?"

Prisoner Snatch

I was involved in three prisoner-snatch operations. My interpreter and the Yards just couldn't understand this. They thought that you ought to kill all the NVA you could find. We once caught an NVA officer. While I was interrogating him, he spit on me. The interpreter cut his throat.

I said, "Why did you do that?"

He replied, "He spit on you—disrespect!"

I told him, "I would have gotten a free trip to Taiwan and a hundred dollars if we had brought him in. He could have spit on me all day!" But by then it was too late.

The last one I caught spilled his guts—told me everything I wanted to know. When we were done with him, I told the interpreter to unlock the handcuffs, take the blindfold off, and let him go. I thought the interpreter was going to shoot him, so I said, "I am telling you, don't shoot him—let him go!"

The prisoner got up, walked off down the trail a little ways, and looked back to see if we were going to shoot him. He waddled off a little more, looked back again, and pretty soon he was gone. The other American with me said, "He's gonna come back, and he's gonna bring his buddies!" But I knew he wouldn't. We moved out of the area anyway, but I knew he was just happy to be alive.

Miller Time with the NVA

I went on another prisoner snatch mission with a captain who later earned a Medal of Honor. We found a trail with a lot of commo wire running along it. We could hear generators at the top of the hill and the bottom of the hill, and it seemed reasonable that there was a lot going on. We decided to cut the commo wire and wait until somebody came along to find the break. We hoped it would be a commo guy, and then we'd have somebody really knowledgeable.

Although I thought it was a bad idea, the captain insisted that we cache our rucks at the rally point before we set up to snatch the prisoner. He and the other members of the team took the stuff while I stayed by the trail. Being lazy and hot, I laid back against a tree, and put my feet out, with the commo wire right across the top and my feet on the trail. As a matter of fact, I reached in my ruck and took out a beer. I always had some beer with me, at least a six-pack.

So I'm sitting there, enjoying my beer, and what do I see coming up the trail but two guys. I thought, Dennis, you goofed up! They wandered up the trail, one with a big sack, both with their weapons slung backwards where they couldn't get to them. They got to me, looked at my feet, and stopped. They looked at me, and I had my weapon pointed at them. First, they smiled. Then you could see it go across their faces: This is an American! I'm sure it never dawned on them that they'd ever see one. I looked down the trail, and there were more of them, and they were moving up toward me. But the rest of the team had moved up into position by now, and I felt a little better.

Another NVA came along, stopped, and saw me. He was a little braver than the others, and I thought, Oh oh, I'm in trouble with this guy! The rest of them were bumping into each other, and this guy started to go for his weapon. I was up on one knee, ready to go. When that third guy went for his AK, the whole team opened up on them. I used my weapon to club the first two, and they went down. I took the weapons away from them and had the cuffs on the first one. There was firing everywhere. I stuck my hand in that big sack—it was *nuc mam* [fermented fish sauce]! I was mad! I figured it was full of money; I thought I was a millionaire! So I punched these two guys, cut them loose, and told them to get going.

We took off down the hill, and then we called in an air strike on the positions and called for extraction. The AD-6s [another version of the Skyraider attack plane] started bombing the top of the hill and began taking lots of ground fire. One of the planes was hit several times.

The helicopters came and got us out with McGuire rigs. It was a horrible ride! Every time I did it, I said, I will never, ever do that again. But then, the next time, I put it on again. You had to have a good pilot. When he plucked you out of that jungle, if he started taking hits and took off, or did anything except go straight up, you were dead.

After I got to FOB-2, I ran six or seven operations and didn't fire a shot. I saw incredible numbers of North Vietnamese, more on one operation than most guys in the 101st would see in a whole tour. If things were going smoothly I didn't have to fire my weapon.

The Prisoner

I was assigned a prisoner snatch mission along the Ho Chi Minh Trail. When we got to the trail, there were lots of NVA, but they were walking in columns so we waited for a chance to snag an isolated straggler or somebody moving along the road alone. We put our Claymores out and just waited.

Several columns went by, and then, sure enough, along came a straggler. He had an AK, but the interpreter and I ran out in the road, grabbed the weapon out of his hands, and dragged him back into the jungle. We handcuffed him, gagged him, and picked up the Claymores. Then we all moved out.

We moved about 300 meters into the jungle and stopped to start questioning the prisoner. Well, he was crying and was really upset. It was sad, and I started to feel sorry for the poor guy. He was kind of wimpy. We pulled out his wallet. It had a couple of minor documents in it, along with a picture of his family—his wife and kids.

I asked him about his job, and he told me that during his training the NVA instructors told them that there were Americans hiding along the Ho Chi Minh Trail, just waiting to snatch stragglers, and now that is just what happened. That's why he was so scared. The South Vietnamese had no use for prisoners at all. They figured that the only good NVA was a dead NVA. I had to handcuff the guy to me to keep from having his throat cut.

Well, the guy really spilled his guts. He was a supply sergeant, and he told me where everything was. He couldn't read a map, but he could describe locations, and we figured out where all his people and vehicles were camped. I said, "Great!" We picked up our stuff and moved out again. Then I called in air strikes on these places, and a flight of A-1Es [Douglas Skyraider attack planes] showed up and clobbered these places. Then over the radio you could hear the pilots—they were ecstatic! They were getting secondary explosions from the NVA ammunition. So I knew the prisoner had told me the truth!

We stayed in the jungle for another two or three days. Then the helicopters came to take us out. The S-2 talked to the guy. He turned out to have a lot of information, and it was going to take several days to interrogate him. Well, we didn't have a proper place to keep a prisoner, so we decided to keep him for three or four days. He slept in my bunker with me, in my little hooch.

I never had a problem with him. In fact, I took him to the club, and he had a few beers. He ate at the mess hall with us. He turned out to be a really nice guy. Finally, it was time for me to go on another mission, so I took the guy to the S-2 shop and told them to take care of the prisoner. They said, "Okay," and off I went.

When I got back from the operation, I had a beer; then I went over to the S-2 shop. "Where's the prisoner?" I asked them.

"You ain't gonna like this," the S-2 said, "but the Vietnamese got him, and they took him to downtown Kontum. There was a kind of riot, and the Vietnamese grabbed him, and they buried him alive."

I said, "That is it for prisoners! No more!" I was furious. The next one I caught after that I let go.

John Kendenberg's Medal of Honor

John earned his Medal of Honor on a mission that I was supposed to go along on. If I had gone, he might still be alive today, and he might not have had to earn that medal.

I was just coming in off a mission. We were walking back in

35

from the helicopters to the compound to be debriefed. John came up to me and said, "Dennis, you've got to come with me—this is a bad one. I need to have you along."

So I said, "Okay," dumped my gear, and went to pick up some more rations.

The sergeant major and the colonel saw me and said, "Where are you going?"

"I'm going with John on this operation."

"No, you're not," one of them said. "We've got something different for you." They gave him another American, a guy on his first mission, and the helicopters picked them up and off they went.

John was killed on that mission, and I think if I had been with him he might have made it out alive. He died because of a stupid mistake.

They made contact that night, almost as soon as they got on the ground. There was a hellacious battle afterwards, and the body count was supposed to be about 2,000 NVA killed, most from air strikes. We never found out what that mission was all about. John's team made contact within 10 minutes of insertion and fought all night long. The NVA brought up two light-armored vehicles, both of which John's team knocked out. This was very unusual for the NVA, because the jets could make it so hot for them once their positions were exposed.

John was able to break contact and get his team out and to a bomb crater. He called for extraction, and when the helicopters came in to get the team, the NVA were waiting. The team climbed on to the helos, but then the North Vietnamese rushed out and grabbed the skids of the helicopter. It couldn't take off; there were so many hanging on to it.

John jumped off to fight them. The new American, who was carrying the radio, was supposed to never leave John's side, but he stayed in the helicopter. John shot the NVA off the skids, beating them off so the helicopter could get airborne. The NVA didn't get him in the crater; he killed them instead. But the helicopter took off, with the radio operator still aboard and John still on the ground. He moved out of the crater to hide, and an AH-1 Cobra gunship came in, firing rockets at the NVA. A rocket hit too close to John, and he died from internal injuries [on June 14, 1968].

The rule was, when the Zero One [the team leader] gets off the helicopter, the radio operator gets off too—no matter what. If that had happened, John would have stayed in the crater, but instead he had to hide out.

The American never came back to the compound from his first mission. They flew him off somewhere else, and we never saw him again. I never learned his name. It was a stupid mission. They should have just dropped bombs on that place.

Tools of the Trade

We made our own LBE [load-bearing equipment, also called "web gear"]. Instead of the regular magazine pouches, we used canteen covers for spare M16 magazines. We carried about 900 rounds of ammunition for our CAR-15s.

Some of the missions were so clandestine that I figured that the only way to survive was to carry an AK-47 rather than M16 or CAR-15. I even started wearing a load-bearing vest like the NVA wore, with pockets for the AK magazines in front and back. We tried to look as much like the enemy as possible, short of wearing their own uniforms.

That paid off for me once. We were on patrol in Laos when an NVA sentry stood up in front of us and said to the point man (in Vietnamese, of course), "If you guys are hungry, just go down this trail over here. The unit's eating dinner down there now."

The point man just said, "No, thanks, we don't need anything now," and we moseyed off.

I tried to explain to the Marines that you just can't use face paint and put sticks in your helmet without becoming conspicuous in a place like that. You have to look like the enemy, wear something like what they wear. We wore a light green uniform that was

37

about the same color as theirs after it had gotten dirty, and we sometimes wore their hats. I always wore jungle boots, though, never those thong sandals—but some of them wore boots too.

We tried to train some Marines to do this job once, and they started putting all that face paint on. I told them, "If you guys want to die, keep putting that stuff on. When you are moving through that jungle you have to look as much like that enemy as you can. Then, when you encounter them, they will sometimes hesitate. That's all you need!"

Half the battle was having the right gear, and the way you walked. What I taught—and still teach—is that you never, ever walk on flat ground. Never, unless you have to scurry across a valley. You always walk on ridges, and you never sleep on flat ground. The enemy is lazy. The enemy walks on flat ground. When he is looking for you, when you get in thick brush on the side of a steep hill, he will go around it. You go where he doesn't want to go. And that's how you live!

Except that there is always an exception to the rule, and one time that rule could have gotten me killed. We had mined the Ho Chi Minh Trail late one afternoon. The closest hillside was on the far side of a valley. We could have crossed it in daylight, but we would have drawn attention to ourselves in the process. I decided to stay in the valley, but instead of setting up on flat ground, I told my team, "We are going to sleep in the river."

We worked our way to the stream out in the middle of this valley and sat down in the water, using the overhang of the bank for cover and concealment. That evening the trucks started moving, and one triggered the mine. They knew what had happened, and they started looking for us. You could hear them moving around, searching for us in the night. Then their artillery started firing—at the hillside where we would have been, ordinarily.

Magnet Ass and the Radio

Mike Tremell, also known as Magnet Ass and Boy Robin, was on a patrol near the Ho Chi Minh Trail. They were taking a little break during the middle of the day. Down below, in the jungle, Tremell noticed two NVA soldiers, also taking a break. They were leaning against a large, man-portable radio—an elaborate and apparently important piece of gear. Such equipment was typically worth a large reward if it could be captured and returned intact.

"Man," Tremell said, "I wonder what I'd get for that radio?" Then, after a moment, he told the other American, "You stay here with the team. There are only two NVA; I'll be right back with that radio."

Tremell snuck down the hill, to within only 4 or 5 feet of the NVA. Only then did he notice that there were not just two NVA but about two hundred or more, all strung out along the trail. He decided to let the two NVA keep the radio. He started to sneak back up the hill as silently as possible, but one of the guards turned around and saw him. "Oh, shit," said Tremell as he opened fire. He hit both the NVA and the radio, too, and then he ran back up the hill to the rest of the team.

The entire team ran up toward the crest of the hill to escape the pursing enemy. At the top they found a large bunker complex built by the NVA, but empty. The NVA were swarming up the hill, so Tremell and the team started throwing hand grenades. Unfortunately, one of Tremell's first pitches struck a tree limb over the bunker and the grenade bounced back, right into the bunker. Despite all the NVA, both of the Americans jumped out of the bunker for a few seconds, until the grenade exploded, then rolled back in. On the way back in, Tremell's assistant, the other American, got hit in the ass.

About this time the recon plane flew over, and Tremell reported the predicament on the radio. The fast-movers were overhead shortly, bombing and strafing the NVA below. Not long after that, the helicopters arrived to extract the team with McGuire rigs.

That evening, back in the club, Tremell's radio operator and second in command was already back from the hospital, almost as good as new, but standing at the bar while giving an informal report on the operation. "I ain't going back out with that guy," he said. "First he tries to kill me with a hand grenade, then I get shot in the ass! And all from trying to steal that damn radio!"

39

BECOMING A GREEN BERET

It has always been extremely difficult to become a Green Beret, although that sometimes hasn't been obvious right away. It requires athletic ability plus intelligence; it demands individual initiative plus the ability to fit onto a team. Rather than the big, brutish Rambo-types, real Green Berets tend to be scrawny guys, built like cross-country runners rather than football linemen.

From the day in 1960 when President John F. Kennedy popularized the group, the Green Berets have had a kind of romantic aura about them that attracts many "wanna-bes." It was true during the Vietnam years, and it is still true today. As a result, the standards for admission were, and are, extremely high. It is not easy to become a Green Beret.

Most people in SF are sergeants, although there is a small, hardcore group of officers who've made it a career. For officers it has often been just another "ticket punch" that is part of the career progression toward senior rank. But for the sergeants, Special Forces is a calling and a career that may last 30 years.

The selection and training process takes about six months today, just as it did 30 years ago. Applicants must already be in the Army, must either have been to "jump" school or ready to go, and have plenty of time left on their enlistments.

There are three phases to the training program. The first is the hardest and isn't really training, but a selection process. Candidates are pushed physically and emotionally from the moment they step off the bus until they either break or survive the month-long initial phase. It used to be common for people to quit within a few minutes of arrival, the stress was so great.

The new SF candidates arrive at the flagpole at Camp MacCall, a remote and decayed facility on the outskirts of Fort Bragg, North Carolina. The men pile off the bus with their duffel bags and they are escorted to their new home—at a run, up a long hill, with a heavy duffel bag, in the oppressive heat and humidity. By the time the last straggler arrives in the camp, the group is already lighter by several men. They've been tested, and some have already failed.

The real purpose of the first month has always been to get rid of the people who aren't up to standard mentally or physically. There is a lot of running, but SF candidates don't just run, they wear rucksacks with a sandbag inside. And they don't just run a measured course, with a finish line, they run from point to point, not knowing how long it will be until they are allowed to stop. Seventeen miles is a common distance for one of these little waddles in the woods. This is a test of emotional and physical endurance, but mostly of resolve. It is brutal to watch. Stress fractures and injuries are common. It has always been common for men to keep running with blood squishing around in their boots. Anything less than a sucking chest wound is considered sissy stuff.

Camp MacCall is the decrepit remnant of a World War II facility. Until recently, trainees lived in old, decayed barracks or in tents. The headquarters building was a tarpaper shack. The latrine, for as long as anybody can remember, has been called the John Wayne Memorial Shitter. The old buildings have been recently replaced with somewhat more modern structures, and the old latrine was replaced by a modern, expensive, politically correct, solar-powered building that doesn't work right but that is still called the John Wayne Memorial Shitter.

—Hans Halberstadt

GREEN BERETS GONE WILD
Russell Mann

*Russ Mann retired from the Army as a master sergeant in 1994
after a long career in the active-duty and reserve component. He
served two "official" tours in Vietnam (which means that he also
went over on "unofficial" assignments that he isn't supposed to
talk about). He was a medic in Special Forces and now works as
an emergency room nurse, where he still gets to work on mangled
bodies and gunshot wounds. These stories are from 1968–1969
and the siege at the old French-fortified position called Khe Sanh,
just below the border with North Vietnam.*

Yards and Grenades

The scariest thing I did in the Vietnam War was to teach Montagnards to throw hand grenades. Montagnards were primitive tribal
people who lived in the central highlands of Vietnam. "Yards," as we
affectionately called them, were an ethnic minority in Vietnam.
Short of stature, stocky and square-faced, they were dismissed as
moi or savages by the Vietnamese, who, by contrast, were slender,
lighter skinned, and lived in the lowlands and cities.

The Yards were easy to recruit. They nursed a smoldering hatred
of the Vietnamese that had been nurtured by generations of prejudice, abuse, and neglect. The opportunity to kill Vietnamese appealed
to them. We tried to ensure that they only killed *North* Vietnamese!

Hand grenades were a problem, however. Montagnards culturally
do not throw. They have no games that require throwing. They
don't even throw rocks at their chickens. Hand grenades are heavy;

each weighs about 2 pounds. They aren't easy to throw, even for athletic Americans.

We had to start from scratch. We began with small stones thrown at close targets and gradually increased the weight and distance. This was all taken in good spirits by the Yards, who were more than willing to humor the crazy Americans as long as they got to kill some Vietnamese.

The final exam in hand grenade training was to throw a live grenade over a 4-foot earthen berm. The student would crouch behind the berm with an American instructor, pull the pin, and lob the grenade over the berm. Not all the students passed this exam.

All too often, a poorly thrown grenade would fail to clear the top of the berm. Instead, it would come skidding and tumbling back down the slope, hissing softly, and trailing a thin spiral of smoke toward the fear-paralyzed student.

The instructor had three courses of possible action, depending on the location of the grenade and the time available—five seconds or less. He could pick up the grenade and throw it over the berm; he could kick the grenade into a nearby trench dug for the purpose; or he could grab the student and dive into the trench. The last option was the least desirable.

The bottom of the trench was knee-deep mud, a mixture of monsoon rains and loose earth homogenized by the exploding grenades. A frantic dive into the trench and the subsequent mud-soaked exit was a source of great amusement to the tribesmen. Any of the Montagnards not otherwise occupied would gather at the grenade range to socialize and to gamble on the outcome of the next student's performance.

As the lowest ranking member of the team, I usually drew the duty as hand grenade instructor. It was a pretty good trade-off: The Montagnards learned to throw hand grenades, and I learned how to stay calm in a crisis—a skill that has served me well since then. I developed a great fondness for the Yards. If it was a slow day, I would occasionally dive into the trench just to amuse them.

As a token of their appreciation for my efforts to teach and entertain them, they presented me with a necklace of rhinoceros beetle carapaces strung together. The village shaman placed it around my neck and solemnly assured me of its protective powers. "VC shoot—no die!" I guess it worked.

I am sure the conclusion of the Vietnam war did nothing to mellow the racial enmity between the Montagnards and the Vietnamese. I wonder if the Yards are still throwing hand grenades?

Khe Sanh

Khe Sanh had originally been a Special Forces camp, with an A-detachment nearby at a site called Lang Vei. The Marines got interested in it because of the airstrip that had originally been built by the SF team and the local tribesmen.

By early February 1968 there were about 5,000 Marines at Khe Sanh, about 4,000 inside the wire, and another 1,000 or so stationed at outposts on hilltops and listening posts in the vicinity.

The Studies and Observation Group (SOG) maintained FOB-3 at Khe Sanh. SOG used the forward operating base to launch teams into the border area surrounding Khe Sanh, primarily to observe traffic on the Ho Chi Minh Trail across the border. These recon teams were small units, just two or three Americans and four or five Bru Montagnards.

The Bru were the local tribe, the northernmost tribe within South Vietnam. They were probably the least warlike of any of the tribes, an agricultural society less interested in hunting and less territorial than other tribes to the south, like the Rhade. They were pretty calm, not as aggressive, compared to the Rhade. But they were competent soldiers, and they worked well in large groups. They were accustomed to working together in teams in their civilian farming activities, so they worked well in platoon-sized units. Like other Montagnards, they were "salt-of-the-earth" folks, very pleasant people. They were rather like Midwestern American farmers, with good work ethics, honest. They'd open their houses to you, and they really wanted to hear what the Americans were preaching about involvement in the government of South Vietnam where they'd been second-class citizens for many years.

The Khe Sanh Cooking School

I had a bunker on the line at Khe Sanh that I shared with two other guys; we had an old M1919A6 Browning .30-caliber machine gun in there that we crewed. Because we were under siege, a lot of rather funny "head" things happened. We couldn't do much, and some of the things that we could do assumed great ritualistic importance. We drew them out. One of these was food.

Food was the only pleasure. There was no sex, no drinking, just a little card playing, so the only really personal satisfaction available to us was food. But all we had were C-rations for about three months.

There are only 12 different kinds of C-rations, and at the rate of three a day, they get old in a hurry. So we got very inventive at taking a little from one and mixing it with some of another and coming up with something entirely different. We actually had contests to see who could come up with the most inventive thing from C-rations.

Meals became an important ritual; when it was time for lunch, we could spread it out for a whole hour of preparation. We had to scrounge all the right ingredients, collect the various cans, trade with other guys, and then open our cans and portion everything out very carefully. We'd add salt and pepper, Tabasco sauce from one of our friends. One of the guys on the team was a Mexican, so he had some salsa; if you really begged and pleaded he would give you a little of the salsa for your meal.

When everything was all lined up, it was time to heat it up. We cooked on an empty C-ration can on top of another can, with a little pinch of C4 explosive for fuel. You'd light the C4, then put one can on top of the other, and that was the stove.

Anyway, I was in my bunker and had completed lengthy preparations for lunch. I had all the cans lined up in the order I intended to heat them, on the sill of the firing slit of the bunker. I had just finished toasting my bread and was almost ready to dive into my meal, when I heard a loud crack from the front, probably 200 or 300 meters away, followed instantly by a tremendous explosion on the front of my bunker.

The bunker immediately filled with dust. When my team members ran in to get me they were yelling, "Russ! Russ! Are you okay?"

I was beside myself with anger. "Those mother fuckers! Those bastards! Did you see what they did to my lunch!" All my cans had shrapnel holes in them, and there was a layer of dust and dirt on top of the food. Although I had just escaped death by a small margin, that didn't seem nearly as important at the moment as what had happened to my lunch.

My Team Sergeant

I'll call him Sergeant "Smith," but (for a variety of reasons) that's not his real name. He was a fabulously interesting character, a person born to be a warrior, unable to adapt to normal peacetime society. Outside of combat he was a drunk, a womanizer—not a person you would like to be around; but in combat he was wonderful. He was a veteran of the Korean War and had gotten into Special Forces at the outset. He had been one of the early SF guys who hid out in First Group. First Group during the 1960s was loaded with characters, and he was one of them.

Sergeant Smith did a lot of interesting things. For example, we had been inside the wire at Khe Sanh for a long time and were getting tired of being shot at. We wanted to do something—anything! Instead of sitting there and getting shot at while doing nothing we decided to go out and "do" a few of them; we'd still get shot at, but we'd at least have the satisfaction of doing something to them.

So we snuck out of our wire with a patrol early one morning, about 0300 and well before first light. We crept out of the wire and managed to get out to the NVA trenches a quarter to a half mile from the wire without being observed.

We had about a hundred Montagnards and about a dozen Americans. As the dawn rose we started to fire into their trench line, and then we and the North Vietnamese traded hand grenades with each other for a while. After a while we thought it was about time to withdraw. We thought this would be a good idea to do sometime before we were flanked and then surrounded. We had gone out and made our statement, gotten their attention, and they outnumbered us by a huge proportion, so it was time to go.

We counted noses; only one man had been wounded. He had splinters from the wooden handle of a "Chicom" [Chinese communist] grenade in his face. I pulled those out, bandaged him up, and everybody was looking pretty good. So Sergeant Smith said, "You know what would really surprise 'em? Let's charge!"

So we lined everybody up, shoulder to shoulder, and roared back to the trenches, whooping and hollering, throwing grenades and shooting. We got to the trenches, shot them up, threw more grenades into some bunkers, and then got the hell out of there before we all got killed! We got back to Khe Sanh shortly thereafter. That was the kind of thing my team sergeant liked to do!

"Don't Bother Me, Boy, I'm Thinking."

We were on another patrol outside Khe Sanh, a small operation with about a dozen Americans and Montagnards and, well, *ambushed* isn't quite the word. We blundered into a group of NVA and began to trade fire with them. As we had been trained, we assembled in a circular defensive position. This was not, under the circumstances, a really smart thing to do.

We were enormously outnumbered. The NVA forces outside Khe Sanh have been variously estimated at between 20,000 and 40,000 men. We were definitely playing on their turf. It didn't take long, only a minute or two, for them to flank us—and then surround us. They were pouring pretty heavy fire into us. We had a couple of folks wounded.

I looked to see where "Top" [an informal and affectionate name for senior sergeants within units] was. I turned around, and there

47

he was, sprawled in the middle of the position, flat on his back with his arms and legs out at odd angles.

Oh, shit, I thought, Top's been hit! So I directed the two guys on either side of me to cover my field of fire and crawled back to him. I reached out my hand to touch his neck, checking for a pulse; as soon as I touched him, his eyes opened and he looked at me. "Don't bother me, boy," he said. "I'm thinking."

I said, "Okay, Top," and crawled back to my position.

After a little while, probably only a minute or so, he stood up—in the middle of all the NVA fire—and gave us our orders. "We're breaking out that away," he said. We all aimed our fire in that direction to clear a path, threw a few hand grenades, and off we went. And it worked. We broke contact and got back to Khe Sanh. There aren't a lot of guys who will lay down in the middle of a firefight, close their eyes to think, and get their mind straight. He was an amazing guy!

Joining the Tribe

I got inducted into the Rhade tribe at Kontum—a monumental tale!

After the siege of Khe Sanh was over, my team was reassigned to FOB-2 at Kontum, again to a hatchet force. We had a company-sized unit of Montagnards, mostly from the Rhade tribe. They were wonderful to work with, aggressive fighters. They liked playing with guns. It was like working with a bunch of 14-year-old American boys; they wanted to get out there and play! And they were anxious to kill almost any Vietnamese, north or south. It was our job to keep them pointed at the North Vietnamese.

After a month or two, the locals decided to induct us into the tribe. It started with about 20 tribesmen playing gongs of different sizes, a bit like watching Swiss people playing bells. The tunes were completely unrecognizable, of course, but the music was very pleasant.

Then we consumed a barbecued water buffalo. Now, we discovered that one of the reasons we got inducted into the tribe was that the locals realized that they could get the Americans to underwrite the cost of a big water buffalo feed, complete with all the fixings, all paid for by the Americans. It was a real win-win situation.

So the buffalo was on the barbecue, and the band was playing, and there were 20 or 30 earthen jugs of their rice wine or beer they called "Ooo." It was made from a rice mash, placed in the jar with a bamboo mesh mat on top of the mash to keep it in place. Water was added and the mixture allowed to ferment. You had to drink this stuff, and it was pretty "green."

There was a little measuring device on the top, and you were required to drink your allotted portion through a long straw. Then some more water would be added and the next guy would have to drink the same amount. You had to keep up and drink your "Ooo." It was a kind of social obligation, and you couldn't lose face. You had to eat all the food, smile and laugh, and drink round after round of the brew.

Well, I was never much of a drinker! The stuff went straight to my head. I finally realized that I was going to be sick, but when the thought entered my head that I was about to be ill, it was already too late. I managed to vomit an enormous amount of barbecued buffalo and rice wine into the lap of one of the tribesmen conducting the ceremony. Needless to say, he was an unhappy camper.

I managed to find my way outside and get myself together some-what, then went back in for the ceremony. They put the tribal bracelet on our wrists, which we also were required to supply. Ten years earlier, in the good old days, the brass bracelets that identified the various tribes were handmade with great care, decorated with mark-ings unique to each tribe. Then they discovered that they had a kind of racket going, with this semicontinuous party as new Special Forces guys rotated into the camp, each of whom would help pay for a water buffalo. So we got brass rings made from welding rod, which we had to supply, that they bent into a circle and gave back to us.

Well, there was an interesting climax to that night. I had been celibate for the entire time I had been in Vietnam—up to that point. My team sergeant had always been after me to join him in a foray to the local house of ill repute, and I had declined. That particular night, however, I was exceptionally drunk, and he recognized a moment of weakness. He made the suggestion again, and this time it sounded like a capital idea to me!

Unfortunately, it was monsoon season, and it was raining so hard that everything was obscured by a curtain of falling water. In addition, there was supposed to be an imminent enemy attack of the compound, so the camp was shut down tight; nobody was allowed in or out. Well, we certainly weren't going to let little things like those stop us.

Since it was hot and raining, we were wearing just cut-off fatigues. We got our .45s and crawled out of the camp, under the wire, through the mine field (although we had no clue where the mines were) and staggered over to Flower's establishment.

Now, Flower ran a house of prostitution that was about 100 yards from our compound. Although it was officially frowned on by the Army, we had Flower and the girls visit our dispensary once a week to be checked for VD. It was much easier to keep half a dozen girls clean than a hundred guys. So Flower already knew me because I'd been examining her and her girls. We staggered up to the door and demanded to be let in.

They realized at once that we were going to be poor customers. We were dead drunk, had almost nothing on, and were outside a camp that was supposed to be shut down tight. "No, no—go away! Come back tomorrow!" Flower said. So we demanded our rights as American fighting men and were allowed inside, perhaps just to shut us up so we wouldn't draw any more attention.

The building was a ramshackle affair built of bits of tin, stolen U.S. Air Force plywood, and other pilfered materials. It was like a rat warren of little cubicles. I was grabbed by the hand in the semi-darkness and led to the rear of the building and a small room with a bed in it.

I was still quite drunk and not in any condition to be the aggressor in this little passion play. So I just fell backward on the bed and was the completely passive partner. The young lady pulled my pants down and had her way with me. When she was done, I detected that she expected payment. It was dark in the room, and I couldn't remember how much money I had brought with me, so I just pulled out whatever was in my pocket and gave it to her. This was probably about 10 times more than the going rate. I asked her then to lead me out, and we negotiated the maze, coming at last to where my team sergeant was sexually engaged with one of the resident maidens.

"Top," I said, "I'm all done, and I'm going outside."

"Just hold on; wait a minute," he said. "I'm almost done."

He concluded this sexual congress, zipped up his pants, and we were about to leave when an MP [military police] jeep stopped outside. The MP got out, walked directly to the door, and we thought, Oh oh, we're in trouble now! We didn't have any identification, we were out of uniform, and we were not supposed to be out of camp.

So we asked Flower where the back door was and made a break for it while the MP was coming in the front door. Then, while he was inside, we made our way to the front of the building—and realized that he had left the jeep's engine running! We immediately thought, Isn't this interesting! Here's a piece of Uncle Sam's equipment that clearly needs protecting. So we got in the jeep and drove back to the camp.

We got to the main gate, where a Vietnamese soldier was on guard. He refused to let us in. We were disheveled, out of uniform, soaking wet, and without identification. We tried all the usual techniques: "You know us! I'm *Bac-si* [doctor in Vietnamese]! You gotta let me in!"

The guard said, "Nope! Orders say, not let anybody in!"

We were getting worried. We figured that it was about time for that MP to come out of the whorehouse, so we both pulled our .45s and pointed them at this guy and told him to open the gate or we were going to shoot him right then and there. He concluded that discretion was the better part of valor and opened the gate and let us in.

We drove the jeep directly to the motor pool, shut the door, and immediately painted over the identification numbers on the bumpers of the jeep with cans of spray paint. By the time we were finished, it was about three in the morning, and we both tottled off toward bed. I hit the bed, and it seemed like I had just closed my eyes when a voice said, "Sergeant Mann, wake up. It's time for guard duty!" I had forgotten that I had guard duty that night. I was supposed to have the shift from 4:00 a.m. to 6:00 a.m.

"God! Can't somebody else take it for me?" I begged.

"No. It's your turn; get up!"

So I got up and pulled my shift on guard duty, but when the sun came up I was one sorry young soldier! And that's how I was initiated into the Rhade tribe.

The Scrounger

Scrounging in the military is a fine old tradition. In Special Forces it's an art form. The scrounger at Khe Sanh was a guy named Craig Rowe. Craig was a good-looking guy, the Hollywood version of a Green Beret: about 6-foot-4, 190 pounds, well-proportioned, with a strong jaw and clear, glinting eyes. He was a persuasive speaker, and he could sell anything to anyone.

As a result, Craig was detailed by the sergeant major at Khe Sanh to go get stuff at depot installations like Da Nang. The sergeant major would say, "Craig, we really need another deuce-and-a-half [the Army two-and-a-half ton heavy truck]. See what you can do."

So Craig would fly down to Da Nang, where he would trade a few Viet Cong flags and a few AK-47s for, say, a jeep. Then he'd take the jeep to, maybe, the 4th Infantry Division, which didn't have any jeeps because we'd already stolen them all. Craig traded the jeep for an ambulance, which he then drove to one of the medical companies where he would say something like, "I know you guys are short of ambulances. You probably don't need that deuce-and-a-half over there; why don't you trade it to me?" And then he'd have the deuce-and-a-half. Then he'd do some more trading, and come up with a supply of booze, sexual favors, or something of similar intrinsic value that was then used to get the crew of a C-130 to transport the truck to Khe Sanh. This was Craig's job, and he was superb at it.

Hangover Repair

Sergeant Smith and I shared a fighting position. He liked to have his medic nearby in case he got hit, but more important, he wanted me around for hangover repair. Although not so much at Khe Sanh, where booze was mostly unavailable, but elsewhere, I could expect to be awakened by my team sergeant telling me that I was going to cure his hangover or he was going to kick my ass!

Our fighting position was just big enough for two men, just forward of the trench, with a step and cutouts for storing grenades. Well, at the sergeant's direction, we had stored about 200 hand grenades in this position, all removed from their little containers and sleeves, ready to throw.

For the floor of the position we had several 20-pound satchel charges that we made from C4 blocks, with 10-second fuses and fuse lighters attached. We probably had about 160 pounds of C4 under our feet in this fighting position. The satchel charges were assembled on the expectation that we would, sooner or later, be overrun, probably by tanks. The camp at Lang Vei nearby had recently been overrun by NVA tanks, and we expected that when the North Vietnamese came—as we were sure they would—we were all going to die.

I was unsure just how we were supposed to die, and asked Top for a little clarification of exactly what his plan for us was supposed to be. He said, "The satchel charges are for the tanks. When they come, we'll just duck down and light the fuses on these things, then stick them up on the tank treads. They'll roll past us and the charges will go off. If they're real close, we can just throw the charges on top of the tank."

"Well," I said, "what about all the hand grenades?"

"When we get overrun, you and I will just hunker down and we are going to take turns throwing hand grenades in all directions. I figure we can hold out for two or three hours this way!" It was not a bad plan. But he was very matter of fact about the way we were going to die.

Coping with Combat

Back when I was a young "buck" sergeant [three stripes, lowest rank-ing real sergeant rank] I was assigned to lead a night patrol out of the wire to set up a listening post. Well, a listening post at Khe Sanh was an enormously scary operation; you were supposed to sit out there and wait for the enemy to overrun you. When they did, you were supposed to make a lot of noise to let the guys in the camp know that you were being killed (delaying them not at all), and the camp could then get ready to be attacked. It was a kind of "throwaway" position.

I had not been in combat before; I had only been in the country for a month or so. I was adrift from all my friends, utterly alone except for two or three other Americans and five or six Montag-nard tribesmen—surrounded by maybe 40,000 enemy. It was a very scary feeling.

The other two Americans were both SF engineers. We all crept out of the wire under cover of darkness, not too far . . . maybe a half a mile or so. We snuggled into the jungle for the night in the only good defensive position around, an old graveyard, a small position about 20 yards across and containing about a dozen headstones. The headstones were the only cover around, and we snuggled in behind them and lay there quietly. One of the other Americans was next to me, our boots touching so that we could warn each other without speaking in the event of danger.

In grand Special Forces tradition, we had taken Dexedrine (a.k.a., "Green Beret candy") so we could stay wide awake all night. We were wired! We were watching intently for any enemy move-ment, hoping that we would have enough warning to call the camp on the radio, report "Yep—they're coming!" and run like hell.

While we were lying there quietly, we heard a tremendous explosion! The explosion jarred me for a moment, and then I thought, "Aw, shit, now they've found us! They're dropping mortars in on us!" I looked around for the guy on my right, and he was gone! I thought, "Oh, no, I'm in the middle of 40,000 NVA, and my sidekick runs off the first time we take fire!"

Then I heard a kind of low moaning sound, which turned out to be coming from one of the Bru tribesmen. I started examining him by touch since this was not a place where I wanted to use a flashlight. During this examination, I discovered that one of his arms was no longer attached to the rest of his body.

I called to the team, all of whom were within a 10-yard perimeter. "We gotta get out of here! We've been spotted. They're mortaring us. We've got to run for it."

I directed the other American to take the Montagnards to another position and set up a base of fire, while I used them as a screen to evacuate the Bru casualty. So I patched this guy up as well as I could, attended briefly to another Bru who had been less seriously wounded, and got ready to go. The rest of the team crawled off as I had ordered them to do and prepared to set up to screen me as I hauled this guy back to base. Well, I knew there was no way I could drag him all the way back to the wire. It was too far to crawl while dragging him. I would have to stand up.

Unfortunately, the noise we created attracted the attention of the guys back inside the wire at Khe Sanh, and they started sending up flares, thinking that they were under attack. That was the last thing that I wanted! There I was, out in a clear field of fire, in a virtual spotlight from the flares. I picked up the Montagnard and threw him over my back and stood up. This was probably the only consciously brave thing I have ever done because I knew that when I stood up I would be "skylighted" and an obvious target. But I couldn't think of any alternative; if I didn't get him back to base he was going to die. So I just gritted my teeth, thought, Fuck it! and stood up with this guy and ran back toward the base.

We all made it, except for the guy who had been next to me and had disappeared. I assumed that he had just cut and run. I couldn't think of any other reason for him to be gone.

During our debriefing, the guy questioning me said, "What the fuck happened to you?"

I said, "Nothing, I'm fine."

"Look at yourself," he said. Only then did I notice that my right side was coated, about a quarter of an inch thick, with hamburger—which was most of all that was left of the guy who had been next to me. I knew it was him, because he was a black guy, and there were little pieces of black skin. I realized that something truly awful had happened.

We went back the next morning, in force, to see if we could find any more of his remains. We recovered his head and one of his legs. It appeared that he had either taken a direct hit from a mortar that had set off the Claymore mine he was carrying under his shirt, or that something else had set it off accidentally.

A lot of the guys theorized that this latter possibility was what had happened. I couldn't believe it myself. He was an engineer, and the use of explosives was his specialty. He wouldn't have been so stupid as to carry the Claymore "primed" [with a blasting cap installed in the device]. I have always liked to think that he took a direct hit from something that set off the Claymore.

Ambush

I don't know how much patrolling the Marines did around Khe Sanh, but we were pretty active outside the base. And we kept getting asked to do these goofy things. Somebody had decided that Special Forces would be the ideal place to test new gadgets.

On one occasion we were supposed to go out and plant some vibration sensors; they were shaped like small trees and resembled foliage. As we were preparing for this mission, somebody came to us with a request. He said, "Since you guys are going out on patrol, why don't you take along these nifty new squad radios? Try 'em out and let us know how they work."

They were really slick little radios and came in two parts. Each was about the size of a pack of cigarettes, with a loop of wire between them. They attached to the shoulder portion of your combat harness, with the transmitter on one side, the receiver on the other, and the wire across the back. We said, "Okay, we'll give them a shot."

"These things are still in the developmental stage," the guy said, "and they are super secret! Nobody knows about these things. This is their first field test. Be careful and don't lose them!"

Well, this was back on my very first combat patrol. I'd probably been in the camp only a couple of weeks. So we got together, planned the mission, and hooked up the radios. They seemed really neat! And then off we went to put in these sensors.

When we'd gotten the sensors installed in the designated spot, we began to work our way back to the camp. We had been taking a little break by the side of the trail and were just getting ready to start back when this little attack began. We were only about a mile out when we started to come under sporadic small arms fire, and then mortar fire, from an enemy force that clearly had a good look at us. It wasn't much of an ambush and wasn't well organized, but they were clearly shooting at us and rounds were coming really close.

Well, we all got up and took off at a dead run toward the base. We had gone about 100 yards when the assistant team leader, a lieutenant, suddenly realized that he had left his radio back where we had been resting. "Shit!" he said, "My radio's gone!"

I was the last guy in line, "tail-end Charley." I said, "Okay, cover me. I'll go back and get it." So I ran back the 100 yards to where we had been. In the meantime, the NVA had moved up on both sides of the trail after us. On the way back, it was like running a gauntlet. They fired at me from both sides of the trail, all the way back. I found the radio, picked it up, and ran back to the rest of the team, all of whom were standing there with their mouths open with amazed expressions on their faces.

I'm sure the NVA were shooting each other while I was running up the trail, but they all missed me, out of sheer luck. When I got back to the group my team sergeant said, "Boy, what the fuck do you think you're doing?"

We got back to base without any casualties and with all the radios. When the enormity and stupidity of what I had done finally struck me, I resolved to never do anything so foolish again. And I didn't.

But when you are in combat for the first time, there is a kind of John Wayne syndrome. We've all seen combat movies, and the good guys never get killed. There is shot and shell everywhere, and yet they manage to get through unscathed. So the first time I was under artillery fire, I was astounded. I just stood there, looking around, saying, "Wow! Look at all this. They're shooting at us!"

Meantime, the rest of my team was all underground, in our bunker. Finally, the senior medic yelled, "Get out of there, you! You dumb son of a bitch! Get in a trench!"

Going Wild

I won't tell you this guy's name, but this is a true story.

A close friend of mine was an SF medic assigned to a team in the highlands, a regular A camp out in the bushes. He was working with the Montagnards, one of whom had become a good friend and whom my friend was training to be a medic. My friend was invited to this guy's house, was made a member of the tribe, and they had a close relationship.

The relationship between the Americans and the Yards was good, but relations with the Vietnamese LLDB [Vietnamese special forces] was uncomfortable. For some reason the LLDB had this Montagnard killed.

My friend became totally unbalanced. He adopted the Montagnard attitude: The only good Vietnamese was a dead Vietnamese. He packed his rucksack, collected his weapon, left the A camp, and disappeared into the jungle. He went wild for several months. He killed every Vietnamese he saw, regardless of what side they were on. If they were Vietnamese, they were dead.

Eventually he was "convinced to return" to American military control. My friend was smuggled out of South Vietnam, was sent back to the United States, and was then promptly discharged from the Army. Special Forces took care of its own. Only an SF soldier could do something like that—disappear into the jungle for months, alone.

Medical Chase

This is a story I try to use today when I train paramedics who whine about the stress of their work. While I was assigned to FOB-2 at Kontum, I (along with the other medics in the camp) had the job of medical chase. This was a dangerous job. When a team was being inserted, across the border or wherever, the last helicopter in the flight was the medical chase ship. If the LZ turned out to be hot, if the team got hit when they landed, then the medical chase ship had to go in to pull the wounded guys out.

This was not like a conventional med-evac anywhere else, where the LZ would be secured before the helicopter could be called in. Anywhere else you'd have one or two companies of infantry fighting off the NVA while the helicopters came in for the wounded. But when our medical ship went in, the LZ was always hot.

On one of these missions, the team was inserted and then was hit pretty bad. The LZ was pretty hot, with fire coming from both sides of the LZ. As we approached the ground I could see the Americans converge where the helicopter was going to land. Well, before the skids hit the ground, while we were still a foot or so in the air, these guys rose out of the grass like apparitions, and they threw their dead and wounded into the helicopter. We were on the ground no more than about five seconds before we were off again, airborne.

I had a half-dozen dead and wounded people on the deck of the helicopter, and that is not a very large space. Even though the seats had been removed from the helicopter to provide more room, I had what amounted to a pile of people to deal with.

I had to decide what to do first. They were bleeding; some were crying out. It seemed like an eternity, but it was probably just a few seconds before I concluded that I must figure out who was dead. I did quick, cursory examinations and identified the dead ones. I put them on the bottom, so I could stand on them while I was working on the living.

You can do all the basic stuff in a helicopter: ensure an adequate airway, stop the bleeding, plug up any chest wounds, and start IVs to replenish fluid volume. About 50 percent of combat medicine involves plugging up holes—holes that are leaking blood, or brains, or lungs. That's about half of it. Then if you can get in an IV, that's a bonus.

But these are young, healthy guys you're dealing with. You don't have to worry about cardiac problems or long-standing cardiopulmonary disease conditions. It's just pure trauma to young, healthy guys. Plug the holes, set up an IV, administer morphine if the guy is in a lot of pain—pretty easy stuff. But you have to get your head in the right place and approach it as if you were a mechanic working on a car. You can't afford to get emotionally involved. You find the problem, fix it, and move on to the next one. You can get emotional later.

And it worked out okay; at least the wounded guys didn't die on the helicopter on the way back. Modern paramedics aren't used to the idea that there are times when you might have to stand on dead people to help living ones.

On Being a Vietnam Veteran

I'm always suspicious when I meet someone and the first words out of his mouth are, "I'm a Vietnam veteran." These are people who've never left the 1960s, whose whole lives are wrapped up in that experience. That's all they are ever going to be, and they believe that they deserve something because of that.

Well, the statistics say that the ratio of front-line combat troops to support personnel was about 1 to 10. And yet, in all my experience, I've only met one or two guys who claimed to be Vietnam vets and would admit to being a cook or a truck driver! They all were combat soldiers! It is bullshit!

I think a lot of the so-called delayed stress syndrome has to do with the extreme youth and immaturity of many of the people who served in Vietnam, along with a lack of training. I can't think of any people within my circle of friends from Vietnam who has anything like delayed stress syndrome. Now, this makes no sense to me because we in SF had some of the hairiest missions over there.

60

The experience for me, and the guys I was with, went in stages. First, there was disbelief that any of this could harm you; it was like watching a movie where you have an emotional separation from the event. It was not particularly frightening. Then the reality gradually strikes home as you become more exposed. It is now scary, but there is still that detachment that tells you that you are not going to be one of the people who gets hurt. You think, It's scary, but I'm not one of the guys who is going to get hit.

Then some of your own friends get killed, and you start to think that perhaps your own death is not as far off as you previously thought. Then you become scared, have nightmares, and begin to worry about what will happen on the next patrol.

If you can get past that, you occasionally get to a point where you start to need a "fix," even though after every patrol you think, I am going to do everything in my power to avoid ever having to do that again. But a week or two will go by, and life begins to get a little flat, somehow. There is something missing. The other guys come back from patrol and tell their stories—with embellishments, of course—and you start to think, Yeah, I could do that again. And before you know it, you're over at the sergeant major's office saying, "I'm ready! Send me out again!"

My team sergeant did that to us once. We had just gotten to Kontum after the siege at Khe Sanh, and we were really enjoying the place. We were digging trenches, building bunkers (we were the camp experts on bunkers), and having a great time. We were going to the club at night, getting drunk, and watching movies; and nobody was shooting at us. It was wonderful.

Well, the team sergeant came into the hooch one night and announced that he had volunteered us for what we all considered a very dangerous mission. We were aghast! Somebody said, "Top, why did you do that? We have just survived a terrible siege; we're getting a little rest now!"

He replied, "I'm bored. We haven't been shot at in two weeks! Let's go do something!"

SPECIAL FORCES MEDICS

If you ever get run over by a truck, pray that the paramedic who reaches you first or the technician in the hospital emergency room is a former Green Beret medic and not a garden-variety doctor. Most SF medics, particularly the ones with any combat experience, are superbly skilled trauma physicians. Many Green Berets would rather have their team medic treat their wounds than risk the uncertain abilities of a "real" physician. That's a bit surprising when you consider that doctors spend years learning their craft while a Special Forces medic is trained in only six months.

The difference, of course, is that the SF medic's training is somewhat limited. Even so, he can perform surgery, administer anesthesia, and dispense powerful drugs. Green Beret medics aren't supposed to open the chest cavity, although they are well qualified to stuff the contents back in if necessary. They can set bones, remove shrapnel, control bleeding, and treat infection. And they are, without exception, the premier trauma specialists; gunshot wounds are their stock in trade.

But how do you take a bright young man and in six short months turn him into somebody who can save your life when your essential juices are draining away? It has always been done through a challenging, extremely intense program that combines academic training with a lot of hands-on training.

Rather than have neophyte surgeons practice on human beings, the medic program originally relied on the use of animals. These were once (but are no longer) dogs from the pound that were going to be put down. Because of the emotional attachment many people have for dogs, this part of the program produced a lot of negative publicity, particularly during the time when the antiwar protests were at their most strident. The program was radically revised, and dogs haven't been used in the program for many years; the pound now just puts them to death.

"Dog lab existed," said one graduate. "It was hidden back in a cluster of old abandoned barracks. The first thing they told you was that you never talked about dog lab! That was the Number One rule.

"Number Two was, you never give your dog antibiotics. They were really serious about that; you couldn't work on your dog without having somebody there to keep an eye on what you were doing.

"We first anesthetized our dog, then inflicted a gunshot wound right behind the femur. Then we took the dog into the operating room and cleaned up the wound, flushed it, and then took care of the dog while it was healing. The instructors inspected the wound every day and critiqued you on the progress of the injury. If it got infected you were in deep shit!

"After the dog recovered, we put it to sleep, but only after we were able to learn several important procedures. It was taken to the operating room, anesthetized, and then we did amputations. Some people learned to put in chest tubes, and I got to do my first 'cut down' [cutting through the skin to find a large vein in order to insert a large catheter] on my dog. One guy in my class did an appendectomy.

"One of us functioned as the surgeon, another as the assistant, and somebody else would monitor the anesthesia.

"I got a pretty good dog, fairly healthy. I fed him well, brought him extra food to get him strong, and he rewarded me by never getting infected or dying.

"It was a learning experience. I didn't enjoy the idea that the dog was going to die, but we all rationalized it because the dog was going to be put to sleep otherwise, and everybody took really good care of the dogs, fed them well, and gave them a lot of attention."

—Hans Halberstadt

PARTY TIME WITH MARTHA RAYE
JOHN PADGETT

John Padgett, like many Special Forces medics, uses his military skills in a civilian medical profession. John is a physician's assistant in a group medical practice. His friends in Special Forces still call him by his old title, the one all Vietnam-era medics seem to own, Bac-si, *meaning doctor in Vietnamese.*

My Wife, the Assistant Machine Gunner

I was with a Mike Force [a quick-reaction combat team of Montagnards led by SF troopers]—4th Battalion in II Corps—and we were moved from Qui Nhon on the coast up to Kontum, up in the highlands. We took over a compound next to the B detachment up there, B-24.

The road from Qui Nhon had long been a treacherous one, up through the Mang Yang Pass, past the graveyard where hundreds of French soldiers were buried standing up, facing France. We drove that road many times and often would see the remains of recently ambushed vehicles alongside the road. I remember coming down out of that pass once, passing a burning gun truck.

At that time I was going with a Vietnamese lady who would later become my wife. She worked in a pharmacy in Qui Nhon, and when we were still based in that town it was easy for me to see her when I was in from the field. But when we were moved up to Kontum it was more difficult, because she still lived and worked in Qui Nhon. But she made every effort to see me.

That created problems for both of us. She normally had to take public transportation to get from Qui Nhon to Kontum, up that dangerous road. On this occasion the section of the road between Pleiku to Kontum was closed because of enemy activity, which did not deter her. She rented a motorcycle and drove up this closed road to Kontum.

But she arrived safely, and I was very glad to see her. We proceeded to spend some private time together. Later, a couple of hours after full dark, an enemy mortar team infiltrated the area and set up between our compound and the ARVN compound about 500 meters to the northwest. This team started lobbing mortar rounds into both camps, some at us and some at the ARVN. Their tactical plan seemed to be not only to harass and damage us, but to get us shooting at each other.

Now, there wasn't a lot of love lost between my Montagnard Mike Force troopers and the ARVNs. They tended to get in fights downtown, to take potshots at each other, and worse. Once, our guys came running back to the compound; they grabbed LAWs, machine guns, grenade launchers. I thought, What the hell is going on? I didn't hear any firing, and it didn't look like we were under attack, so I asked what was up. It turned out that they had gotten in a fight with the ARVN, and the ARVN told them they were going to go get their tanks, and they were going to assault our compound. Apparently they meant it! We got on the radio to the ARVN advisors, and they shut that down; but tensions were high. So when the enemy mortar team started lobbing rounds in both directions, they apparently were trying to use the bad feelings in both camps to their own devices.

As soon as the first rounds went off our alert warning sounded, and we all went to our fighting positions. I told my girlfriend to get down and to stay put. My fighting position was a machine gun in a bunker on top of a wall, and it faced the area where the enemy mortar was firing from. Of course it was our policy not to fire automatic weapons after dark at an assumed target, but in this case I could see the mortar's muzzle flashes and I knew where he was.

I started "firing him up," using short bursts to try to silence the mortar. An M60 machine gun is a crew-served weapon, normally operated by a gunner and an assistant. I was dimly aware while I was firing that my assistant was keeping me supplied with ammo and doing a good job. Finally, the mortar stopped firing, and I looked over at the assistant gunner. It was my girlfriend. We were not yet married, but I thought, this has got to be the woman for me! And so, after another difficult year of courtship, I married her.

Bong Son was my first camp, and it was a neat place. It was in the middle of an area that was allegedly pacified, and it was decided that it was time for us to pack up and move and to let the First Cav take it over. So we were closing it down and getting ready to move to Ha Tay. But for the few months I was there, some very entertaining things happened.

We had a quite good internal security net in the camp. At one point we learned that an assassination plot was in the works, that some of the Vietnamese in the camp were going to try to kill the Americans. The security guys "tumbled" a CIDG [Civilian Irregular Defense Group] member who was in on the plot, and he was interrogated. He gave up the others, including the leader—one of our hooch maids, a 16-year-old girl.

This girl was delivered to the Vietnamese interrogation specialists, who started to question her. Suddenly, from out of nowhere, she produced a bottle of poison and consumed the contents before anybody could stop her. Guess who was then brought to the dispensary for the medic to work on? I didn't have any Ipecac syrup to induce vomiting, but I put together something from scratch. It did the trick.

I can remember thinking a couple of things while I worked on her. In America, 16-year-old girls are thinking about prom dates and dresses, and this one was planning an assassination. What kind of society is it that selects and trains its children to do this kind of thing? Second, this girl looked at me—while I was trying to save her life—with such intense hatred that I will never forget it. This young girl, an otherwise probably sweet, somewhat attractive young woman, hated me. If she had had access to a weapon then, she would have killed me first, then herself.

But I brought her back around, and they took her back to interrogation. I don't know what happened to her after that; I think she was turned over to the national police. I prefer to think that she was. But this is what we learned from her.

She had been trained in North Vietnam for about a year. The plan was simple. They were going to wait until the wee hours of the appointed night, which happened to be the very next night. Then they intended to shoot the guards on our team house and bunker, then roll grenades inside. If anybody got out, they would be hosed down with machine guns. They would stand their ground as long as possible, then split. Fortunately for us, they never got the chance.

Honorary Jarai

The city of Qui Nhon was taken by the Viet Cong during the Tet Offensive in February 1968. When the place was retaken by a force of Montagnards (after an attack by the ARVN and the Koreans failed), it was decided that the place needed its own Mike Force. For political reasons, this Mike Force was going to be a two-company battalion, including a recon platoon and a headquarters element. One of the companies was to be made up of lowland ethnic Vietnamese and one of tribesmen from the highlands. I was one of four Americans assigned to go up to the highlands to recruit this company from among the Jarai tribe.

We trained them for about a month in weapons and small-unit tactics, but most were already experienced in paramilitary operations and were natural soldiers. We had to teach them about "fire and maneuver" and introduce them to some crew-served weapons like the mortar and machine gun, but they were already familiar with the carbine. They learned to use the M79 grenade launcher, and other, more effective weapons. Then we took them out on training combat patrols in the vicinity of the camp, and they did very well.

We were very happy with them. Well, they were sufficiently impressed with us that they wanted to induct us into their tribe, to make us honorary Jarai.

On the appointed day, we put on our best and cleanest uniforms, put on our berets (which we normally never wore in the field), polished our boots to a high luster, and marched down to the village. The ceremony involved a visit to each of the tribal elder's homes for a drink of rice wine—a large drink. The proper and traditional presentation is in very large ceramic urns. Rice is placed in the urns, some water is added, a layer of banana leaves is placed on top, and the top is then sealed. The urn is buried for a while, and the stuff ferments. When the time arrives, it is dug up, water is added, and it is ready to drink. It is a very potent brew!

The wine or beer is drunk through a long straw, and each man's portion was measured by a carved ceremonial stick placed across the top of the jug. Your mission, as a new member of the Jarai tribe, is to drink until the surface of the wine in the jug clears the bottom of the stick. That is about a quart or more of this exotic potion—at each house.

After the fourth or fifth visit, getting up the little ladder to the long house became a challenge. The floors of Montagnard houses are about 6 feet off the ground, a lattice of bamboo that allows a kind of natural ventilation and that keeps everything up out of the mud and dust. These ladders, though, are just logs, notched for steps, propped up against the end of the house.

After all that alcohol, climbing the logs became very difficult! But we made our round of social calls, talked and visited. At one point, I remember vividly, one of our group said, "Excuse me for a moment," went to the side of the house, and barfed his guts out. Then he came back in and took up where he had left off.

Finally, it was time for us to be initiated into the tribe. We were asked by the shaman to remove our boots and socks. Then he placed an old bronze ax head on the ground. We gathered around the ax head, and he put the bracelets on the ax, then our bare feet on the bracelets. He took some of the rice wine, and, with some raw local cotton, he began painting our feet, the bracelets, and the ax head, all in one continuous motion.

68

During all this he was chanting incantations, and the painting process was repeated several times for each of us. When he was done, he placed the bracelets on each of our wrists, telling us that they would protect us from bullets. And—interestingly enough— none of us was ever struck by a rifle bullet, although we were all peppered with shrapnel, and one guy lost his leg to an artillery round. But, as he promised, none of us was hit by a bullet!

After the ceremony, we all proceeded to get even more drunk. When we finally headed back to our camp later that evening, our fatigues had somehow been replaced by Jarai loincloths and cere- monial hand-woven shirts. That's how I became a member of the Jarai tribe, and I still wear my bracelet today.

Chase Medic

Before I moved across the river to take over the C&C Central remote dispensary in the old Mike Force compound, I was a "chase" medic for C&C Central, working out of the main com- pound at Kontum. My job was to get on the first helicopter going in to extract a team that had been in contact with the enemy, to start treating casualties on the ground or in the air. The wounded were picked up first, everybody else after they were out.

During Operation Tailwind, I was sent out to pick up a team that had been in heavy contact with the enemy and had a number of wounded. The helicopters and crews were supplied by the Marines, two big Sea Stallions out of Da Nang. They staged out of Dak To, picked us up, and we headed into Indian country to collect our guys. These particular Marines, though, had never heard a shot fired in anger. They had simply been ferrying cargo from ship to shore and back out again, low-stress logistics supply "milk runs." They had never done such a mission, but they had been tasked with this mis- sion, and—like good Marines—that's what they were going to do.

On the way in we started to see something I'd only encoun- tered before in the movies: flak. There were little puffs of flak going off, just like in [the Gregory Peck movie] *Twelve O'Clock High*.

The other SF medic and I told these guys, "Look, when you go into that landing zone, go in hot; fire up the tree line. You don't have to have a target. Just don't hit any of our people, who will all be in the immediate vicinity of the LZ. Anything beyond that is fair game. Fire it up!"

Well, when we got to the LZ, the pilots started a slow, deliberate approach, just like they were used to doing on to the landing platforms of ships. While we SF medics laid down fire with our CAR-15s, the gunners didn't fire a shot. Then, many bullet holes began to appear in the fuselage, in rapid succession.

While we were still in the air, a few feet above the LZ, I was trying to reach a patient who was being handed up to me, a wounded guy wrapped in a poncho. The ground fire must have become too intense just as we were about to land, because the pilot pulled pitch and rotated a little to his right. As we started gaining altitude, a B-40 [NVA rocket-propelled grenade] came through the bottom of the helicopter and up through the fuel tank. It didn't explode, but it punched a big hole in the tank, and now fuel was gushing out, all over the inside of the helicopter.

The crew chief was looking out the window and didn't notice. I banged on him to get his attention, then pointed to the fuel. His eyes got very wide. He reported all this to the pilots who were trying to get us out of there. We only lasted for 2 or 3 kilometers, then crash-landed. The other SF medic and I grabbed our weapons, and as soon as we were on the ground, we dashed out and tried to set up some security. This was a good thing since, as we soon discovered, we had landed directly on top of some NVA bunkers (which were, thankfully, unoccupied at the time).

I looked back at the helicopters, and the Marines were all huddled around the tail of the aircraft, looking rather bereft and forlorn. So the other medic and I had to go back, tell them to get their machine guns, and set them up in defensive positions in some sort of perimeter around the aircraft.

It seemed like an hour later (but was probably more like 20 minutes), when another helicopter finally arrived to get us out of there. They dropped a rope ladder from a hover. We hadn't received any unwanted guests during the interim, but when the second helicopter dropped that ladder they also started receiving fire. The Marines didn't want to climb the ladder, but I thought, The hell with this, I'm getting out of here, and I started up the rope ladder. I held on with one hand and tried to return fire with my rifle with the other. Even over the noise of the helicopter, I could hear the .51-caliber rounds from the NVA hitting it, but finally everybody was hanging from the rope ladder, and off we went.

But the helicopter was damaged enough that we only got 20 or 30 kilometers with this one before it, too, had to land. Finally, a third helicopter arrived and picked us up and carried us back to Dak To.

I was really upset. We'd been through all that and still had to leave the wounded guys out there. We rescued them later, but at that moment I didn't know what would happen to them. I dumped my flak jacket, CAR-15, web gear, and aide bag on the floor. When I took off the flak jacket I noticed a shrapnel hole, right over the heart.

Party Time

The medics liked to party as well as anybody else. When bad weather closed in, or when we had no teams out in the field, we knew that there wouldn't be any incoming casualties—and that was our signal to start partying! We took the precaution of having a "designated medic," like the designated driver of today, who stayed sober just in case, but the rest of us kicked back and had a drink. A favorite cocktail was canned orange juice from the mess hall combined with medicinal alcohol to make a screwdriver. But, one thing about military men when they start drinking, they start thinking about women!

We tended to combine our cocktail parties with visits to the local "ladies" who were loaded up in the back of our ambulance and transported back to the camp for "dermatological studies." The next morning we loaded them back in the ambulance and made another medical run back downtown to take them home.

Phase II training for medics, when I went through the OJT [on-the-job training] part of the program, was assigned for the first time to Fort Gordon, Georgia. But the people at Fort Gordon didn't really know who we were, what we were doing, or what to do with us young Special Forces medical trainees.

The hospital at Fort Gordon at that time was a complex of long, wooden barracks buildings connected by what seemed to be miles of covered walkways. We were provided with one of these barracks for our living quarters. It was great; we had comfortable hospital beds, we had our own kitchen, and it was all our own. And it was particularly interesting when we first opened it up because it hadn't been used since the Korean War, and in the bedside tables we found a lot of magazines from the early 1950s that made amusing reading.

When we graduated from the medic OJT program at Fort Gordon, my class had a real knock-down, drag-out party. We had a good time! We had water fights and everything! But the next day we were all supposed to leave, to go back to Fort Bragg for Phase III [a team exercise in the woods], the last phase of SF training after which we would finally become real Green Berets. A couple of us looked around at the mess and said, "We gotta clean this place up! This place is a disaster!"

Of course, as might be predicted, we were met with a chorus of "Fuck you!" The consensus seemed to be that there were plenty of "legs" [people who weren't jump-qualified] around. After all, we were almost Special Forces. We could walk on water, and we didn't have to clean up after ourselves!

Well, I wasn't about to do it all by myself. Since we had already signed out, they couldn't do much to us unless they actually caught us—so we left! Some of the guys got on busses, some of us climbed in our cars, and we "exfiltrated." But I will never forget that, just as the last two of us cleared that messy building, the hospital's first sergeant was walking across the facility toward our barracks with fire in his eyes! As he was headed up the stairs, we made our getaway—and we didn't look back.

"I Love You, Bac-Si!"

Here's a story about one of my favorite patients. When we moved to the new camp at Ha Tay the first thing we needed to do was to secure the area, and that means that the security patrols go out immediately. While I was putting my dispensary together, one of these patrols came back in one day with an eight-year-old patient. He looked five. He was malnourished with a protruding abdomen and very thin arms and legs. The patrol had found this child hiding in what was left of a village.

The Viet Cong had gone in four or five days previously and, as an object lesson, wiped out the entire village. They apparently decided that the people were a little too cozy with the government, or they weren't sufficiently supportive of the VC, or whatever reason, so they killed everybody they could find. Then they killed all the livestock, and they left the place. This one child managed to find a place to hide, and he escaped death. He had survived for those four or five days on what little grain and foodstuffs were around the bodies of his parents and neighbors.

When he arrived at the dispensary he had pneumonia, parasites, and malaria. But slowly I was able to bring him back to health. The child quickly became a regular fixture of our camp. The ladies who we hired to do our cooking took him under their wing; they made sure he was fed, and they began to teach him reading and writing. Gradually, he came around.

He was fascinated with the running water in the showers we had installed. He would stand in there and turn the water on and off endlessly. He loved taking baths and did so at any time of the day, so he acquired the name *Tam*, which means bath in Vietnamese. The team sergeant more or less adopted him at that point, and it was time for me to move on to another camp.

A year later, my assignment was with the Mike Force. As it happened, our new unit's first really big toe-to-toe fight with the North Vietnamese Army was in the 506 valley, right at the edge of the area of operations for the force in the SF camp at Ha Tay.

We were called in because the NVA were building up for a hit on this camp. We went out there and found them, and they found us! It was a real epic battle, with one company of camp Strike Force and one company of Mike Force against two battalions of North Vietnamese.

I was actually on another operation with the other Mike Force company across the river, but we were ordered to stop our mission (a raid against the NVA secure areas) and come back to camp to get on helicopters to go out to take part in the battle. We were lifted onto a ridge overlooking this battle and had to wait all night before we could come down from the mountain to try to relieve our people.

It was interesting. You could see our guys' positions below, surrounded by the muzzle flashes and tracers of their weapons firing outward and the positions of the NVA firing in. With all the artillery and air strikes, it was quite a light show. But at first light we moved out and were able to break through to them. The enemy had pretty well dissipated with the light. They knew the gunships would be able to see them, and they left. When we broke through, that was the final straw for them, and they broke contact.

We resupplied, got the wounded out, and rested for a while before moving out. The plan was to move up, out of the valley, to a plateau where the helicopters could come in and extract us. So now the remnants of the camp Strike Force, Mike Force, and the group that I had brought in were all together. As we moved out of the valley, the NVA let the first group through, then opened up on us from their bunkers.

I had joined one of the groups of Montagnards that had been hit pretty hard, and now they were getting hit again. My recon platoon leader was right beside me. He got up on one knee to give the hand and arm signal to order his unit forward—and was immediately hit by one bullet in the arm and two in the chest. I dragged him to cover and started treating him (he survived, by the way), but we all reached the same conclusion at the same time. We were not going to be able to hold the position. So we started retreating back down the mountain. I put the platoon leader on my back and moved out.

When we got to the valley floor it was obvious that we were surrounded; it was kind of like Custer's Last Stand. Luckily, we got some close air support on scene, and they dropped their ordnance between where we were and where our other company was, on the hill above. The FAC [forward air controller, a coordinator for artillery and air fire support] called me up and said, "You've got a lot of movement around you. There are a lot of people moving toward your position from the west. There are some to the south, too!"

I thought, Shit! I started looking around, and I was looking for a place to die—a place to make a stand and to make it count. We headed for a little rise, a little high ground. We wanted to get there before the other side. That was going to be the place I would be killed.

Then I heard a call on the radio: "This is so-and-so . . . I've got eight slicks and two gunships. Can you use us?" One of the gunships was brought down by enemy fire, but they managed to get all of us out of there, and they dropped us all at Camp Ha Tay—the camp that I had helped to build. We got off the helicopters, and after the debrief, I headed for the club.

I walked into the club with my CAR-15 in one hand, the aid bag in the other. My fatigues smelled like smoke and sweat, and they had blood all over them. I sat at the bar and ordered a beer. There was a little commotion from the back of the room, out of my line of sight, and I heard, "Bac-si! Bac-si!" It was little Tam, who remembered me from a year or so before, when I was treating him. He crawled up on the stool, planted himself on my lap, threw his arms around my neck, and said, "I love you, Bac-si!"

When people ask me why I spent four tours in Vietnam, that's the story I use to explain my attachment to the place and the people.

Later, I learned from intel sources that we had killed more than 250 of the NVA and wounded many more, so we pretty well decimated the two enemy battalions—but at a price for us too.

Martha Raye Kicks Butt

The first time I encountered "Maggie" was by radio, right around Christmas or New Year's 1968. Maggie was traveling around Special

Forces camps with a few girls, putting on shows for the guys, and I had the radio watch when she called me up from the helicopter.

"Hi, Doc," she said, "I'm gonna come up to your camp and bring my show." I told her that sounded great, and she was welcome anytime.

"I have some problems with transportation," she said. "You'll have to be satisfied with the old broad!"

I radioed back. "Maggie," I said, "an old broad is better than no broad!"

"You sorry son of a bitch," she said. "I'm gonna come up there and kick your butt!"

I said, "You know we love you, Maggie!"

"I love you too, but I'm still gonna kick your butt!"

And that was my introduction to Martha Raye.

A couple of years later I was down at C&C Central and ended up being one of Maggie's unofficial escorts. She had a lot more freedom of movement than other visitors and could go just about anywhere she wanted. We ended up over in the recon team's billets about midnight, drinking and telling war stories and drinking some more. The last thing I remember was that Maggie was still going strong, and I was down for the count!

Happy Hour at the Hospital

After the war, Captain Arnie Estrada joined the reserves. He broke his back in a training jump accident when his reserve shoot deployed prematurely and sucked him out of a C-130; he struck the tail. He ended up in a full body cast at Letterman Army Hospital.

Arnie maintained an illegal stash of liquid refreshment under his hospital bed, and every afternoon at the usual hour he would have a cocktail. Arnie and one of the nurses became friendly, in a kidding, teasing sort of way. For Arnie at the moment, this was about as friendly as he could get.

The nurse had a supply of popcorn, and Arnie wanted some. The nurse knew about his bar and told him, "If you can come up with the drink I want, I'll let you have some popcorn."

"Okay," Arnie said. "What will you have?"

"I'll have a beer," replied the nurse. "And not just a beer, but a cold beer!"

"No problem!" Arnie said, and he handed her a cold one.

Well, Arnie did a little "intel" work on this nurse, and he found out what her favorite drinks were. So the next day the nurse came in with the popcorn and the same demand. Only this time she said, "Today I want some wine, and the wine I would really like to have is Mateus."

"No problem!" said Arnie, and out came a bottle of Mateus. Arnie got his popcorn. The nurse was impressed.

On the third day the same nurse came in at happy hour again and said, "Okay, if you can repeat your performance again, I will keep you in popcorn for as long as you're here. You will never want for any popcorn!"

"Okay," said Arnie. "What'll you have?"

"Today, I want a margarita."

"No problem," said Arnie. He produced a glass from the bed stand, some ice from his ice chest, a little lemonade and orange juice, then pulled a flask of tequila from somewhere, and assembled the margarita. After that Arnie had all the popcorn he could handle.

Sergeant Psycho and the Alien Life Form

Several of us from 3rd Battalion, 12th Special Forces Group, were tasked with training some ROTC [Reserve Officer Training Corps] cadets from the University of New Mexico in small-unit tactics— raids, ambushes, and patrols. Several of the senior NCOs, myself included, were assigned teams of these trainees. After several days of joint training, we each took our teams on training missions out in the desert.

Those of us in 3rd Battalion knew Staff Sergeant "Rod" had a short fuse. So, naturally, we did all we could to provoke him. We enjoyed ambushing him on occasion and harassed him just to get him started.

One night we were operating in teams of 10 or 12 out in the desert, three or four teams, far from civilization. My team encountered something extremely strange. The point element reported back to the main body that they had something odd in sight, so I did a little "leader's recon" and went forward to investigate. The point team was on a slight rise of ground. Ahead of them, in a slight depression, was a very strange green metallic glow. Behind the glow we thought we might be able to see another shape, but couldn't tell for sure.

I came off the berm and consulted the other NCOs. It didn't seem to be part of the training program; it was too strange for that. Staff Sergeant Rod was called on the radio, and he and his troops moved to our position. I led him to the top of the berm and showed him this phenomenon. He couldn't figure it out, either. We studied this thing for a while, and none of us could make any sense of it.

Finally, in his typical, well-reasoned, diplomatic way, Staff Sergeant Rod declared, "Fuck it! Let's assault it!" He put all the troops on line, and down the hill they all went, blazing away at whatever this thing was!

I was thinking, this looks like a UFO to me. If this is our first contact with an alien life form, we are not going to make a good first impression.

Well, the assault was unopposed. When we got down to the glow, it turned out to be a reflection from some streetlights of the camp, miles away, from the polished blade of a bulldozer parked in this little depression, miles from nowhere. But that was his style. He didn't have the slightest idea what it was, but he was going to kill it anyway.

We camped that night nearby, in the open desert. The next morning, as we prepared to move back to camp, the cadets started calling him "Sergeant Psycho." So I asked them, "Would you guys like to know what would really piss Sergeant Psycho off?"

"Yeah!" they all said with eager anticipation.

"Let's ambush him!"

So we planned our route back to camp to intersect his. Just as he and his team departed the bulldozer site, we hit them. He was really angry. "Dammit, you aren't supposed to do that!" he screamed.

We said we were sorry and we wouldn't do it again.

Then we hit them again, about 2 kilometers back toward camp. He got so mad that, if he had had any real ammunition, he would have shot me.

JOHN WAYNE AND RAMBO

A lot of Americans have learned everything they know about the Special Forces community through films like *The Green Berets* (starring John Wayne) and *Rambo* (starring Sylvester Stallone). The consensus in the community is that the first portrayal is okay and the second sucks.

The Green Berets is actually a pretty accurate description of SF work in the highlands. Unfortunately, John Wayne's character is a colonel, but they have him doing sergeant's or captain's work. Although there were certainly a lot of bad actors in Vietnam, *The Green Berets* makes things look even worse than they were. This movie has some of the worst acting in the history of motion pictures—except for Wayne, who was a pro. The rest of the cast appears to have been selected by somebody standing on a street corner, asking, "Hey, buddy, wanna be in a movie?" Even so, the SF community liked Wayne (who actually visited Vietnam and the highlands) and the movie for its attempt to accurately describe the missions and situations of people in the camps—for part of the movie, anyway. Wayne became extremely popular with Green Berets in Vietnam, though, because he wore the tribal bracelet ever after, even in his cowboy movies! The Montagnards loved his heroic roles, and with that bracelet . . . well, they were fired up, big time!

Rambo, on the other hand, has the same type of bad actors plus a story line that is just plain silly. That would be okay, except that the story is alleged to be about the SF community, and a lot of people think it's a documentary. Green Berets mostly hate *Rambo* and are quite fed up with being associated with this story and its bone-headed, renegade central character. Oddly, though, the *Rambo* movie and the commie-killing Rambo character are extremely popular in (I'm not kidding) Russia!

—Hans Halberstadt

THE BOY CAPTAIN
KENN KUBASIK

*Kenn Kubasik left active duty after a long and varied career
but still serves in the Texas National Guard as a lieutenant
colonel. He operates a private investigation business with his
wife and is active in Special Forces Association and Special
Operations Association.*

"We Are All Dead. Out."

It happened on my birthday, December 29, 1964. I had been in
the country for about a month. I was a somewhat green second
lieutenant, the XO at Camp Ben Cat.

There were three of us in the camp who took the patrols out:
Captain Andrew "Buzz" Erickson, the commander; myself, the
executive officer; and the team sergeant, Sergeant William Segrist.
We took turns in rotation, so every patrol had one of the three senior
leaders. A patrol was scheduled to go out on my birthday, on
December 29, and it was my turn to lead it.

We had a Strike Force made up of Nungs, Cambodians, and
Montagnards, and these troops hadn't been paid for a long time.
They refused to go on any more patrols until they were paid, so
this issue became an important one. It was my job to be paymaster.
Since I couldn't pay the troops and get ready for this patrol at the
same time, Sergeant Segrist and I traded turns.

Segrist, Sergeant Reino Peanula, and Sergeant Roy Jacobson
took the Strike Force out, about 300 men total. They got to the little
town of Ap Ban Dong So. Sergeant Elliot Wilson took another

element around to the north, toward a town called Bau Bang. Some Vietnamese Special Forces—the LLDB—went too.

Sergeant Segrist's Strike Force got to Ap Ban Dong So about twilight, and they decided to spend the night in the town. We were all pretty new to this stuff and didn't know or use the tricks we did later on that might have saved them. They decided to camp right in the middle of town, and when they did the Viet Cong came up out of their holes, formed skirmish lines, and attacked.

Sergeant Segrist called me on the radio. "Sir," he said, "put 300 rounds on top of our position!"

"I can't do that," I told him. He was asking me to kill him and all the strikers too.

"Sir, please, you have got to put 300 rounds of artillery on our position, NOW!"

"I cannot do that!" It was hard to communicate with him, for several reasons. One was the VC started mortaring our camp just as they hit the Strike Force. Their shells used VT [variable time] fuses, set for air bursts. These things were going off outside, right at rooftop level.

While all this was going on, I was on another radio, talking to a major in Saigon, trying to get some air support and some supporting artillery. I had Segrist yelling at me on one radio, and this major down in Saigon telling me, "Calm down, now, lieutenant, get control of yourself. You're getting overexcited; the VC don't even have VT fuses."

About that moment one of the rounds detonated right over the ARVN regimental commander's house and took out the whole roof. The local Vietnamese artillery unit was doing its best, but the air bursts from the incoming mortar rounds produced a kind of metal rain that was falling all around us. That made it virtually impossible for the ARVN gunners in our compound to fire their guns, although they tried hard and managed to get some rounds downrange. Whenever there was a little break in the attack, those gunners got off a few rounds. We didn't get any support from anybody until the next morning, and by then it was all over.

I gave up on the major in Saigon and hung up on him. Then, Sergeant Segrist called the last time. "Sir, they are coming through the gates now! Put 300 rounds on top of our position. We are all dead. Out." That was the last I heard from him. The radio went dead, and so did he.

Buzz Erikson, the commander, was in Saigon drinking and whoring around when this happened, so I was in charge. I flew in to Ap Ban Dong So the next day. I had a gunship overhead to provide cover, and I didn't let anybody else go in with me at first.

There were bodies everywhere (our bodies only; the VC had removed all of theirs). The VC took the boots from all our guys. I had tried to get Peanula to leave his pistol and save the weight, but he had taken it anyway. They had emptied it into his face. He and Sergeant Segrist were lying together, inside the town. Jake [Sergeant Roy Jacobson] had wandered out of the jungle, alive but without his boots or weapon. The Vietnamese LLDB commander, Lieutenant Toi, had survived without a scratch, which made us all wonder about him.

With the gunship overhead covering us, I got the surviving Nungs and Cambodians to start loading bodies on the other helicopter. We sent out about 15 helicopter loads of bodies. The strikers had to load the bodies of their friends on the helicopters—the wounded first, the dead second. There were 30 dead, 30 wounded, and 30 captured by the VC.

I was very upset about the whole thing. It was a patrol that I was supposed to lead, and I didn't lead it. I had liked Sergeant Segrist. He had been a good man and a good soldier, and now he was dead instead of me. He had told my wife, when we left, "Don't worry, Mrs. Kubasik, I'll bring your husband home, safe and sound." We had been over there for a total of three weeks, and I had let him down. He had a wife and two daughters. It was as if I were responsible for his death, in a way. I had big problems with this thing for a long time. And they focused on Sergeant Jacobson.

When he showed up, it was without boots or a weapon. He had been hiding in the jungle. It looked to me like Jake was a coward, had run and hid in the jungle instead of standing with the other guys and fighting. When Jake got the Bronze Star, I refused to attend the ceremony. It really bothered me. It ate at me all these years, until the 1993 convention in Nashville.

I hadn't seen Jake since I left Ben Cat. He had looked me up and called me a couple of years ago, but I didn't say anything to him about the way I felt. All I said was, "Jake, someday we'll have to talk." But I made up my mind that, if we ever met at one of these conventions, I was going to ask him about it, face to face.

Thank goodness Joe Stringham (Brigadier General Stringham now) was there. I asked the two of them to take a walk with me. I wanted Joe to hear this, too, because I hadn't talked to him about this before. I don't mind telling you, I cried my eyes out. I faced the man and told him that I had carried with me all these years the idea that he had been a coward. Now I wanted to hear from him directly what had happened that night.

It turned out that they were all heroes, including Jake. What he told me was that they were all running together, trying to get to cover, when Sergeant Peanula and Sergeant Segrist ran back for something. Jake didn't know for what or why. And then I started putting the pieces together, and a picture of what might have happened appeared. [Sergeant Roy Jacobson's account of this battle and his escape are presented later in this book in the story "Bad Day at Ap Ban Dong So."]

The Littlest Guy in SF

Tully Strong was quite a character. He was supposed to have been the shortest man in the Airborne, and somehow he managed to end up in Special Forces. I was working for The Agency in early 1968 as a USAID employee, a captain in civilian clothes, when the NVA offensive struck during the Tet holidays. I was the CORDS [Civil Operations and Revolutionary Development Support] advisor to the PRU [Provincial Reconnaissance Unit], the Revolutionary Cadre, and the Census-Grievance Committees [three of the programs from which the Phoenix program was developed]. During the mop-up after Tet, my sergeant, who was the PRU advisor, was killed, so I was sent a new replacement NCO, who turned out to be Tully Strong.

A CV-2 Caribou landed at the strip at Song Be. I was standing there, looking for something that looked like a PRU advisor, and this little thing gets off the plane and comes up to me. He says, "My name is Sergeant Tully Strong, and I am here to kill Viet Cong!" He had a Cambodian woman with him, and I don't want to say anything bad about her, but she looked like five miles of bad tank trail. But he loved her, and that was his business. Nobody had told me that Tully had a little trouble with his drinking.

There were two military compounds—the SF facility at one end of town and another camp, the old SF camp that had been overrun years before—and a USAID compound in Song Be. We lived in the USAID compound, but often ate and drank and watched movies at the old camp, now used by MACV [Military Assistance Command Vietnam]. The MACV compound was in the south, the USAID compound in the center, and the new SF compound in the north.

Until Tully arrived, I had a jeep, a Bronco, and a moped to get around my province. One night, not long after Sergeant Strong had arrived, I was down at the MACV camp for dinner and a movie when I got a phone call. It was Major Nelms, the commander of the B-team [the company-level command and control]. He said, "Come down here and get your PRU sergeant. He is trying to tear up the camp."

I arrived to find Major Thompson, a very big, good man, with his one hand on Tully's head, holding him off. Little Tully was trying to fight him, but his arms were too short. It looked like something out of an old comedy film, with Tully yelling that he was going to whip Major Thompson's ass. I collected Tully and took him outside, told him that he was a bad boy, and that he couldn't do that sort of thing.

Less than a week later, I got another phone call. "You better come and get Tully," they said. "He just put your Bronco into the wire." Sure enough, Tully had gotten drunk and had driven my Bronco off the road and into the wire. It was destroyed.

"Okay, Tully, we can't have this sort of thing anymore. This has to stop," I told him.

But not long after that I sent him off somewhere on my little moped, and then the phone rang again. "The medic is down here working on Tully," they said. "You better come down and get him." Drunk, he'd run the moped off the road and into the concertina wire, and he'd gotten both stuck and cut quite badly. He had now ruined my little moped.

"Okay, Tully, that's it. No more driving for you." From then on Tully was restricted to walking or using a bicycle.

Not long after that a new sergeant arrived. He had just arrived in country. On the evening of his very first day, he was walking down to the MACV camp for the movie when he noticed a moaning sound coming from the moat around the camp. He stopped to investigate. Down at the bottom was this tiny little figure in an American uniform, moaning, "Help meee . . . help meee. . . ." It was Tully, drunk again. He had run his bicycle off the road, into the moat.

The new guy went to the mess hall where the movie was going to be shown, and he said to me, "I want to go home. I've seen enough of Vietnam! I've had it! I just saw a midget trying to get out of the moat!"

Everybody looked at me. "Kubasik," one of them said, "you better go get Tully." So a bunch of us went out there and looked in the moat. It was about 10 feet deep. There Tully was, trying to climb up out of it, calling in a pathetic, drunken voice, "Help me. . . . "We pulled him out and sent him to bed. That was the end of the bicycle.

Shortly after that the town was under threat of attack by the NVA, and we started making preparations. I was looking for Tully, to get him out in the field to see what was going on, but I couldn't find him. We were out by the airstrip, talking about it, when the interpreter started laughing.

"What the hell is so funny?" I asked him. The rest of the Yards were laughing, too, but they didn't want to tell me why.

"Andy," I said to the interpreter, "give me the straight scoop. Where's Tully?"

He said, "Sir, first goddamned plane in, Tully take his wife, he get on plane, and he *di-di-mau!*"

Only then did I discover that Tully, who was beloved by the PRU, never went on the three-day operations that I had sent him on. Instead, he sent the PRU off while he went behind a building somewhere and crashed. When the PRU got back, they gave him some information and he gave it to me, completely fabricated. We never saw him again, but his memory lingers on. Even today, when those of us who were there get together, the guys kid me about Tully. I swore I would kill him if I ever got the chance. We put out a chair for Tully, just in case he shows up.

The Boy Captain

Joe Stringham would later become a brigadier general, but when he was my boss at Ben Cat, 30 miles north of Saigon, I called him the "Boy Captain." Joe didn't really know how to play cards very well, so we used to lure him into card games and take all his money.

We were playing poker one night in the team room. A young sergeant from the MACV compound across the road was visiting and playing poker with us. He was also a Stringham (no relation to Joe), so we called him "Joe Jr." We played several hands when, in the distance, we heard the unmistakable sound of an enemy mortar firing: Whump! Whump! Whump!

Now, under normal circumstances, we would all start running immediately because we all knew that, in about 15 seconds or so, those mortar rounds were going to come back to earth, probably in our compound. But the Boy Captain kept studying his cards. Since he was the senior man, nobody moved. Joe Jr. started to look a little apprehensive.

"Uh, don't you think we ought to go to the bunkers, sir?" Joe Jr. asked.

"We'll get there," the Boy Captain said, still contemplating his poker hand.

We were all getting a little shaky at this point. I'm not that brave to begin with, but I was not going to leave until somebody else did. The Boy Captain continued to ignore the prospect of imminent death.

After another eternity, Joe Jr. meekly asked again, "Sir, are we going to go to the bunkers now?"

"NOBODY MOVES UNTIL THIS GODDAMN HAND IS OVER! Do you hear me?" the Boy Captain roared.

Joe Jr. was really getting worried now, because the impact was due any second. He pleaded with the Boy Captain again.

But this time Elliot Wilson, our weapons sergeant, said in his slow, southern drawl, "I'll tell ya how it is, Stringham: We'll probably go to the bunkers when we see the Nung guards doing hand-to-hand combat with the VC at the doorway."

Captain Stringham said again, "Nobody moves till this hand is over!"

And then the first three mortar rounds hit, not too far away: Blam! Blam! Blam! Now the Boy Captain was a little shook up. "Everybody lay your hands down on the table! Nobody touch them till we get back!" And we all took off for our bunkers.

We were back in 45 minutes. Nobody got killed in the attack, not a lot of damage got done, and we picked up the game where we left off. We'd been playing Deuces Wild. Joe Jr. turned over his cards; he had a straight flush, normally a winning hand. But one of the other guys laid out five aces and beat him. He had figured that he'd finally get back all the money we'd taken from him, but he lost again!

And Joe Jr. never ever came over to play poker again.

"I Think He Wanted to Kill Me!"

A guy came wandering down the highway and into our camp one day, asking to speak to the American commander. He had a note and handed it to our interpreter. They talked for a minute, then Joe Stringham asked the interpreter, "Well, what does the note say?"

We all knew that interpreters didn't like to tell us bad news. They didn't lie, but they would avoid answering if they could. The guy said, "Oh, no problem. Nothing to worry about."

Joe said, "What is in the letter?"

"Nothing important," the interpreter said. "No big deal."

This just made Joe highly suspicious. "I want to know what is in the goddamned letter!" he said.

Finally, the interpreter opened the note and read: "To the American commander of forces in this area. If you take any more troops and attempt to move north of Lai Kai plantation, we will cut you off and annihilate you." It was from the VC commander in the region.

Joe turned to me and said, "*Te-uy* [Vietnamese for lieutenant], that son of a bitch can't threaten me like that!"

"Joe," I told him, "don't do it!"

"Goddammit, they can't tell me to stay home! I'll show them!"

The interpreter and the guy who brought in the message were shaking in their boots. They thought we were going to kill them. The interpreter said, too, "*Dai-uy* [Vietnamese for captain], this VC commander, he means business!"

Joe said to me, "I am going to go up that road, kick some butt, and take some names. They are not going to do this to me!"

Joe had to go, but he wasn't stupid about it. We had a good ARVN artillery unit in the town, and Joe developed a very detailed fire plan for his mission. He took it down to the artillery unit and went over it with their advisor, in detail. This fire plan covered the entire route from our camp north for about 5 miles. Anyway, Joe took a large force (about half the camp) out on the road and up to the north.

They had been gone only about three hours when, off in the distance, you could hear the Whump! Whump! Whump! of artillery and the sounds of machine guns and rifles firing. Then Joe called me on the radio. "Send in the preplanned fires!" he said, giving me the coordinates. His fire plan gave him covering fire all the way back. Joe and his force were coming back to camp, on the run.

While I was working the radios, coordinating the artillery support, a helicopter carrying Lieutenant Colonel De La Pena, the detachment commander, arrived. He had a new major with him, his XO [executive officer]. This major, new to the combat zone, was trying to make sure that military courtesies were observed. "Where's the camp commander?" he demanded of my sergeant.

"Well, sir, the commander is in contact right now, but Lieutenant Kubasik is in charge of the camp."

The major came over to me while I was still on the radio. "Lieutenant," he said, but I cut him off. "I'll be with you in a minute, major," I told him.

"I want to talk to you now!" the major said.

"I'll be with you in a minute," I told him again. "My commander is in trouble!"

"Do you realize that the colonel is here?"

"That's great. I'll talk to him later!" He was telling me that I was supposed to be standing at attention, and I was telling him to get out of my face. He was saying that he was going to have me court-martialed when Lieutenant Colonel De La Pena grabbed him and pulled him out of the way.

Well, it took Joe and that force of his three hours to move up the road, but it only took them 45 minutes to get back! They must have run all the way. Joe was sweating heavily when he finally arrived. When he caught his breath, he said, "You know what, *Te-uy*, that goddamn guy out there was serious! I think he wanted to kill me!"

Ambush at the Rubber Plantation

We sent out a patrol into the French-owned-and-operated Michelin rubber plantation at Lai Kai. Of 72 guys on the operation, 69 were killed, including one American. We were mad. We figured the French knew about the ambush and could have warned our guys, but they wanted to avoid trouble with the VC and didn't.

We could hear the firing. It was only a couple of miles from the camp. Joe Stringham wanted to take a relief force out, but I wouldn't let him. The VC routinely prepared ambushes for relief forces in situations like this, and it got lots of guys killed unnecessarily. If we could have gotten air support, it would have made sense, but not otherwise.

"If you try to take a force out of camp, I will take command and have you detained," I told him.

He didn't go, thank goodness. Then, afterwards, we had to go out and collect the bodies.

There were two towers at the plantation. One was a radio facility, and the other was a lab. Joe and I both figured that they used the radio to signal the VC. We all felt the French were in collusion with the VC.

I don't remember just whose hair-brained idea it was, Joe's or mine, but we decided to blow up the radio tower as a warning to the French plantation owners not to let this happen again. But of course we couldn't actually do it ourselves; that would not have been nice. So we paid our Cambodian soldiers a hellacious amount of money to do it for us. They collected their gear and off they went.

It was about midafternoon when the explosion went off. A huge cloud of smoke and debris filled the sky above the plantation in the distance. Even at that range, we noticed a large quantity of what looked like paper floating in the air. I don't know how much C4 they placed in the tower, but they certainly blew the hell out of it.

Within minutes the Frenchman who ran the plantation arrived in his ancient Citroen, waving American fuse-lighters and blasting materials in our faces, insisting we were responsible.

"Don't be silly," we told him. "We've been right here all afternoon, and besides, the VC have more of those things than we do!"

He departed, and then we finally figured out that the operation wasn't quite the success we had thought it had been. The Cambodians became confused and set the explosives in the lab, not the radio station.

The Boy Captain, Part II

Our camp at Ben Cat got hit pretty hard one night, and Joe Stringham and I and the radio operator were all in our hole. Well, actually Joe was standing up beside the hole. He would never get down, no matter what was happening. Stringham wanted air support, even if it was the middle of the night, and he wanted it now. He was yelling into the radio, "I want to talk to Ben Hoa . . . I want to talk to Ben Hoa!"

He wasn't getting any response at all. "Goddammit," he roared, "I can't hear anybody!"

The RTO, Staff Sergeant Pressler, was normally a rather excitable young man, but he looked up from the pit at Joe standing above. "Well, Sir," he drawled, "if you'd get your goddamned foot off the antenna we might be able to communicate with somebody."

BDA Mission

We got a mission to go in after a B-52 strike to do BDA [bomb damage assessment]. It was just like in the movies: sealed orders to be opened only at midnight. Well, our maps were old, our smoke couldn't get through the triple-layer canopy jungle, and we were lost the whole time we were out on this operation. The VC seemed to know just where we were, and where we were going; they were coming up out of their holes to snipe at us all during the mission.

There were three groups of us led by Spargo, Stringham, and me. And we were separated by a few hundred meters. Spargo called on the radio, "I'm making contact now. I'm pushing them to the east."

Well, that was toward Joe Stringham, and then Joe calls, "Yeah, I see 'em. Maybe I can push them over that way too."

That's when I chimed in, "Dammit, why don't you push them straight ahead. You're pushing them all toward me!"

Finally, we made it to the pickup zone, and we could hear the choppers inbound to get us. I could hear firing from the other two sectors, but mine was quiet. I figured that I had a clean pickup zone. I had the helos in sight in the distance and "popped smoke." Then I heard the voice of Colonel De La Pena on the radio: "I see your smoke. We'll be there in zero five."

Well, the VC actually had us surrounded and were just waiting for their opportunity. As soon as the helicopters came in over the tree line, all hell broke loose. I waved them off with the only smoke grenade I had left—WP, white phosphorus. The helos pulled up and out of there, and I called, "We are in contact. We need help!" I started yelling for gunship fire support. "If you see my smoke, I need fire put 50 meters to the north!"

"I can't do that, sir," one chopper pilot called. "We have to maintain a 100-meter buffer!"

"I want it 50 meters to the north of that smoke!" I told him. "I don't want you to put it behind them and chase them toward me. I want you to chase them away!" But he wasn't going to do it.

Then the voice of Dick Jarret came on the radio: "I'll take this mission. That's a friend of mine down there. If anybody's gonna kill that son of a bitch, it ought to be me!"

The White Star Program

I started out in the White Star Program in Laos as a radio operator and as an advisor with the 14th Mobile Combatant of the Royal Lao Army. We were trying to develop 100 guerrilla companies to operate across the southern portion of Laos. We were trying to build up the forces and take back the villages that had been captured by the Pathet Lao.

I also worked for Captain Elliot Sydnor as his radio operator in the jungles of the Plateau du Beaulevens. We trained and equipped guerrilla companies—tribesmen in loin cloths, with crossbows. We trained them to use World War II weapons. They were primitive, but they weren't stupid! I remember giving one of these men a BAR [Browning Automatic Rifle—a very heavy weapon], and he just couldn't manage to hit a thing with it. Then we gave him a carbine, and he hit every target. We figured he just didn't want to lug the BAR, but we made him carry the BAR anyway.

Rest and Relaxation

Ben Cat was a real hole of a camp, and we tried to get out whenever we could. Normally, that meant a trip to Saigon about once a month. Since we always had to have at least one officer in the camp at all times, that also meant that Joe Stringham and I alternated. And when I went, it was usually with Elliot Wilson. We tried to go on a Friday afternoon, and planned on catching a flight back on Sunday or Monday.

We didn't drink in camp—or at least, I didn't—so that was an important activity for our first night in town. Willy and I got down there, and we had a ball! On Monday we went out to the chopper pad at Tan Son Nhut, and there were no helicopters to take us back to Ben Cat. So we went back to town, had a drink, and stayed another night. Our interest in returning to camp began to diminish.

Messages started arriving at all our local Saigon haunts (the SF camps and offices where we might possibly drop in, as well as at our regular "safe bars") from Joe Stringham, instructing me to call the camp to report on our status. We didn't think this was tactically sound, so I didn't do it. We spent the week partying.

Lo and behold, we came staggering out of a bar, and down Tu Do Street marched Joe with fire in his eye. It was one of the few times I have ever seen him really mad at me. "Goddammit, *Te-uy*, we have been trying to get you everywhere. I had to come to town for a meeting, and there isn't an officer in the camp!" We were standing on the corner of Tu Do and Louis Pasteur streets, in the shade of the many tall trees that lined the avenues of that part of town.

"Gosh, sir, I'm really sorry," I said, "but we tried and we tried but we just couldn't get a helicopter! We tried, every day." Joe started to calm down, and he even looked like he might be beginning to believe me.

But Willy ruined that. "Goddammit, *Dai-uy*," Willy slurred drunkenly. "Do you have any idea how difficult it is to get a goddamn helicopter at this intersection?"

Joe suddenly began to lose confidence in our sincerity. Willy continued, "We come out here ever' mornin', look up at those trees, figure ain't no helicopter gonna land, an' we go back in the bar to wait till tomorrow."

"You son of a bitch!" Joe roared. "You get your ass back to Ben Cat—if you have to walk!"

I was really scared. Joe was sincerely angry; but it was late in the day, and there really wasn't any practical way to get back to Ben Cat until the next day.

Willy looked at him. "We can stay the night?"

"Well, you can't get out tonight, so of course you can stay the night. But I want you out at the helicopter pad first thing tomorrow morning!"

Willy looked at me. "Sir," he said, "the old man says we can stay in town tonight. Do you think he'll loan us 20 bucks?" We were both broke by now.

"Uh, sir," I said to Joe, ". . . . uh, do you think you could loan us 50 bucks?"

Joe blew up again, but he pulled out his wallet and loaned us the money.

Trade Bait

I flew into Tan Son Nhut airport one time in 1965. While I was waiting for a vehicle to pick me up, I noticed a large number of air conditioners stacked up on the ramp, down the flight line. Now, we didn't really need any air conditioners, our hooches were just screened-in enclosures, but they would make excellent "trade bait." So I was standing there when an Air Force chief master sergeant came out and said to me, "Can I help you, lieutenant?"

"Yes," I said, as casually as possible, "I was supposed to pick up some air conditioners, but I don't see them."

"We've got them for you, sir. They're right down there, at the next loading dock. Did you want to pick them up?"

"Well, I can't right now, but we'll be back for them."

So I sent a sergeant downtown to Camp Goodman to pick up a 2 1/2-ton truck and a clipboard. He came back with the truck and the clipboard, and we went back to the Air Force logistics office. The chief master sergeant wasn't around this time, and I had to start over. Another airman came over and said, "What do you need, lieutenant?"

"I was supposed to pick up twenty air conditioners, but I don't see them. They told me they'd be at Dock 65." We were at Dock 20.

"Well, sir," he said, "they must have given you the wrong dock. We've got air conditioners here. How many do you need?"

"Twenty," I said.

"We've got two hundred; they must have made a mistake on the paperwork. These have to be yours!"

"Okay," I said. "But it will take us a while to load these things."

"Don't worry about it, sir," he said. "We'll get you a forklift." Within a few minutes, the guy had loaded 20 of someone else's air conditioners on the back of my deuce-and-a-half, and we were out of there.

We took those things and traded them for steaks and beer and stuff for the camp. It started out as a joke, but when everybody fell into place, I figured that 20 air conditioners were good trade bait.

The Mutiny

Do you want the true story, or the funny story about this that I tell? Okay, this is my version of events. In Morley Safer's book, *Flashbacks*, he said that Joe Stringham was the bravest man he'd ever met, and I'd agree with him. But the incident he described didn't quite happen the way he remembered. Here's the way it really happened:

Ben Cat, remember, was so poorly protected that we would have given it to the NVA if they had just asked for it politely. It was theirs for the taking. Our normal routine was to batten down when the lights went out, and we prayed for daylight.

Morley Safer and his cameraman, Alex Briar, were visiting, and this happened just before it was time for them to leave. The local Vietnamese special forces, the LLDB, got a brand-new second lieutenant as a commander. This guy was a jerk; that just goes to prove that second lieutenants are the same in every army.

Our camp population included two major groups, one of ethnic Chinese Nungs and Cambodians, the other of Vietnamese. There were two companies of each. These two groups were billeted in buildings facing each other across a square. The two groups didn't get along at all.

The Nungs were mercenaries, and they got paid better than the Vietnamese. That made the Vietnamese angry. The Chinese Nungs didn't care who they killed. They had no love for the Vietnamese at all, even before the new lieutenant arrived.

The new lieutenant (in the tradition of his breed) went downtown and encountered some of the Nungs. He decided that they were out of uniform and started chewing them out because they didn't salute him. The Vietnamese officer was offended and angry, and he returned to our camp. He had all the Chinese fall out into the square, on the north side of the plaza, into formation, and started raising hell and chewing them out. The Nungs responded by laughing at him.

About this time Morley and the cameraman started filming. They knew there was going to be trouble.

This dumb-ass lieutenant drew his .45 (I didn't see this part) and was about to fire into the formation. His first round went over their heads, which was all the excuse the Chinese needed. They came up shooting! They nailed him, right next to the building. He went down, but he was still alive.

I was coming in the gate when all this started. I was wearing my tiger-stripes and carrying my M16 and walking toward the group when the shooting started. Joe screamed at me, "Throw that weapon away!" With the weapon, I would look like a natural target to either side, and anybody could shoot me. Suddenly, it felt like a red-hot poker, and I threw it in the air. It landed in the back of a truck.

I dove into our storehouse building for cover. Two of the other guys, Jake [Sergeant Roy Jacobson] and Bac-si [Sergeant John Burns], went out to the lieutenant. The Nungs were screaming at them. They didn't want to kill him; they wanted him to die slowly, and they didn't want anybody interfering. Finally, our two guys got back inside, and then the shooting picked up again. This time it was the Vietnamese troops from the other side of the compound who started firing up the Nungs.

We really didn't want to be involved. I went into the supply room for cover. I used some of the piles of empty sandbags (the ones that Colonel Jeff Wilson wouldn't let us fill) for cover. Somebody's machine-gun bullets came through the window. I didn't know this at the time, but they hit a bunch of big number 10 cans of ham and lima bean rations that were stored in there. The big cans were falling on me, and the thick juice was running out, all over me. My eyes were closed, so all I really knew was that I was getting hit with these solid impacts, and I could feel something wet. I really thought that I was being killed! I thought I was being shot and I was bleeding, when actually it was just the cans falling on me, leaking their juice!

Well, I decided it was time to make a break for it, and I dashed out of there, headed for the MAAG compound. When I got outside, I ran right into one of the Vietnamese officers giving orders. I ran over, screaming, and crashed into him. The collision shook him up, and it shook me up too. That collision stopped the fight. The Nungs stopped firing because they didn't want to hit me, and the Vietnamese stopped because they didn't want to hit their commander. I was yelling at him, and he finally ordered his men to cease fire. Joe Stringham went over to the Nung commander, so Joe and I were now between the two forces, and that calmed the situation down.

A couple of days later my father-in-law was sitting in a bar in Philadelphia and was watching the news on the TV over the bar. He was watching the report from Morley Safer. "That guy looks familiar," he said. Then, they tell me, he fell off his bar stool when he recognized me.

Later, back at Fort Bragg, I was called in to see the commanding general, and I was presented with the Soldier's Medal, the highest decoration you can get for an action that does not involve the enemy. The citation makes me sound like a real hero, but I was actually one mighty scared SOB!

MONTAGNARDS

I've never met anybody who knew the Yards who didn't love them. They were tiny, tough, cheerful, smart, honest, and faithful—and in sharp contrast (sad to report) to the dominant culture in South Vietnam. They were, besides all this, the victims of many centuries of oppression from the lowland Vietnamese who call them moi, meaning savage. The motto of Special Forces is De Opresso Liber, or Free the Oppressed, and it was pretty much love at first sight between these two communities. When one of the big Green Berets led a gaggle of them off on patrol, it looked like the Boy Scout troop from hell, what with all those guns and grenades, and they looked like they were going to have some fun!

There are (or at least were in 1973) 11 major tribes in the highlands, including the Hmong, Jarai, and Rhade. The Montagnards are ethnically different from the Vietnamese. The Montagnards' origins are Malayo-Polynesian. They are different, too, in language, culture, architecture, and religion, and the Vietnamese remind them of this constantly. The dominant Vietnamese loathe them, and since the victory of the NVA over the ARVN and the Republic of South Vietnam, the Yards have been slaughtered by the tens of thousands, their language and tribal culture suppressed, their lands taken away by the lowlanders. Most SF people I know didn't especially care about the fall of South Vietnam— the lowland Vietnamese people of the south just weren't willing to fight for their cause. But the Yards were a different story.

—Hans Halberstadt

SLOGGING THROUGH DONG XOAI
Roy Jacobson

Roy Jacobson, Joe Stringham, and Kenn Kubasik all served together at Detachment A-301 at Ben Cat, north of Saigon along Highway 13. Roy, a sergeant, was the only American survivor of the company-size patrol that was ambushed on December 29, 1964, by what was probably a brigade-size force of hard-core VC. He spent most of the period from 1964 to 1972 in Southeast Asia, including several years in the employment of the CIA's Air America in Laos and Thailand. The first story is a good illustration of the problem ARVN units had, and why SF teams generally disliked working with the lowland Vietnamese. (In the story "We Are All Dead. Out," Kenn Kubasik tells about this same disastrous mission from his perspective, back at Ben Cat listening to the calls for support from the team sergeant on the radio.)

Bad Day at Ap Ban Dong So

We had only been in country a couple of weeks. We had very little experience in combat or in Vietnam. Although the team senior radio operator had been in Korea, and Kenn had been with White Star in Laos, neither had been in really heavy combat.

Our team leader at the time, who shall remain nameless, was a real son of a bitch and was shipped back to the states early. He didn't provide team leadership. Kenn had to do that as a new second lieutenant. Kenn had 10 years as an enlisted soldier, but there is a real difference between being a staff sergeant and being the officer in charge of a team in a combat zone.

100

Things were so bad at Ben Cat that we weren't even patrolling when we first got there. The team we were relieving had only been at Ben Cat for a couple of months. Instead of the deliberate transition period that became SOP later, the other team just pulled out when we arrived. Bang—there we were, new as a team, new to the country, all by ourselves with an incompetent commander.

Our first patrol was a short, unambiguous excursion that didn't accomplish much, but the second one was done with the Vietnamese LLDB. The whole operation and the Vietnamese company was led by an LLDB lieutenant named Toi.

Our team sergeant had been around for quite a while. He was a senior master sergeant and a decent enough guy, with a lot of time in 10th Group in Europe. "Top" (as we called him) was in the nominal position of command, advising the LLDB captain.

Sergeant Reino Peanula was the other guy; he and I had gone through demolitions training together.

I was an E-4, and I had command of 346 Company. Despite my low rank, our team leader gave me command of this company of ARVN infantry. Their lieutenant was a guy named Nguyen-something, but I called him "Cowboy." He spoke decent English and was a nice guy, and the lover of the Vietnamese nurse in the camp. He was kind of a wise guy, and maybe I was assigned to him because I was young and a wise guy too. We got along fine, although it was a very short-lived relationship, because the company got wiped out.

I have strong memories of that patrol. We moved out of camp at night and marched to the east of Highway 13, through the jungle toward Ap Ban Dong So. It was not a silent move. We had a head-quarters element with Lieutenant Toi, Top, and Reino, then a heavy weapons platoon with mortars and machine guns, and the two companies of ARVN infantry. We left Ben Cat and marched north.

But the march was typical of the ARVN—transistor radios playing, pots and pans banging, laughing and smoking. An occasional sniper shot would stop us for a few minutes, then we would move north again.

During a smoke break, about halfway to Ap Ban Dong So, Reino was fooling around with his AR-15 and lost a part of the bolt. He wasn't really concerned about it; he still had his Browning Hi-Power pistol. Although Reino wasn't worried about his rifle, I was, for a different reason. Mine kept jamming, and after this operation I turned it in for an old M2 .30-caliber carbine.

Another thing I remember was our march rations. The troops used to get a piece of very fatty pork rolled in sticky rice, all wrapped in a banana leaf. I changed that for my ration. I had them give me a piece of well-cooked chicken instead of the pork fat.

Sergeant Elliot Wilson had a company of ethnic Chinese Nungs, 349 Company, and with him was one of our medics, John Burns. They moved independently of us, around to the north to a town called Bau Bang.

We arrived at Ap Ban Dong So in late morning, posted guards, and went to a little restaurant. Dong So was a nice town, clean and pretty, and people were friendly enough. It was on the northern edge of the huge Lai Kai Michelin rubber plantation. We drank beer and had some noodle soup. It's funny what comes back after 30 years. I remember thinking how beautiful it was—nice smells, a clear, crisp day.

I remember the spicy cooking smells, the interpreter kidding me as I brushed my teeth. I was with Peanula, Top, and Lieutenant Toi in a small house in the town. After we ate dinner, posted guards, and scheduled guard duty among the Americans, we turned in.

About midnight the interpreter woke me up to tell me that there were many VC around the town. He had some weird, concocted story: The VC had Thompson submachine guns with red-painted stocks! They were led by a white man on a white horse! Then runners came in from around the town with reports for us.

There were only about 120 of us in this company, not very well trained, not very heavily equipped or organized around quite a large perimeter.

We were aware that there were VC on at least three sides of us at that point. We got reports from the north and east and the south of sightings and contact with the VC. There was a hell of a flurry of activity then. Within minutes we were being shelled by mortars and rifle grenades, right there in the center of Dong So.

We were out of range of our own mortars back at Ben Cat, and we heard artillery firing somewhere to the south. We figured that the camp was getting hit at the same time we were in contact. Top contacted Denzel on the radio. I was in the same room with him and the radio, and my company and I were all part of this big, loose perimeter. I didn't know where Cowboy was. In minutes, we were under extremely heavy fire. All of a sudden we had a lot of casualties. I hauled a couple of wounded guys into the building where we were, which turned out to be no good, because we had to leave them, anyway, when we took off.

The troops were firing into hundreds of VC running right down the middle of Highway 13 and the middle of the streets. I later heard a Vietnamese report that there were 4,000 enemy soldiers attacking us, and I don't doubt it. They were pouring though the town gate, roaring into the place. They were moving into the place in a kind of continuous stream.

I don't think they really knew where we were because many ran right past us. Initially there was a lot of firing and confusion. I didn't know where Peanula was, but I did know Top was in the building behind me. We threw hand grenades. Then I went back and told Top, "The VC are among us in town!"

He and I talked, and he called in artillery as I was standing there. Then he told me, "Throw a grenade under the radio," and we both rolled grenades in there. At that point he and I both took off from the house. The fighting from then on was very fragmented and leaderless, just individuals or groups of two or three. And it was over very quickly.

About that time some heavier artillery came in, and there was a tremendous series of explosions right in front of us. I don't think I was knocked out, but the artillery disoriented me. When I regained my senses, I noticed a large group of VC running north, right up the highway. I don't know why they did that, if they were reacting to Willy [Sergeant Elliot Wilson] who might have been moving to react to the attack with his Nungs. But one large group was obviously moving under the control of somebody, and they moved right past us, without searching the houses for us. They headed for the north side of town.

Then Top, Reino, and Lieutenant Toi came running past, and the LLDB were with them. Top hollered that we were going to move toward the west. Lieutenant Toi reported at the same time that there were no VC to the west. At that point, as far as I could tell, there were VC everywhere. Reino gave me all the magazines he had for his useless AR-15; I put about six in a sack and another two in the cargo pocket of my pants. There were bullets cracking around us, but we'd lost our night vision and couldn't see anything.

We were walking away from town, to the west. We were moving through a pig pen when an automatic weapon opened up on us from about 50 feet away. There were about 12 of us, marching single file in a column. The sudden fire split the group into two sections. That was the last time I saw the other two Americans alive.

Now there were five of us, still marching to the west, with shooting all around. The sound of firing was very loud, with loud cracks from the bullets going by. The cracks meant that the bullets were really close!

Then Andy, the interpreter, fell headfirst into a well. He screamed, "Help me, Jake!" I had two of the other guys hold my ankles, and I reached in and hauled him out. At that point we realized that we'd been separated from the rest of the group, and we agreed between us that we would continue to move toward the west. By this time, we were in "escape and evasion" mode, and we decided to move into the jungle and wait for daylight.

There were groups of VC moving around us, in both directions. While we moved to the west, Vietnamese air force fighter-bomber planes arrived on the scene and started dropping bombs around Dong So. Well, at that point the VC were in the town. The strikers who were still alive were in the jungle, so our guys were getting bombed.

We made it to the edge of the jungle about 3 kilometers from Dong So. There were VC everywhere, moving in groups of two or three, moving along. We crawled into the jungle, and I took an assessment of the group. Nobody was unscathed. We had cuts, bruises, bleeding, concussions. Andy was bruised and cut all to hell from his fall into the well; he thought both his arms were broken.

I had an AR-15 with about a half-dozen magazines, including the ones Reino had given me. Andy had an M1 carbine with one magazine. There was one tall striker from the 346 Company, and he had an M1 rifle with a half-dozen eight-round clips. The other striker had no weapon or ammo. We had one hand grenade.

We all lay in the jungle in a star formation. The unarmed striker started to cry. Andy, the interpreter, was lying next to him. He took his bayonet and put it to the guy's throat and told him to stop making noise, or we would all die. He stopped crying.

Then we heard engines coming. We were only a few feet from the edge of the jungle, and we happened to be near a place where a VC unit was exfiltrating from the battle. The noise was coming from many little Vespa-type scooters. Some of them were halted just beyond where we were.

One of the VC gave a series of orders to the others, then stepped over to the edge of the jungle to take a piss. He hit both Andy's and my boots! Then he and the little scooters left, back in the direction of Dong So; they were clearly hauling something out of there, to the edge of the rubber plantation.

We just laid there until first light. Then we moved back to the east, toward Dong So. We saw workers leaving Dong So, heading to the rubber plantation—the start of another normal day, I guess! And as we walked toward the town, I had one of the Vietnamese (a civilian who'd been along to crank the ANGR-9 radio generator) flag down a bus. This guy was in civilian clothes. I pulled the pin on that last grenade and gave it to him, with instructions to hold the spoon firmly down unless he had to throw it in the bus.

He got the bus to stop. The driver said that everyone was dead in Dong So, including two Americans. There were no VC, he said, but there were some "imperialist" soldiers still in the town.

We saw Lieutenant Toi and a few of the strikers, and we moved into the town. Lieutenant Toi took me behind the house where we had been the night before. Top and Reino were both there. It was obvious they were both dead; they were gray and stiff. Both had bullet holes in the head.

The little restaurant was still there, and it was open! We went in, and I ordered beers for the guys. We had Beer Larue, not *Ba Muy Ba* ["33" brand, the Budweiser of Vietnam]. About that time, Kenn came over in a helicopter and landed. He told me that he'd been in the town earlier that morning and that nobody was alive.

I remember the battle vividly, but after that things go blank in places. I remember riding back on the helicopter with the remains of Top and Reino. Kenn and I had words because I thought the wounded guys ought to go out first, before the dead Americans. But, in hindsight, that didn't matter. By then nobody was going to die who hadn't died already.

I was taken by helicopter to a Vietnamese LLDB compound called Thu Dau Mot, a brigade headquarters. I recounted my story, essentially what I have just told you. I was there for a few hours and was interviewed by a Special Forces major. I was sent to Ben Hoa, where our C-team [battalion-level command and control] was, and then to a TOC [Tactical Operations Center] in Saigon, where I repeated it again. By this time I was getting sick of it.

Finally, after they were done with me, a master sergeant from the intel section took me out drinking and left me with a pretty girl for the night. It was a good way to heal. She was a nice young person, and we were married for the night. It was just what I needed at the time, a good load of beer and a girl. When I got up in the morning, I went back to Ben Cat.

I had some questions about the whole thing when I went back. Lieutenant Toi said that Top and Reino went back to try to find me, apparently after we got separated. I have a hunch, not based on any real proof, that Lieutenant Toi was VC. Of the two times in my life where I have come very close to being killed, and where a little bad luck would have made the difference, both involved Lieutenant Toi. Both times he looked very surprised when I showed back up again. Besides, I thought it was bad form on his part to be reporting me captured when I hadn't been.

I have no survivor's guilt about that operation. The battle probably lasted about four minutes. Actually, there was no battle. It was an immediate, overwhelming annihilation. I was very young and inexperienced. Knowing what I knew then, and now, there wasn't anything different I could have done.

<u>Bad Day at Ap Dong Xoai</u>

Captain Joe Stringham and I were the only two survivors of six on this patrol. We were the Mike Force. We were so new to the program that we didn't yet have the recon team, but were simply sent in to augment camp security at the camp at Dong Xoai (pronounced "Dong Sway") after an entire Vietnamese airborne ranger unit was decimated in June 1965. It was quite a battle, and one of the Americans at the camp earned a Medal of Honor.

After the battle, we went in with two companies of Mike Forces, with no recon team element, as was normal later. Joe took Willy and me with him. We were the only Americans. We arrived late in the evening, and we awoke the next morning to discover that directly beneath the thin floor of our hooch the ground was covered with scorpions.

The camp was still being built, but we were putting out patrols. We made one patrol to the north; the memorable part of that one was wading neck-deep up a creek. We found large quantities of weapons from the battle that had annihilated the ARVN airborne unit. The more influential of my Nungs came away from these patrols with AR-15s, helmets, and other equipment left on the battlefield; it was quite a cache.

We went on a patrol to the west of Dong Xoai: Joe and I, two Cambodians, and two Vietnamese. We'd received information that elements of the VC 325C Regiment were present about eight or nine klicks from our camp.

We'd become accustomed to hearing warning shots during these patrols; they came from VC who observed us and marked our progress and location by firing their rifles. That was disconcerting, but we got used to it.

When we reached the assigned area, we approached a house in an open field. The two Cambodians went forward toward the house. The two Vietnamese were about 50 meters to the south of the house, and Joe and I were to the north at the edge of the clearing. As the two Cambodians approached the house, we all came under sudden and intense automatic weapons fire. The Cambodians were killed immediately, shot down right in front of the place. The other pair took off to the southwest, and Joe and I took off almost directly into the attack, where they'd least expect us to go. That was actually the only thing we could do.

We ran hard for the first few hundred meters. We could hear the NVA yelling to each other; we understood enough of the language to tell they knew we were Americans. I remember tripping and getting my feet tangled in a vine. Joe asked, in an almost conversational voice, "Could you please hurry up?" I chuckled at that, even then.

We made our way back with minor contact with the enemy. The other two guys, the Vietnamese, were killed by a patrol of strikers from our own camp. They were in black pajamas and didn't identify themselves properly and weren't recognized. Joe and I also had trouble entering the camp, but ultimately we identified ourselves and made it back inside.

The same Lieutenant Toi appeared at Dong Xoai, and this was beginning to be too much of a coincidence. Once again he looked surprised to see me. It was one of the closest times I have ever been to death, even more than at Dong So, which was much more intense. At Dong So the confusion and darkness provided a kind of cover; at Dong Xoai there wasn't any protection at all. Joe and I ran the whole way back, about 8 or 9 kilometers!

Dong Xoai Cooking School

The camp wasn't yet set up to support the multipurpose reaction force. At the beginning we didn't get a proper resupply of food. We did manage to get one planeload of ammunition, but after a few days we were out of rice and everybody was hungry.

One day a vendor appeared with a supply of sugarcane on the back of a little horse, and I bought the whole load for the strikers. Every single person in the force was soon chewing on chunks of that sugar cane. The vendor started to complain about the price; he had decided that he ought to have bargained for more money. But he stopped when I started looking at his little horse in a way that we might want it, too, for dinner. The troops were very annoyed that the horse walked out of town!

We got on the "horn" [radio] and finally got through to the B team and convinced them to get Captain Bob Saltzman [the S-4 logistics officer] to send us some supplies. The troops would rebel if they weren't paid or if they didn't have food. So, finally the Caribou flew over and dumped several pallet loads on the camp. We got enough C-rations for one meal for everybody, about one day's food for each man. The strikers weren't familiar with the little P-38 can opener, and for the next few days we had a lot of guys with knife wounds to the hand, received when they tried to open the cans with bayonets. The Nungs didn't like the ham and lima beans, or the cold scrambled eggs and ham, any better than the Americans did. We radioed back to headquarters and said, "We've got to get better food!"

The next day another Caribou flew over and dropped us some chow. We got a pallet of Aunt Jemima pancake mix, a pallet of canned salmon, a pallet of asparagus tips, and a pallet of Tabasco sauce! The Mike Force strikers were very disgruntled as we gave them their pancake (cooked on a section of tin roofing material), a can of salmon, a can of asparagus, and a bottle of Tabasco sauce. Off they went to stab at the damn cans again, mixed with Chinese cursing as the guys flung the cans as far as they could throw them. It became so serious that we finally called for an evacuation; we'd been there long enough that the guys were really pissed!

Ambush at Tieu Ea Da

Our Mike Force got called to the airstrip at Tieu Ea Da one day, and you could tell that something was up. There was an urgency in the air. A Vietnamese artillery lieutenant with three "tubes" had been assigned to set up his battery to provide supporting fire for a Delta unit operating near the border. He took a wrong turn and ended up at a wrong set of map coordinates. It was at the same time that a Vietnamese airborne ranger battalion was being committed and later annihilated.

One of our FAC spotter planes noticed the VC converging on these tubes, and we got the call to urgently get out to this little unit to get them some support. We took off and moved to the west of the camp, 6 or 7 kilometers. I took my recon platoon, and we ran down the highway. On the way we investigated some potential ambush positions along the highway. I wanted to put a reinforced platoon in one of the most likely places, a banana plantation, but got overruled. We pressed on to find the artillery.

When we arrived a big argument developed. The lieutenant didn't think he ought to be taking orders from an American NCO. It took all afternoon to convince him that he ought to leave this position. Both conditions—the lost little lieutenant and the attitude—were typical problems we had to deal with.

I sent my platoon on a patrol. At that moment we were light on manpower, and both my team sergeant and interpreter were unavailable to me. My platoon at that point was only 18 other guys, all Nungs. We had a few compasses and no good radios.

The biggest hazard to the teams was getting shot by our own guys as we reentered the perimeter, so we had ways to minimize the hazard. One method was to come back in at a certain point at a predetermined time. I elected to stay at the rally point, alone.

While I waited, I thought about how beautiful this particular area was, how much it reminded me of the part of Wisconsin where I had grown up. I resisted the desire to take a nap in this beautiful, peaceful place. Even the roads reminded me of the logging roads back home. I was lying behind an earthen berm, motionless and virtually invisible.

The first team was due back in and was supposed to enter from due south of my position. I saw a guy walking toward me on the right azimuth at the right time, and carrying the right weapon (a U.S.-issue M1 carbine). What I didn't notice at the time was that he wasn't carrying a rucksack or other gear. He kept walking until he was quite close to me before I moved slightly, and then he noticed me. At the same moment, I realized I was looking at a VC, and he realized he was looking at an American. We looked at each other. We both tried to bring our weapons to bear, but he disappeared before I could get a shot off at him. I don't know if he was lost and looking for his unit, or had come up out of a hole, or what, but he was alone and that was the last I saw of him. I fired one shot in the air to alert the boys. We used the same technique as the VC.

The patrol came in shortly thereafter, crawling because of the warning shot. They hadn't seen the lone soldier, but they had seen large numbers of VC massing in the area. The VC knew where the artillery tubes were, and they seemed to be getting ready to take them.

We headed back to camp, slogging through rice paddies and then through the banana plantation. There were fresh foxholes everywhere. We reported the holes over the radio, and we were told to press on. We proceeded, but off the road, in the cover of the plantation.

The artillery finally started to move—right down the road, without any flankers out for support. As they were driving down the road, a VC recoilless rifle opened up on them and shot up the Vietnamese unit very badly.

We got pinned down by a fairly small force and took cover in a rice paddy. I thought we'd have to wait till dark, but some gunships and fast-movers arrived, and at least one of the gun tubes was fired into the ambush by an American sergeant.

GREEN BERET WEAPONS

The basic weapon issued to Green Berets was the CAR-15, a compact version of the M16 with a shorter barrel and a collapsible stock. It fires a high-velocity bullet about a quarter inch in diameter, singly or in bursts. It, like the M16, is fussy about ammunition and about cleaning; problems with either result in stoppages. Stoppages in combat, I can tell you, are not a lot of fun.

One quite popular weapon with SF is the AK-47, and it didn't come through the normal supply channels; if you wanted one you normally had to kill the guy who had it first. It is a very different weapon from the M16, and much admired by Green Berets for its reliability. This seemed a little odd at the time, since everything the Russians made was supposed to be crude, coarse, and unreliable copies of U.S. technology. Its major flaw may have been a noisy safety; whenever SF teams heard the distinctive metallic klatch coming from the underbrush they knew the next few minutes were likely to be filled with action-packed adventure.

Another favorite tool was the M79 grenade launcher, a little shoulder-fired 40-millimeter artillery piece. It looks like a rifle that has been in a bad accident; it's short, with a big barrel and a funny stock. It throws a kind of grenade up to about 300 meters in an arc, and with it you can beat up on the opposing team way over there, behind the dike. Besides the high-explosive warhead, the M79 fires smoke, illumination, tear gas, and the "bean-bag" projectile. This latter device was no more than a bag with sand inside, but if you needed a prisoner and wanted a live one, the bean-bag round delivered a solid punch that would knock a guy down for the count without having him leak all his essential juices. Then you could invite him back to meet the folks at home and to have a little chat with the intel weenies.

—Hans Halberstadt

EXTRACTING WATER BUFFALO
CHARLES BERG

Charles Berg served two and a half tours with Special Forces in Vietnam before losing a leg in combat. He left the Army as a captai, and now works for the Veterans Administration.

Studies and Observation Group

My first tour was with the Mike Force, working with Nung tribesmen, mostly out of Nha Trang, before they became the Mobile Strike Forces assigned to each of the four corps areas. These were the soldiers that later went on to the projects—Omega, Sigma, and the rest.

The idea behind the Studies and Observation Group [SOG] was using the Mike Force system, but with the Yards as well as the Nungs. In fact, by the time SOG got started, the Nungs had been pretty well used up. A lot of them were starting to think that the war might not be such a good deal. I can't blame them.

SOG missions were usually five days long. A soldier can't carry enough food for longer than that, and that's about the limit of endurance for a man in that kind of situation. After five days of humping through the brush, off the trails, you could get pretty well worn out. And once you got compromised, you just ran, even with that rucksack on, to get away.

Water Buffalo Don't Die Easily

My first mission with the Mike Force was just outside of Nha Trang on what was supposed to be a relatively safe operation. During the night, while we were in our positions, we started hearing a lot of noise moving toward us. The Nungs had good fire discipline, though, and held their fire. It sounded like a whole company of NVA moving through the jungle toward us. The Nungs finally opened up, and somebody sent up a flare. Then we could see the "enemy": a herd of about 20 water buffalo. Well, let me tell you, water buffalo are big, and they don't die very easily.

When the sun came up the next morning there were all these water buffalo in various stages of demise. I thought it was awful, but the Nungs were delighted! They were trying to finish off the animals with the little M1 carbines they were issued at the time, but the bullets were bouncing off the buffaloes' skulls.

They butchered the animals, and we called for the helicopters to come in and get us. The Marines showed up with CH-46s, dropped the ramps, came down, and then all the Nungs started coming aboard with what looked like bloody, mangled bodies. The crew chiefs were looking at all this blood and raw meat—and happy, smiling Nung faces—and just didn't know what to make of it.

The aircraft commander knew that we'd called for extraction and figured things had gone sour in a big way. Then we all came aboard with what looked like a lot of mangled bodies. When he found out what had really happened, he was pissed. He hauled us back to the FOB and landed right in the middle of the compound, creating a huge dust storm that engulfed the whole camp.

Unfortunately for the aircraft commander, though, a delegation of senior MACV officers was inspecting the place at the time, and the dust storm was not appreciated. As a very junior NCO, I took this opportunity to exit stage left and tried to become invisible. We took a lot of kidding about that operation for a long time.

OP 34 and 35

I had been back in the States for about five months when I realized it was about time to go back to Vietnam. I volunteered and went to work with SOG. I was assigned to OP 35A, 35B, and 34 [these were experimental, super-secret programs in covert operations].

One of these involved our training Vietnamese hoodlums and gangsters, straight out of prison. We taught them basic military skills and how to function as small, three- or four-man teams. Then we took them up to North Vietnam, where they were parachuted into enemy territory. While our success rate with these guys wasn't very high, it was pretty good under the circumstances. Some of them lasted quite a long time and did some good work. But others were "rolled up" right away—they were either captured or they immediately surrendered to the NVA.

The actual operations involved these hoodlums teamed with Vietnamese airborne or rangers. The gangsters were well paid, and there wasn't a whole lot of choice for them; they had to go into the Vietnamese army one way or another, or stay in prison. Most of them became pretty well motivated, although one-third of them were VC infiltrators. They were weeded out, one way or another (Detachment B-56 or -57 court-martialed a couple of guys for their "weeding" techniques). You dealt with them the best way you could, including telling the Vietnamese to take care of them, which they did, by killing them. I don't know if many Americans did that.

In theory and in fact we really were advisors in this program because we didn't jump in with the teams, we just took them up there and dropped them off. There was a Vietnamese team leader for each operation, and the only control we had was the radio. Once they were inserted, though, I didn't have any more contact with them. Any communications with them were in code. I never saw any of the guys I trained come back out.

Most of them were compromised, often by a lack of logistic support. And, it really wasn't too tough for the NVA to figure out what was going on when the bombs started dropping on their convoys and troops in the jungle. The teams were operating in the NVA's back yard, and it didn't usually take the NVA too long to beat the bushes and find the teams. These guys were dropped with the old, hand-cranked radios, and the only way they could get out of North Vietnam was to walk out.

One of the ARVN sergeants I worked with in the program had walked out of North Vietnam three times! He told me, "You fight and then go home. I have been here all my life. I have to fight, and then fight again."

It was a different perspective than we had, and I can't blame some of them for being reluctant to keep at it. They were in a meat grinder, and they knew it.

I worked with these guys for four or five months before being assigned to a recon team up at FOB-1. I did that for a few months, and then I got assigned to Special Projects at Khe Sanh, just before the Marines took over. While on a recon in Laos in February 1967, I got wounded in the legs and was med-evaced back to the States for an obligatory two-and-a-half month hospital stay.

Khe Sanh

I was in-processing in Da Nang and discovered that SOG had grown up while I was gone; they now had launch sites all over the place. Even so, I had just about convinced the guy behind the desk that I ought to be assigned to NKP when I heard a voice behind me say, "Welcome to hard times!" It was Sergeant Major Dick Piegram, a man who had about six years in the country by that time and was already a living legend. He said, "I got a job for you up at Khe Sanh." I whined and sniveled, but he said, "Let's go," and off I went.

It rained and rained at Khe Sanh. It was muddy, and it got muddier. It was miserable. The siege began. That was in January 1968, and it was incredible. There we were, in the trenches. I was thinking that it was just like World War II. This was not what I went into Special Forces to do. It was awful.

The TDY teams from Okinawa started coming in to support and reinforce us. Russ Mann [his stories are elsewhere] was one of these, and so was Sergeant Bob Scully. We watched the town of Khe Sanh get hammered, day after day, and then finally overrun.

116

We were living in the trenches and bunkers, getting hammered by the NVA artillery night and day. We could listen in on the NVA artillery spotter's radio traffic, and it was clear that they not only had us surrounded, but they could also see everything that was going on inside the camp.

There were a lot of wounded, and artillery coming in, and we got a report of an American getting hit and needing to be collected and brought back to the casualty evacuation station. Bob Scully and I grabbed a stretcher and headed out of our bunker. These bunkers were well constructed, designed to take a B-52 strike, since we intended to call them in on the camp when and if it got overrun.

We got about 12 steps out of the bunker when I heard the artillery coming in on us. When the rounds are close but not right on you, they have a kind of distinctive warbling, whistling sound— but the one I heard didn't. I knocked Bob down with the stretcher, and then the round went off right in front of me. I was knocked flat on my back.

When this happens to you, you go through a little checklist, working through your systems one at a time. I opened my eyes, and I could see. I checked my ears, and I could hear. My nose was okay, my arms were okay, my right foot was okay; but my left foot didn't move too well. I knew I had a problem. Then I looked down and could see that I was badly hit.

I crawled back to the bunker and just fell down the steps. I went down head over heels, and when my leg came around and hit me on the back of the head, I knew I had a serious problem. The leg was just attached by just a little skin at the front of the thigh, the bone shattered at the hip. I looked up at young Sergeant Mann, who had just arrived at the camp, and heard him say, "You're going to be okay!"

And I remember telling him, "No, I'm not!" Bob Scully and Russ Mann did the amputation, and they did a super job, right at the hip. When I got back to the States, the doctors were amazed that I had even survived. After a year and a half in the hospital, I got out of the Army, went back to school, and got on with my life.

SPECIAL FORCES: A SHORT HISTORY

There are two major parts to the history of U.S. Army Special Forces: before John F. Kennedy and after John F. Kennedy. The parentage of the modern organization is officially traced to World War II and two rather different units, the Office of Strategic Services (OSS) and the U.S. Army Rangers. The OSS mission was highly clandestine; tiny groups of men and women were parachuted into enemy-held territory where they help organize, coordinate, and direct the efforts of resistance groups, mostly in France and Burma. There was nothing very covert about the Rangers, a small infantry combat organization selected and trained for the most challenging missions. Entire Ranger companies were consumed by the German defenses on D-Day. The OSS and Rangers were never popular with the Army's senior staff and were disbanded after the war.

The real birth of Special Forces happened at Fort Bragg's Smoke Bomb Hill in 1952, and Colonel Aaron Bank was the proud father. Bank didn't buy the notion that future wars were going to be just like World War II, but with even more tanks, airplanes, and nuclear weapons. Bank had been an "operator" behind the lines in France during the big war and was sure that there were some lessons to be learned from the experience, applicable to whatever war the United States might fight in the future.

Well, the Army didn't think much of these odd, unmilitary people when they were called the OSS, and they hadn't changed their minds. The new unit, christened the 10th Special Forces Group (Airborne), was a bastard child, unloved by anyone except the lunatic fringe. Naturally, the unit attracted every hardcore oddball in the Army—and there were plenty to choose from. Bank insisted on the unit being all-volunteer (no draftees, thank you) and all Airborne (that means "paratrooper" to all you "legs" in the audience). Volunteers needed to have several years in the Army and be on at least their second enlistment. This was quite different from the massive formations of two-year draftees in their starch and polish, counting the minutes until they were discharged.

Just as the conventional force generals feared, 10th Special Forces Group instantly became home to every weirdo in the ranks, people who just refused to play by the program designed by and for very conventional strategies and tactics. Colonel Banks' little rat pack was often used to play the role of adversaries in war games, and in highly insubordinate fashion, refused to fight fair or by the script. The "guerrillas" used all sorts of ruses and disguises to sneak up on the commanders of the conventional units, then "killed" or "captured" the generals and destroyed the battle plans. It drove some officers, particularly in the 82nd Airborne Division, nuts. God, it was fun!

When John F. Kennedy became president in January 1961 he learned of this organization from an aide. He was intrigued and fascinated; it was just the sort of novel thinking that matched his own. He visited Fort Bragg to inspect both the 82nd Airborne and Special Forces. He knew about the prohibition of the green beret at Bragg (it was worth a court-martial), but as commander in chief, he had the power to change that, and he did.

Kennedy sent SF to Vietnam as a kind of experiment, to see if the basic theories that the OSS used in France and Burma would work against a communist enemy in an unconventional war. It quickly appeared that it did, especially with the tiny mountain tribes who lived on the key terrain to the conflict. Kennedy championed and protected SF from the rest of the Army, then he was assassinated. He is still revered and mourned within the community, particularly among the old soldiers, and that visit to Bragg more than 30 years ago remains a benchmark moment in SF history.

Since the end of the war in Southeast Asia, the Army's interest in special operations has waxed and waned, and the emphasis on the unconventional warfare mission has ebbed away to near invisibility.

119

Since then Special Forces have largely retreated from the limelight, into the shadows of covert operations. But small SF training teams still assist the armies of many nations around the world with professional development—the same kind of instruction offered by those OSS operators in Europe and Burma half a century ago.

The ranks of today's active-duty SF companies and teams include few veterans of Vietnam, but many of the attitudes and traditions of the organization remain. It still cherishes its characters, and it is still a place where individual integrity is the prime qualification for admission.

—Hans Halberstadt

THE LEGEND OF THE GREEN BERET

The green beret has always been a symbol of a guy who was a bit different from the people in other Army units. Over the years it was a symbol that had to be earned the hard way, by each individual. Then, in the new kinder, gentler Army of the 1980s, somebody decreed that everyone assigned to a Special Forces unit, qualified or not, wore the same headgear. That policy has recently been revised back to the traditional Q-course graduate limitation.

The first berets came from a ladies' apparel shop in Fayetteville, North Carolina, in 1952 and looked just darling. A trio of young sergeants bought them to wear out on maneuvers against the 82nd Airborne; they were playing the role of partisans and wanted to dress the part. Berets were definitely partisan uniform issue during World War II. A guy named Don Gabe got the green one. Green is the traditional infantry color, and green berets were items of uniform issue in the Canadian, British, French, and other armies of the time. Somehow the idea caught on as a kind of private little tradition for field operations. Then guys started wearing them in garrison, and the poop hit the propeller.

Wearing a green beret at Fort Bragg was worth a court-martial right up until about 10 minutes before President John F. Kennedy arrived in 1961. He'd heard about the prohibition and (earning the undying gratitude of the community) ordered the SF soldiers he was to inspect to wear the beret. Somebody made a mad dash to Canada, and the Canadian Army supplied the 800 berets.

It is a rather useless piece of headgear, except for impressing women or getting into fights. It doesn't keep the sun out of your eyes, it doesn't keep your head warm, and it makes "liberals" wonder how many babies you've killed this morning. It is never worn in a tactical environment, and when you see photos of people sneaking through the brush wearing berets, you can bet it is only because the visiting idiot civilian journalist has sniveled and whined, "But nobody will know you're Green Berets if you don't have them on!"

The beret does have one useful function: When you are bouncing around in the back of a C-130 on a low-level insertion mission and you start to get airsick, it makes an excellent barf bag.

—Hans Halberstadt

DUMB STUNTS
GERRY SCHUMACHER

Gerry Schumacher retired as a colonel in 1997, after 32 years of service with the U.S. Army and U.S. Army Reserves.He spent over 20 of those years in Special Forces. Like many career SF officers, he started out with a tour as an enlisted soldier, went to OCS, and then built a career in Special Forces.

First Blood

I came into Vietnam as a 21-year-old captain and was assigned to a MAT [military advisory team] team. I'd previously served a tour in Korea as an enlisted man, then, following OCS, spent several years in Germany as a platoon leader and company commander. In spite of my young age, this background gave me a fair amount of experience, more than most young officers coming out of OCS going straight to Vietnam.

My first combat operation was a night ambush with a platoon-minus (about 20 PF [Popular Forces] soldiers) plus my interpreter, my American NCO, and myself. The setup was classic: We set up about eight or nine at night, just at twilight. Then about ten we shifted positions into our final ambush location. We were lined up as an inverted L along two trails. Because of the terrain, we were prevented from setting up as well as we might have on one side.

My NCO was a veteran of the Korean War and already had a couple of tours in Vietnam by that time. He was taking me under his wing, teaching me the ropes, trying to keep me out of trouble. He and I were at the corner of the ambush, in the center.

About two in the morning I noticed a figure standing above me. He was dodging side to side, obviously trying to look at me. I thought at first that it was one of the South Vietnamese—the squad or platoon leader—who had come back to talk to us. While I was trying to figure all this out, about the time I realized I might be looking at an NVA, the guy tried to fire on me. But he had a stoppage of some sort, an empty chamber or a jam, because I heard the click as he pulled the trigger, and I heard the bolt go back to clear the weapon.

In a split second I concluded that this must be what it is all about, and in my sharp fear and terror I unloaded the entire magazine of my .45-caliber "Grease Gun" into the guy. I hit him with nearly all the 30 .45-caliber rounds. He literally went airborne. He was raised off the ground by the impacts.

The rest of the ambush team then pivoted to their rear and started firing in our direction, right back at me, the NCO, and interpreter. The NVA took up their own fighting positions and started shooting—also in our direction! The three of us were trying to dig holes in the ground with our teeth at this point. There were hand grenades flying over us from our men, the NVA were shooting B-40s back into the position, and there were tracers coming from everywhere. I thought, "This has got to be hell."

Well, the NCO was a big guy, and he happened to be on top of the radio at that moment. I was trying to get to the radio to call for illumination, to make some sense of what was happening, and to call for some artillery. It was the only thing I could think of to do right then, but I could not get this guy off the radio! I finally had to brace my feet against him and my back against a tree to push him off the radio so I could get at it!

When the shooting stopped there turned out to be a couple of casualties on each side, far fewer than all the firing had suggested—although it scared the living crap out of me.

But the next day, when we got back to the compound, the NCO was telling everybody what a hero I had been, how I had killed about four of the VC myself, and how I had led the reaction—none of which I had done! I didn't deserve any of this praise. It took me a few minutes to figure out that the NCO was mortified because he had lain across the radio, and I couldn't get him off. Even though almost none of the praise was true, at least it helped establish my credibility with the team.

Ambush

We got intelligence that a large NVA unit was going to come into a village, and we mounted a large operation to ambush the enemy force. We put in six or seven ambush sites around the village. I went out with the RF unit that night. We moved into our designated locations, the preliminary one about nine o'clock. Then we started the shift to the final position about eleven. It was a black night; you couldn't see the hand in front of your face.

I was following a Vietnamese soldier. We moved for what seemed like a very long time—far too long. Normally a shift took only about 15 minutes, but we moved for at least an hour. I began to worry about the six other ambushes set up in this general area, any one of which we might be walking into. So I tapped the little Vietnamese guy on the shoulder and asked why we were still moving. He replied that he had lost sight of the guy in front of him about 45 minutes earlier and was trying to find the ambush position.

Well, I had no idea where we were now; we'd made all sorts of twists and turns in sugarcane fields, thickets, and underbrush. I said, "We are staying right where we are!" The little Vietnamese guy said he couldn't do that; his squad leader would kill him the next day if he didn't link up with the rest of the squad.

Behind me was the interpreter, my NCO, and three of the RF soldiers. We were the tail end of the ambush force. So we stopped—the NCO, the interpreter, and I—and all the Vietnamese insisted on going ahead. I thought it was pure suicide to proceed, and we sat down right where we were and waited. Not more than five minutes later, the four stumbled into the ambush position set up by the Korean White Horse Division soldiers, and all four were killed.

Meanwhile, though, the NVA battalion that we were after had gotten into the village undetected. When the Korean ambush started shooting, three or four of the others opened up as well, even though they didn't have targets. But the NVA in the village concluded that they had been discovered, and they broke and ran. And guess where this battalion decided to run? Right at the three of us, sitting there in the weeds, trying to stay out of trouble!

Somebody fired some illumination rounds, and now we could see—far too well! Suddenly we saw all these guys in pith helmets, with AKs, charging toward our position. I thought, Well, we have had it now! We lay as flat as we could and watched them stream past. Some of them ran past, then stopped to turn and fire back at the ambush sites.

A couple of the NVA dove into the bushes beside us, got off a few shots, and got back up to run again. As one was departing, he said the Vietnamese equivalent of "Come on, let's get out of here!" to us.

I told my NCO, "Don't shoot anybody!" It would have just drawn attention to our position, from both sides. So we stayed put all night, and at dawn we were still right there, with our eyeballs wide open. There were a few dead NVA around us, all casualties from the ambush. That was quite a feeling, to have a couple of companies of NVA charging all around us.

Pet Monkey

I had a pet monkey that I kept with me in my hooch. Whenever there was an attack, this monkey would quickly climb on me, wrap his arms and legs around my head, and start pissing on my face! I could not pry this damn monkey off my head. So here I was, running to the old French bunker that I used for a command post, with this monkey on my head, claws dug into my skull, pissing like hell on my face! Somehow, I just never got used to that.

126

"What Took You So Long?"

Two of my NCOs were assigned to a Montagnard compound that got hit one night. Most of the Yards broke and ran—and were shot in the back—but these two sergeants stayed in their position and kept fighting, alone, all night long. The NVA overran the entire compound. These guys had an M60 machine gun; during the fight they burned up one machine-gun barrel after another. The NVA dead piled up in front of their hole so deep that they had to go out at intervals and clear away the bodies to maintain their field of fire. They were surrounded by the NVA—dead NVA!

It took us all night to get a reaction force together and to get out there to their compound, fighting some NVA on the way. When we arrived, these two guys were still sitting in their hole, still surrounded by bodies, drinking beer.

"What took you so long?" one of them asked me. They were unscathed. These two guys were just about the only survivors from the entire force. They were quite nonchalant about the whole thing.

Ruff-Puffs

I worked with many foreign military, paramilitary, and local militia units in Vietnam. There were the "Ruff-Puffs" [RF-PF, Regional Forces and Popular Forces], the People's Self Defense Force, the Revolutionary Development Cadre, the Provincial Reconnaissance Units, the Montagnards, a Korean army battalion from the White Horse Division, and to a lesser extent, the regular Vietnamese army. I didn't really work with U.S. Army units. In fact, outside of our team members, we rarely saw other Americans.

My first assignment to Vietnam was to MACV, subassigned to MAC Corps, and assigned as a MAT team leader. A MAT team was set up like a Special Forces A-team, only smaller: a heavy weapons specialist, a light weapons specialist, a medic, an assistant team leader, and a team leader (five guys as opposed to twelve on an A-team). We were supposed to do with the Ruff-Puffs what the A-teams were doing with the Montagnards: advise them, train them, take them on operations. The ops were more militia-type missions, protecting villages and patrolling, than the long-range recons that the Yards were doing.

After I had served as MAT team leader for four or five months, I was assigned to be district senior advisor. That was a pretty good assignment for a young, 21-year-old captain—a job that would normally go to a 38-year-old major or above. It was the largest district in South Vietnam, and it was in many ways a showcase district, with demonstration hamlets and a lot of attention.

Things started to change in my compound, an old Chinese fort with a moat, a big wall, and big gates at the front and back. You could fire a missile through the front gate, and it would sail right through, out the back gate. The place was indefensible.

Inside were the quarters for the district chief, his headquarters staff, his guards, and the largest Special Forces A-team ever assembled, Detachment A-503, with 35 men. Two of my MAT teams came in from time to time, but normally they were always operating outside the camp. Finally, we had a district team in the fort, too, with the intelligence people and the folks who ran the teams on operations.

We supervised 34 villages and 14 hamlets. The villages each had a PF platoon guarding it, plus three Regional Force [RF] companies. These RF companies were each set up in classical triangular compounds, with barbed wire and firing pits all in exactly the same place in each one, just as the French had designed them many years ago. Also within the district were 12 CIDG [Civilian Irregular Defense Group] companies that were mostly managed by the SF A-team inside my compound.

The A-team had built a compound within the compound because the Yards didn't trust the Ruff-Puff Vietnamese at all. The whole compound wasn't more than three or four city blocks from one side to the other, only about 400 meters across.

As part of the defenses of the compound, we had a 100-kilowatt generator inside the SF compound to power a series of big spotlights that illuminated the perimeter at night. Well, many of the Vietnamese brought their families into the compound with them, and almost all of them were tapping into the output of this generator. Inevitably, they would overload the generator, and it would go out. We would then be attacked by the VC, and we couldn't turn on the lights! The district chief literally threatened people with execution for tapping into the lines, but they continued to anyway. And you could bet that, just as soon as we had a blackout, the VC would attack.

All in the Family

I had a Ruff-Puff soldier who told me that he knew that the VC were going to visit a particular village that night, where they were going to be resupplied. So we took the Popular Force platoon out and set up an ambush. When the VC showed up, we killed about 10 of them!

The next morning the district chief flew out to pin medals on this platoon, especially the guy with the information. This was a big deal for them, and three or four got medals for their bravery.

We had killed these VC near a house that they had gone to for supplies. I discovered that one of the PF soldiers in my platoon lived in that house, and that one of the VC we had killed was his brother! While we were decorating this guy, his family was weeping over the body of their other son, his Viet Cong brother, just a few feet away!

Another incongruity: We had an old woman in our district with cancer. Even though her son was a notorious Viet Cong leader and on our Phoenix hit list, we took her into Nha Trang for regular treatments. Sergeant Sattamore and I drove her to Nha Trang about 15 times for radiation treatment to reduce her tumor.

The war was like that for me, much more personal than for other Americans. We knew the enemy, often by name. The enemy knew us by name too. I found my name on one of their hit lists one time; they had their own Phoenix program.

Tet

It is a Vietnamese tradition that the first visitor of the new year brings luck, good or bad. So it was the district chief's new year routine to visit the village chiefs in each of his 14 villages on Tet, the Vietnamese new year, and he took me with him.

The problem with this was that you had to have something to eat and drink with each and every one. None of the chiefs would let you leave without drinking some of his special brew and eating some special delicacy. We would eat and drink and visit for maybe half an hour, then leave to go visit the next village.

Some of these villages and hamlets were pretty safe, but many were virtually VC communities. Normally, the district chief was very cautious about moving around and visiting these places, but for some reason, not on Tet. This district chief had been a member of the Viet Minh and had fought against the French. I later learned that he struck deals with the VC, and I believe that he was striking deals that day while we were visiting.

By the end of that day, he and I were so drunk that we couldn't see straight. I have never been more sick, or more drunk, in my life. I ate countless fish heads and chicken eyeballs, and drank more rot-gut booze. I'm surprised that I didn't die of alcohol poisoning! We were staggering into E hamlets (the least pacified, virtually enemy controlled), and the VC could have shot me with an RPG [rocket-propelled grenade], and I wouldn't have felt it.

Miles from the Closest Meatball

While the regular SF camps were on the end of some sort of supply line, MACV completely forgot about those of us in the CORDS program. If we wanted a steak or spaghetti and meatballs, we had to go over to the A-team compound and beg a plate. We didn't get anything from the American food supply system except C-rations. When I asked them where our chow was, they replied, "You're on per diem." But what the hell was per diem out in the hamlets, 200 miles from the closest meatball!

The MACV attitude was, "Send them out there, and they will figure out a way to survive." I really resented it. Not once in my entire time out there did I get even one warm American meal sent to us by MACV! So we got them the old-fashioned Green Beret way—we stole them!

Every time we picked up an NVA pistol, an SKS carbine, or any other booty, we took that right into Cam Ranh—and we made sure that we had a real good war story to go along with it! In fact, we had a little mama-san sewing up these VC and NVA flags for us. We shot chickens and let them bleed all over flags; the guys in the rear area were real suckers for that. Actually, the best technique was to pull the chicken's head off and let the blood just squirt out on to the flag; there were fewer incriminating feathers that way.

Our favorite story to go with the flag was that three enemy soldiers came running up the hill and tried to plant this flag in our compound, but that our guys got them all and the flag was booby-trapped, and two of our men died taking it down! Well, the mess sergeants would just eat all this up, and we could trade that flag for all the steaks, fruits, and vegetables we could carry. That was, honest to God, how we had to operate. That is exactly how we got American food!

If, for whatever reason, we couldn't get anything and were out of C-rations, we ate what the Vietnamese ate—rice balls with leaves and stuff mixed in. Now, my wife tells me when we go out to exotic restaurants that I'm not very adventurous because I prefer steaks and hamburgers to things like dolmatis [a Greek dish featuring rice and lamb wrapped in grape leaves]. I have had all the adventurous food I want, thank you.

Throwing the Book at the NVA

When you worked with the Ruff-Puffs, you were at the very bottom of the priority list for air and artillery fire support. The NVA knew this. So when we got into a battle with the NVA, we were not only fighting with a less-skilled force than an American unit, we could expect little or any support from artillery or the Air Force. In a way, though, that gave us an advantage that many American units didn't have. The enemy didn't avoid fighting us.

While some people might say that is a disadvantage, we didn't have the frustrations that the Americal Division, for example, did. When they made contact, the NVA broke off and disappeared right away. They would leave large quantities of booby traps behind them, and these American units would take large numbers of casualties from the booby traps, without even the satisfaction of a good firefight. Their frustration levels built accordingly, to the point where their behavior as units was sometimes erratic because they wanted revenge on an enemy who had been hurting them, unseen, for years.

But in my case there was a kind of catharsis in our ability to meet, engage, and defeat the enemy—to shoot them and kill them. We had some fairly long (for Vietnam) engagements with the NVA. It was not uncommon to fight it out with them. These engagements were typically at night; only three or four of my engagements were in daylight.

One of these, though, was rather comical. We had cornered some NVA in a rice paddy. (Well, on second thought, if they were here telling the story, it was they who had cornered us.) I called for close air support, but the available aircraft had already expended their cannon and machine-gun ammunition. They still had some napalm and some 500-pound iron bombs, though, and dropped that for us. The two fast-movers went back to rearm while the FAC stayed overhead.

When the close air support aircraft left, the NVA decided it was a good time to close with us. They started coming across the rice paddies at us. This kind of behavior—a daylight, prolonged engagement—was completely unlike what they would do with an American unit. It was obvious that they thought they could take us.

The FAC could see that we were in trouble, serious trouble, and even though he didn't have any fast-movers to control, he made runs on the NVA, firing his marking rockets among the enemy soldiers in the open. This confounded the enemy. They knew what the marking rounds were, but they didn't see any fast-movers, so they kept coming.

The next thing I knew, the FAC came flying by, 100 feet off the deck, firing his little .38-caliber revolver out the window! He started throwing anything in the cockpit at them. He made pass after pass at the NVA, dropping smoke grenades next. In fact he threw the book at them—his aircraft log book!

As desperate as the situation was, I will always remember looking up from that attack and watching all that paper fluttering out of the sky. The poor FAC must have been mighty frustrated, because he was taking hits on every pass. After about a half hour of this, while the NVA were closing in and we were trying desperately to break contact, a flight of four F-4 Phantoms arrived on station. They started laying napalm on the NVA and fried a bunch of them. Our goose would have been cooked if they hadn't arrived.

But that behavior shows the kind of love and brotherhood that we had for each other, even between the Army and the Air Force, in Vietnam. You sometimes hear about the "fragging" and the protests and the other problems of the Vietnam era, but incidents like that one are, to me, much more indicative of how we got along with each other. Never before in my life, and never in my life again, will I experience that kind of brotherhood and mutual support. It infuriates me to see Vietnam described so often in a negative way, when so often people really cared for each other.

People's Self-Defense Force

We got a call one night that one of our PSDF [People's Self-Defense Force] hamlets had been hit by the NVA. Now, the PSDF was a program I personally thought was stupid. It gave guns to old men and children who didn't know how to use them; they were supposed to be able to defend their own communities, but they just managed to get themselves into trouble.

Anyway, the PSDF in this particular hamlet made the serious mistake of firing on the NVA and were getting their butts kicked as a result. They had a lot of women and children injured, and we had to go try to help them.

Somebody had to go in to mark an LZ so the "dust-off" [medical evacuation] helicopter could come in and get the wounded out. According to the report, the NVA had broken contact, and the engagement was over.

We got airborne from our compound—just myself, one of my NCOs, and my interpreter. But the PSDF were so unskilled that they couldn't even mark the little courtyard where we were supposed to land. We were flying around in the dark trying to identify our LZ. Finally, we spotted what we thought was the right place and came in. Just at treetop height, prior to landing, the pilot turned on his landing light to make sure that we weren't going to hit any wires or obstructions. I could see 30 or 40 VC and NVA soldiers with AK-47s, SKSs, and I realized that we were landing in the village school yard, rather than the courtyard where we were supposed to go.

It was obvious to me that this was where the enemy had regrouped after the initial attack. We were only about 2 feet off the ground when I realized what was happening; I opened up with my M16 on full auto. The VC and NVA were apparently in shock as a result of the helicopter attempting to land directly in their midst. Even so, they recovered quickly, and some started to fire on us.

But the helicopter door gunner didn't understand what was happening. He mistook them for the PSDF villagers and tried to take my M16 away from me, thinking I was trying to kill innocent civilians; we nearly had a firefight between the two of us. Only when he noticed them firing at us did he get his cue and open up with his M60.

We pulled up and out of the school yard. The pilot called that he thought we had taken some hits. He managed to find the right LZ this time, and we settled into the courtyard where the PSDF villagers were.

The villagers rushed the helicopter. Everybody was trying to get aboard: women—some with babies in their arms—children, old men. They were all trying to get on. But they weren't wounded, and we were there to get the casualties out. While we were trying to sort out the wounded from the uninjured, the VC and NVA attacked again. So we were tossing civilians off the helicopter because they weren't wounded, and then, right there in front of us, they were getting hit! I pulled one guy off the helicopter, and right while I was holding him, he got shot in the head. Half of his brains spattered all over my face!

Finally, a couple of gunships came on station and started putting some suppressive fires on the enemy force. The NVA assault petered out, and we were able to effect the dust-off. We were afraid to leave anybody in the village, so all of them were evacuated.

I was on the last chopper out. The flight back to Nha Trang and the hospital was weird. It was a hot night, humid and rainy; everything was wet, sticky, and uncomfortable. Finally, we landed at the hospital helo pad, and Sattamore and I walked into the emergency room. There were lots of wounded everywhere, some missing limbs, some with sucking chest wounds, others with brains leaking out of head wounds, others with less critical injuries, all waiting for attention.

The uninjured villagers were there, too, milling around without any guidance from anybody. They had been ejected from the emergency room, and now they were squatting on the tarmac in front of the place, talking and crying. Inside the hospital were babies, old men, children, grandmothers—injured, dead, and dying. It sent chills through me. I thought, How sick this whole war is!

I looked at my interpreter, a South Vietnamese soldier. He looked at me and asked, "What now, *Dai-uy*?"

There was a club nearby for the doctors and nurses (although open to other American personnel), a place called (I think) the Operating Room. So I took the interpreter, and we went down the street for a beer. As we got close to the place, we could hear the music—"I Can't Get No Satisfaction" was playing, as I recall—and we went in.

There were lots of American nurses and doctors dancing, everybody in their party clothes, the women in short little mini-skirts, all having a wonderful time. Of course, they had probably been up to their armpits in gore an hour or two before, and other doctors and nurses were busy up the road.

But the incongruity of it all was devastating. Just 100 yards away were kids, old folks, babies, a grandfather with his intestines hanging out—and they were in there dancing! Just a little earlier I had been out in that village with the NVA, with the gunships and the dust-offs. I thought about the NVA. They were off in the bushes some place, nursing their wounded too. We raked them with those Cobra gunships! And here the nurses were, in their tight, abbreviated little tops, dancing and laughing. It was very, very strange.

When we had gone into the village that night, there had been seven serious casualties; by the time we left there were forty-five. I was thinking, I should have just let those seven die, or left them there till morning. Maybe the NVA would have left. Maybe the only reason all those people got hurt was because we showed up, and the NVA responded to an opportunity. Did I make a mistake? I don't know. Of course, the NVA could just as well have finished off the whole village too. I will never know.

Dumb Stunts, Part I

I watched some Vietnamese do incredibly stupid things. One was on a patrol of our perimeter at night. We were moving down a trail, and, in the light of the illumination flares that the camp mortar team were sending up, you could clearly see a section of trip wire across the trail. I watched this little Vietnamese soldier go up to the trip wire. He looked at one end, he looked at the other, and then he reached out and pulled the wire! The last thing I saw of him was a fireball that enveloped him, blasting his body sky high. Everybody knew what that trip wire meant! Everybody was trained to avoid booby traps. It was so stupid.

Dumb Stunts, Part II

We had one guy on the A-team who had just arrived from Fort Bragg and the Q course and was out on a patrol with me. I guess they were pounding out Green Berets faster than normal, and he was one of those people who were run through a little too quickly, because he was not quite up to speed.

We moved down the trail behind the guy on his first real time on "point" [walking first in line in the patrol; the first target for the enemy]. He did all the hand and arm signals with crisp and dramatic precision and flare. Apparently this guy had watched a lot of war movies, because he scowled a lot on patrol.

He encountered a cave that needed to be cleared. With textbook precision, he directed the patrol to spread out in a skirmish line, then to drop down to the ground. He moved to the edge of the cave mouth, produced a hand grenade, and pulled the pin. He deftly chucked the grenade into the cave, just the way they teach at Bragg. Then he stepped to the cave mouth and fired a burst of full-auto into the cave, when the grenade detonated pretty much in his face. He had done everything by the book, except the little part about waiting for the grenade to go off.

The poor guy was not badly hurt; the grenade had rolled fairly far back into the cave before it went off. But when he turned around and came back to us, he had shrapnel sticking out of a cheek, little pieces in his chest, his arm. They were all little fragments, and none were at all serious. Once we determined that his injuries were slight, the whole team just rolled down the hill, laughing.

THE LATE, GREAT WALT SHUMATE
DOY MCPHAIL

*Doy McPhail retired from the U.S. Army as a sergeant major
after a long career in Special Forces.*

Sergeant Walt Shumate died of cancer in 1993, but he became one
of Special Forces' many living legends while alive, and his legacy
will linger for a long time. He asked that his ashes be spread on a
drop zone at Fort Bragg. Before he died, Walt prepaid a substantial
bar bill for his friends to get drunk in his honor. Most, but not all,
of Walt is now a part of that DZ, but one famous component is still
U.S. government property. In fact, Walt is still a visible presence at
Fort Bragg if you know where to look (I'm not going to tell you
where), because when he died, his mustache was removed with great
ceremony and is now framed and displayed on the wall of . . . well, if
you don't know, it's because you don't need to know.

I was a platoon sergeant in the 501st Battalion of the 82nd Airborne Division when one of the other NCOs from the 505th told
me, "If you're looking for a good soldier, get Walt Shumate. He
raises hell, but he's a good trooper. And they're trying to '208'
['undesirable' discharge] him out of the Army."

I started doing some checking, and the more I heard about
him, the more I thought he ought to be in my unit. It turned out
that he was always studying weapons and that kind of thing, and
he worked hard at soldiering. But even so, he was being brought
up before a 208 board.

At the conclusion of the hearing before the board, the colonel
said, "Private Shumate, is there anything you would like to say

to the board before we make our decision about what we'll do with you?"

"Sir," Walt said, "ever since I was a little boy, I always wanted to be a soldier. But it seems to me, ever since basic training, I know more than the sergeants. They resent it. . . ." He went on, and he just about had the colonel in tears. The board made its determination, and Walt stayed in the Army. The colonel promoted him to specialist 4th class and transferred him out of the unit. That's how I got him.

He and I ultimately went to Special Forces. He made three trips to Vietnam. He was a remarkable person. He had a way with people; they either hated him or loved him.

He retired as an E-9 in Delta [theU.S. Army's elite counter-terrorist force, commonly called "Delta Force"], then was a GS-13 safety officer here at Fort Bragg. He died in 1993, of cancer, and he left $500 in his will for the bar at the Green Beret Sport Parachute Club here to underwrite a party. He had everything worked out. He was Catholic, so they had a mass for him. After the service, we all went out to the drop zone and spread his ashes, then everybody adjourned to the bar.

MONTAGNARD MUTINY
VERNON GILLESPIE

The long years of anger and oppression finally boiled over on September 19, 1964, when the Montagnards rebelled against the South Vietnamese. Captain Vernon Gillespie's camp at Buon Brieng was the only one that didn't participate. That was because he saw it coming and acted to prevent the crisis.

Gillespie, Major Edwin Brooks, and several other SF officers, managed to suppress the rebellion with minimal loss of life. This was accomplished at great personal risk and was documented by National Geographic's legendary writer-photographer Howard Sochurek, who happened to be present when the mutiny began. These officers were rewarded for their gallantry by the U.S. Army in the traditional way when politics and integrity collide: They were sacked and censured.

Major Brooks alone confronted several hundred angry rebels and ordered them out of their positions and back to their compounds— and they went. As a result of this courage and initiative, his military career was destroyed. Vernon Gillespie describes the events.

Major Edwin Brooks was a B detachment commander in II Corps and his headquarters was in Pleiku. He commanded a number of A-detachments in the II Corps tactical zone, including the one I commanded, the camp at Buon Brieng. Major Brooks commanded the A-teams, but the actual command of the camps themselves was assigned to the Vietnamese Special Forces, the LLDB.

We recruited and trained strike forces. My camp had about 700 Montagnards under arms at Buon Brieng, a battalion. We trained, armed, and equipped these forces to secure the small portion of South Vietnam that surrounded our camp (primarily jungle), which contained infiltration routes used by the Viet Cong and, later, by the North Vietnamese Army to conduct operations in South Vietnam. The two tribes in the area were the Rhade and Jarai. Our camp at Buon Brieng was right between the two tribal areas, and I had recruits from both tribes. They worked well together and got along well with each other. I didn't have any trouble with them.

Our primary mission at my camp was running reconnaissance missions down toward the Laotian and Cambodian border to interdict the NVA infiltration routes. We also rescued captive Montagnards that the VC were using as laborers and porters at their way-stations. We brought those people back to Buon Brieng to get them away from the VC and deprived the VC of this source of labor.

There's one thing about Montagnards: Once you are accepted by them, they won't lie to you. So if you ask them leading questions, and they don't want to answer, they just won't tell you anything, which provides an answer of its own.

We noticed that something was wrong in the camp at Buon Brieng in late July and early August 1964. We didn't know what was wrong, but the tension was building among the Montagnards. Sometime about the middle of August, I briefed Major Brooks on the situation, and he believed me. Then I went down to Nha Trang and briefed the group commander. I had a friend in the CIA, and I told him too. He went to Saigon to brief the J-2 [Joint Services level intelligence officer] at MACV. The essence of the information that I passed to the higher headquarters was that tension was building, and it seemed that something would happen about the middle of September. That information was ignored by everybody except Major Brooks.

On September 19, all hell broke loose. The rebellion actually began the night before in our camp, and we were prepared for it. By the next morning we knew that the rebellion was occurring over a much wider area. The leaders of the Montagnard battalion at

Buon Brieng were receiving orders over our regular radio net to take specific actions.

I told the Montagnard battalion commander (a guy named Y Jhon Nie) that I was taking command of the camp and that the Vietnamese Special Forces in the camp were under U.S. protection. Any move against the Vietnamese would be considered a move against the U.S. government, and we would fight. Y Jhon kept the camp pretty much out of the events that followed. Once we put down the rebellion in Buon Brieng, Y Jhon and I got on a helicopter and flew down to Ban Me Thuot to see what we could do about the rebellion in that area.

I ran into Major Brooks there; he had flown down from Pleiku and had put together a rag-tag collection of U.S. Special Forces people from the liaison team at Ban Me Thuot and formed us into a group. We tried to get support from the local U.S. MACV personnel in the town, but they just stayed hunkered down and wouldn't give us any help at all.

On the afternoon of September 19, Major Brooks, completely on his own, took this little force and went to the radio station where the rebel commanders and about 100 Montagnard soldiers were sending orders to the rebel units around the highlands. I was part of a small force that secured the gate to the compound, and Major Brooks and the rest of the group went into the radio station and dragged the rebels out. Although I didn't see it myself, one of the guys who went in with him reported that he walked in and said, "Okay, get your asses out of here!" And they left!

They came out of the radio station. We tried to get some trucks from MACV to take them back to their compound at Bon Sar Pa just outside of Ban Me Thuot. When it became apparent that MACV wasn't going to furnish any trucks, Major Brooks ordered me to take a few of the other guys and march the rebels down the highway back to Bon Sar Pa, about 20 or 30 miles away.

At several places on the march we encountered Vietnamese army units in blocking positions along the highway. They had orders to prevent the rebels from getting into Ban Me Thuot. I went up to the Vietnamese commanders and told them what I was doing and told them not to fire on us. We were allowed to pass. Nobody really knew what was going on. We finally reached Bon Sar Pa, and Major Brooks arrived in a jeep. He told me to stay the night in the village, which I did, along with Y Jhon Nie, to try to keep track of what was going on.

By that time Special Forces had the rebellion under control throughout the region. The next morning, after everything was finally over, MAAG finally decided to get involved, and "Fritzy" [Colonel John] Freund moved in to take over. The Special Forces people were sent back to their camps.

Major Brooks was now in trouble. Out of six Montagnard camps, five rebelled. Only mine didn't rebel. There were a lot of questions asked and a lot of people in MAAG and MACV saying, "It was out of our control. We couldn't do anything about it." But then other people pointed out that Gillespie's camp didn't rebel, that it could have been controlled.

All the Special Forces camp commanders were relieved in the camps except me, although I was relieved two or three times later. And that's when Major Brooks started to fight. He was fighting for his commanders, to keep them from being relieved.

There was also an attempt by Special Forces headquarters down in Nha Trang to whitewash the whole event. Brooks fought the whitewash attempt too. Brooks went to bat for his A-detachment commanders against Colonel Spears, the commander of 5th Special Forces Group, and to prevent the cover-up. That's how Brooks got relieved, about a month later.

They brought in a new B detachment to run the operation out of Pleiku. Colonel John Spears was sent out to Vietnam by General Harold Johnson, then Army chief of staff, to bring Special Forces back into the Army. Spears was a damn good officer, but he was undoubtedly under all kinds of political pressure to get Special Forces under control.

An After-Action Report was written on the event, a document that was about an inch thick when it was finally published, classified secret. They presented the draft to me in late November and asked me to approve it. I read the document, and it was so inaccurate that I told them there was no damn way I could approve it. I insisted that they include a copy of my own After-Action Report as an annex to the document. If they were willing to do that, I told them, I wouldn't object to the report's publication.

The report was published and distributed to the Army worldwide as a "lessons-learned" document. Shortly thereafter, a *National Geographic* article was published. There was such a disparity between the official report and the *National Geographic* article that the inspector general of the U.S. Army conducted an investigation in January. My team and I were back on Okinawa by that time, and the investigation team visited us there. As a result, the original report was withdrawn, worldwide, and all copies were destroyed.

MEN, WUSSIES, AND BUMMERS
OTIS HEDGES "BANE" ASHLEY III

Otis Hedges Ashley III, nicknamed "Bane" by his mother ("You are the bane of my existence!" she is reported to have said) retired from the Army as a lieutenant colonel, then trained to be a veterinarian. He and his wife (also a former Army officer) spend a lot of time training for and competing in triathlons. Bane is working on a book about his many adventures.

"We Need Men, Not Wussies!"

If you were born a redneck, with a name like mine, you had to be ready to whip every single kid on the school bus every morning! I come from a long line of rednecks and criminals, moonshiners and gunrunners. I was abandoned when I was 14. I came home from school one day, and my parents weren't there. They never came back! I raised myself from then on, and life actually improved once I got in Special Forces. Combat was no big deal after my childhood! I lived out of an old car for a while, got out of school a bit early, and went to a scumbag recruiter and told him, "I'm 18. I need to be in the Army."

He said, "Right!"

I was 5 foot 3 1/2, 117 pounds, and 16 years old. The recruiter showed me how to juggle my birth certificate, and I went in the Army in January 1962. While I was in basic training, the recruiting team from the Airborne school came swinging through the windows during the sixth week, doing chin-ups and being manly. They pointed at me—the little "wussie" in the front row—and said, "We need men, not wussies like Ashley here!" Naturally, I immediately signed up. The same thing happened during advanced individual training, but with guys wearing berets. It was during the time when it was possible to sign up [for Special Forces] right out of basic, as a private, unlike later.

I am terrified of heights—still am, always will be, but I was very fortunate. I was the first third-generation military parachutist to go through the program at Fort Benning. Then it was on to "Special Forces" and Training Group, where I arrived as a wide-eyed 16-year-old. I was impressed with everything that moved or hopped or crawled. I fell in love with the whole military experience.

I was trained as an engineer and attended the HALO [high-altitude low-opening, the military free-fall parachute technique that involves jumping from a high altitude and waiting until you are about 3 feet above the ground to deploy your canopy] course. Shortly thereafter, I attended the Ranger School as a private first class. I made honor graduate at Ranger School, something of an accomplishment when you consider that we started with 156 people and 59 graduated. I think I was very fortunate to have served in combat in Vietnam with both the Rangers and with the Green Berets.

I went to OCS as an E-5 and was fortunate enough to make distinguished graduate there. Then I was sent back to Bragg and Smoke Bomb Hill to the newly formed 6th Group.

Hill 875

Shortly after I arrived in Vietnam as a 19-year-old freshly qualified Special Forces second lieutenant I was assigned to Detachment A-245, a team that was supposed to set up a camp at Dak Seang. The monsoon season made that momentarily difficult, so half of us were sent to Dak Pek, and half (including me) to Dak To. We staged out of these two camps with the teams assigned to those camps. While waiting for the rain to let up, we went on operations with the teams from these other two camps, A-244 and A-243.

146

My first real operation was a seven-day patrol that ended up putting us right on top of an element of the 304th NVA Division. We took out three platoons of Yards, the local guys we were training to go into Dak Seang with us. The other platoons got more experienced Americans, but the guy who went with me was a guy named Dunn [Specialist 4th class Creighton Dunn, killed in action October 29, 1966, at Dak To].We were both 19, but he looked 12, with blond hair and glasses, a nice guy but TDY from Okinawa. Neither of us had a lot of experience, although I had been to OCS and Ranger School by that time (having already been in the Army for three years).

The Yards in my platoon came from four different tribes, Banar, Sedang, Rhade, and Jarai. It was fortunate that among them was an old recruit who showed up with bits of his old French army uniform, complete with decorations and a kepi; he became the assistant platoon sergeant. The presence of this old colonial soldier just added to what was a very surreal climate on the patrol. The Yards were having a swell time for the first few days, sliding down hills, falling in the streams, laughing and enjoying themselves.

On the fourth day out, though, that changed. I was called up to the point, at the edge of a narrow and deep stream. The point man indicated a flat rock on the far side; on this sun-baked rock was the clear, dripping imprint of an NVA sandal.

That was the very first time that I realized that this was war, for real; it wasn't Camp Darby at Benning. I remember the feeling vividly: I realized that, until now, I had just been playing soldier. I was a teenager, dumber than a sack of hammers, and until then, I had felt indestructible. It never really occurred to me, until that moment, that someday I might really have to engage in combat. When you play those games in the Army schools, it's just like being back on the old playground. You just know that the referees will be along sooner or later, the "dead" guys will get back up, you're going to be critiqued. I had boxed, and you could get hurt. I had gone to jump school, and you can get killed there. But this was the real thing in a way that nothing else before ever was.

We started across the stream, and now the Yards were really quiet and serious. Everybody "locked and loaded" [chambered rounds]. Then, just at dark, we made contact.

The point man was no more than 30 meters ahead of me; first one, then two, and then three AKs opened up on us. Then some SKS semi-automatic rifles started firing, too, and I heard some of our .30-caliber carbines firing. My blood absolutely ran cold, it frightened me so badly! Later I was in worse situations, but I have never been so scared as I was that day.

I could feel the muzzle blast of those weapons, they were so close. I thought I could feel the ground shake from their concussion.

Several grenades detonated; I could tell from the sound that some were ours and some were theirs. Then from out of nowhere, some clown fired an RPG-7V into our midst; it detonated in a tree about 15 meters behind me. The guy who fired it was so close that I heard it launch and then the impact almost immediately. Fortunately, the shrapnel sprayed away from me, but the detonation was just deafening!

Everybody was yelling now. Then I saw something pretty incredible: The Montagnard next to me actually used his teeth to pull the pin on a grenade! It was odd enough that I thought, Man, does his dentist have any idea what he's doing with those molars? But he threw the grenade only a short distance to our front. I crawled over and tried to tell him in Vietnamese, "Don't throw that thing unless you can actually see people to throw it at!" Then I looked up and realized that, in fact, he could see somebody out there. The NVA were right there in front of us. That was the second big jolt; I could actually see them, about 30 meters away in the jungle! The Yard didn't come close to them, but he had the right idea.

It became one of those slow-motion things. They knew where we were, we knew where they were, and they knew that we knew! I couldn't function. I was completely confused and disoriented. I was ducking and trying to save my own hide. It was really disappointing, later on, for me to consider how badly I performed in those first minutes.

We started to take fire from the rear and from the right, as well as from the front. We were just about surrounded. The bullets were whistling through the trees, ricocheting off things, and it was almost impossible to find a target. I was basically trying to hide.

Then, very shortly after all this started, two Montagnards were hit to my right. It wasn't like in the movies. They dropped their weapons and were writhing on the ground, within 10 feet of me. One was shot just below the nose, and the bullet took off part of his upper lip. In the cowboy movies I used to watch, that never happened. You never saw any blood. This was Attention Getter Number Three, and the day was just rocketing downhill, getting out of control.

I started crawling around. It finally dawned on me that the cracks I was hearing were bullets going right by me; I had heard about the sound from the old-timers, but this was the first time I experienced it for myself, and it was frightening.

There was a little lull in the firing, so I tried to tell the Yards to calm down and be quiet for a moment, trying to get them to not draw any more NVA fire. Unfortunately, I said that rather loudly—and the whole world came apart as the NVA opened up on me! I remember looking down at that old Montagnard who served with the French; he looked up at me and just shook his head in disbelief at what I had just done.

Now we could hear the NVA talking, yelling commands, firing and maneuvering. My teeth were chattering from excitement and fear. It was very surreal, and then I realized that the whole platoon was looking in my direction. They were looking at me to lead them. I was an officer in the United States Army, an Airborne Ranger, a fully qualified Green Beret—and they were looking at me because I was in charge. It was the darnedest thing for a child to figure that out, and to be factual, that's what I was at the time, a teenager.

I had a flashback to an incident a few days before. Brigadier General Joe Stillwell came out to see my team leave Fort Bragg, and he shook hands with the A-teams as we boarded the aircraft.

When he got to me he noticed a black eye I had acquired while intervening in a squabble the night before; he said, "Ashley, I was going to tell you to take care of these men, but obviously you can't even take care of yourself!" The whole thing, at the time, was a game, but it occurred to me then that Stillwell's words came true at that moment.

The old Yard started crawling around, organizing the platoon, indicating fields-of-fire for the soldiers, something I should have been doing.

All this transpired over an extended period of time—maybe 30 seconds or so—and although the point men had returned fire, I hadn't done anything. People started returning fire and throwing a few hand grenades. Finally, I started crawling around to the men, directing their fire, but I was very confused about where the enemy actually was. Were they in the trees? Were we surrounded? What was going on?

After crawling only 5 meters or so, a bullet hit the stock of my M16 right at the hand-grip, splattering bits of fiberglass into my face and left hand. Another round in the same burst of fire hit my rucksack, striking a little camera I carried, and chunks of that went into the back of my neck. That was a severe attention-getter. Then, everything went silent for a moment, but when I started crawling again I drew fire again.

My radio operator crawled over, and I reported, "We are in contact. We have casualties!"

The guy on the radio responded that the other two platoons had already reported that they could hear the firefight. He said, "Are you sure you aren't engaging friendlies? Monkeys? Gibbons?"

"No," I told him, "I am hit, Dunn is hit, and at least two of the Yards are hit—and not by Gibbons. I need artillery, and I need it right now!"

He passed me off to the fire support battery co-located at our base camp. "Fire mission!" I called. ["Fire mission" is the first phrase of the "call for fire" or a request for artillery, a very ritualized procedure learned by all young combat-arms officers in the Army.]

After a pause, he responded, "Great, glad to oblige; what's your location?" I couldn't tell him. I didn't know! I had not been paying attention; I had been playing army. It was the sort of behavior that makes dead people in wholesale quantities. This was just another little lesson in my professional development course, a program that was evolving at what seemed to be light-speed.

Some A-1E Skyraiders appeared over head, and we finally established where we were when I could tell them exactly when they flew over our position. They radioed that back, and it turned out later to be about 4,000 meters from where I thought we were; I wasn't even in the ballpark. But now I at least knew where we were, and that was a start. And we got some help from the Air Force, too, who brought in an FAC to coordinate things. I asked him, in essence, "Get us out of here!" I was thinking, but didn't mention, that I had decided that I had seen just about enough combat for the next 13 lifetimes, and they could skip the decorations if they'd just get me out of there alive.

"Okay," the FAC called, "I'm going to direct you to an LZ so we can try to get out your wounded."

About then I started getting control of myself and started moving around the platoon, directing people, and it seemed to be working. We moved off, with me in the number four position from the point; we had gone only about 150 meters when the whole world seemed to open up on us. We had gone from what might have been just a squad outpost of NVA, then turned around and bumped into what was probably a company of NVA in bunkers on Hill 875.

Relatively speaking, the first engagement of 30 minutes before had been child's play. RPGs fired into us, and then we heard new sounds of the little NVA "burp-guns"; but the Yards reacted well this time and fired back effectively, even though all we had were old Grease Guns and M1 carbines from World War II and the NVA had modern weapons. One of the Yards took a round right below the eye and dropped to the ground, dead.

It was dark now, and the FAC overhead called with some cheery news: "By the color of the tracers [NVA weapons usually fired green tracers while U.S. weapons fired red tracers], I can see that you've really stepped into something ugly." We were in a three-sided crossfire at the time, and I had already reached the same conclusion, even without the intervention of the referees for the war-games I was accustomed to at OCS and Ranger School.

I tried to break contact; we had moved about 40 more meters when mortars started dropping in on us, my baptism of indirect fire. Now, since we're discussing what a wimp I am, my fear of indirect fire and of heights are ones I have never fully mastered. They can get you anywhere! But fortunately we were under some triple canopy jungle and some of the mortar rounds were detonating in the treetops.

The FAC called to report that a battalion of ARVN infantry was moving toward us, but they were 9 kilometers away and advising us to hold tight. I told him we'd try, but we needed some relief. Since he didn't know precisely where we were in the dark, I told him I'd fire up a flare.

"Do you really want to do that? Then everybody will know where you are," he said.

"The NVA already know where we are," I told him, and so I put up the flare—mistake 53 for the day. A world of fire rained down on us, but the A-1Es came in and started dropping some pretty heavy fire all around us, and that slowed the NVA fire. The FAC reported that a lot of fire was also coming from hills nearby. We were being engaged from about 1,500 klicks by NVA heavy machine-gun fire, .51-caliber stuff.

We hunkered down and, after taking a lot of rockets, mortars, and heavy machine-gun fire for a while, it all slacked off and things quieted down. There were F-105s and F-4s overhead and our engagement was turning into something significant. I managed to fall asleep somehow. When I awoke, it was light. I set a new leech record; there were 13 of them attached to me. We spent the whole day just hunkered down, waiting for relief.

The sounds of a tremendous firefight could be heard in the distance late in the afternoon. The FAC reported that the ARVN battalion trying to reach us stepped into something nasty and was apparently wiped out. "But, no problem," the FAC called. "The Screaming Eagles [troopers from the 101st Airborne Division] are coming to get you!"

We had been out six days now, and we were getting very hungry and thirsty. But I had calmed down, and I started to feel more competent and confident that I knew what I was doing. For the first time, I started to believe that we would make it out of there alive.

We heard helicopters in the distance, putting the 101st into LZs a couple of hills away. Firing picked up in the distance as the NVA engaged the 101st. We took some mortar fire, too, from so nearby that we could hear the rounds drop in the tubes before they fired. We could hear the NVA moving around in the undergrowth, maneuvering on us.

We crawled about 150 meters to the edge of a little clearing where we hoped the helicopters might come to pick us up, but the heavy machine guns on Hill 875 picked us up first and started firing on our position. This was an entirely new experience because you just can't get away from those big bullets by ducking behind some bamboo. Those .51-caliber armor-piercing rounds are just horrific, and they were hitting all around us, sending up geysers of dirt. Several hit in front of me and my first thoughts were that they were dud RPGs from all the dirt they kicked up. Other rounds ricocheted into our position, and you could watch them coming at you. I saw two of them, tracers, that tumbled slowly right toward me—and I actually started to put my hand out to catch one! If OCS actually knew how one of its graduates was doing out here I think the place would have been shut down, the curriculum revised, or the entrance requirements tightened.

The FAC was reporting that the 101st platoons were getting closer, warning us to avoid firing on them. The A-1Es dropped some napalm nearby, and that was impressive. On the radio, I could hear by the call-signs that every colonel in Southeast Asia was overhead, trying for an Air Medal and the Good Housekeeping Seal of Approval. They were all circling overhead, putting each other in for awards. The sky was black with helicopters, and I desperately wanted them to put one or two of them down so we could get out of Dodge.

By now we had 3 dead and 13 wounded Yards, and both of us Americans were wounded—more than 50 percent casualties. We could hear M16s firing now, though, and that was nice, although they sounded wimpy compared to the sound of the AKs. Finally, the 101st's lead element crawled over to us and we effected a link-up.

The first American guy I spoke to was a big black soldier. He looked at the two Montagnard soldiers beside me and said angrily, "Who are the fucking gooks?"

I hadn't realized till then how attached I had become to the little guys, and I contemplated jamming the muzzle of my rifle up his nose.

"Do you have Americans here?" he said.

"Yes," I told him, "there are two of us."

"Everybody else is a fucking gook?"

I tried to briefly explain to them that these weren't ethnic Vietnamese, but Hmong-Khmer tribesmen. He said, "What's the difference? A fucking gook is a fucking gook!" I pointed out to him that they were the only reason I was still alive, that they had fought for days, and that they were still fighting and were at that moment holding the flank of his position, keeping his platoon from being overrun. I also told him that most of us were wounded, and that seemed to adjust his attitude a bit.

One of the 101st soldiers crawled over and asked me, "Do you have a medic with you? Our platoon leader's been hit."

"Yes, I'm one," I told him. I wasn't a Special Forces trained medic, but I had been cross-trained and was qualified.

We started crawling over to their position. The soldier asked, "Do you guys have an officer with you?"

"Yes, as a matter of fact we do," I told him. "Why do you ask?"

"Well, he must be a fucking idiot. Do you know how many NVA are out here? Do you know what he got you into?"

"He didn't mean to," I said, "and besides, he's good looking and a really nice guy. And I'm him." The soldier looked at me—I was, remember, only 19 and wearing the shreds of a uniform with no insignia on it.

"No, I don't have time to fuck with you, I need to talk to your officer!"

"Trust me on this," I told him, "I am the officer!"

We finally got to the wounded platoon leader, and I got a good look at him; good God, it was a guy named Bob, one of my OCS classmates! It was awful. He looked at me—a 10-day growth of beard, an eye swollen shut, a hand that wasn't working too well, and a mouth that was messed up; not quite the way I looked in OCS.

I looked at Bob's fatigues in the area where he was wounded; the blood was pumping out of his hip so fast that the fabric moved with every pulse. We cut the pants away; the wound was horrific. The femur was broken. The wound was too high on the leg to put a tourniquet on so we tried direct pressure; I ended up standing on the wound, trying to put enough pressure on it to stop the flow of blood. The pain must have been incredible, but Bob never made a sound.

"I need a cigarette," Bob said.

"I didn't know you smoked," I told him.

"I just started."

The wound was fatal, and he knew it. I remember just how he looked: a cigarette in his right hand, his arm draped across his knee. He never took a puff from that cigarette, and I remember standing on him, with my bare heel pressed against the exit wound. I was dead tired, almost to the point of hallucinating, and I was watching that cigarette because I didn't want to look at his face. The cigarette slowly turned red; blood was trickling from somewhere down his arm, soaking into the cigarette. It went out with a hiss. Then it dropped from his hand. Bob was dead.

I crawled back to my platoon. We got some LAWs from the 101st to use against some bunkers we'd found. I had three of these things. I cocked one, put some stuff in my ears to protect against the noise, and crawled forward to try to fire into the bunkers. I pushed the button, but it was a dud. I went back for the second, and dashed out, John Wayne style, and tried it—but it was a dud, too!

But I guess the entire NVA division had been waiting for this target, and they all opened up with a mass of green tracers. I managed to get back, and this time decided to just shoot the third one from behind a log we had as part of our perimeter; that one was a dud too! I was zero-for-three at bats with the LAW.

Finally, we got the word to pull back to the clearing. The NVA must have pulled back by then because the firing had stopped and several CH-47 helicopters were already on the ground. We brought out the dead Yards in ponchos slung on poles and placed them on the ground next to the body bags of the dead ARVN and 101st already in the landing zone. Someone from the 101st came over and told me to move my dead. They didn't want our dead soldiers alongside their own. That was very upsetting to me. There were three rows of body bags. It was the most dead Americans I had ever seen, or ever would see, in one place.

Finally, they were ready to put us on a helicopter; the wounded boarded first, Dunn with them, then the unwounded, and I stayed with the bodies, intending to return with them. They put me and the bodies aboard a helicopter, and I still wasn't getting much respect. Of course, I was burned black, I was in tiger-stripes, and was otherwise pretty much a mess. Some ARVN soldiers, very badly wounded, were also loaded on the helicopter, and they weren't getting any respect, either. I went over to one and asked in Vietnamese what was going on, only to discover that they were all NVA prisoners!

"Do you realize these are enemy soldiers?" I asked the flight crew.

"No, how can you tell?" one answered.

"I asked them."

"Do you speak gook?" the crewman replied.

"After 37 weeks in gook language school, I should hope so," I said, trying to imply that I thought he was a screaming asshole of a jerk. But I was able to talk to these enemy soldiers, and that seemed to make an impression.

At last, as I was about to depart, one of the 101st guys grabbed me by the back of the shirt and tried to pull me off the helicopter.

156

"This helicopter is just taking dead, wounded, and officers!" the guy said.

"As I have been trying to explain, I are one!"

They let me on, and put me in the last seat, right by the ramp. Then they put on 13 dead in body bags. The bodies were stacked like cordwood, with heads and feet alternating. Then they brought aboard a wounded American; he looked like Dunn, apparently about 12 years old, in a 101st uniform. It was obvious that he was pretty badly wounded, and it took two people to support him as they carried him aboard. They sat him down among the body bags, with his legs over some of the bodies. I thought, "Man, that's weird; they ought to at least strap him in."

We lifted off and headed back to Dak To, jiggling along through the sky. This guy just sat there, no more than 3 feet in front of me, staring down at the body bags. He looked very, very tired. I asked him, "Are you hit?" He didn't respond but just kept staring down at the body bag on the deck. I asked him some other questions over the noise of the helicopter: Was he part of the unit that went up Hill 875? Still no response. Then, as we banked to make the approach to Dak To, he fell over, right on my feet. Only then did I realize that he was dead and had been dead for a long time. He must have died in that seated position and stiffened up before he could be put in a body bag.

When he fell over, his arm fell across my boots and I noticed he was wearing a Mickey Mouse watch and a wedding ring. I still remember just what it looked like. I thought, Man, he doesn't look old enough to be married.

We landed, and when the medics came out I tried to help pick him up and carry him out of the helicopter. But my left hand wasn't working very well, and I dropped him and his head hit the deck of the helicopter. "Oh, gosh, I'm sorry!" I told him, but he was about as dead as anybody ever gets. His eyes were still open, though, and he still just looked very, very tired.

Some other people came out and helped get him out of the aircraft; they placed him on the helipad in a sitting position. I went over to check the name tape on his uniform, just to see who he was, and the Mickey Mouse watch had already been stolen by someone.

I got shipped off to the hospital for a while, then came back. Dunn was later killed in action [on September 23, 1966] right there at Dak To. Two of the other Americans with me on the operation but with the second platoon, Drummond [Staff Sergeant Emanuel F. Drummond] and [Sergeant First Class] Warren Cobley were also killed [on July 8, 1966] there at Dak To, even before we could get to our camp at Dak Seang. A third American, who had been with the third platoon on this operation, a guy named Welsh [Sergeant First Class Thomas Welsh] also was killed [on May 16, 1966] before we left Dak To. The place started out ugly and went downhill from there.

I thought I had experienced the worst that was possible, but later on [see the next story] things, in fact, got much worse. It took about three days for my heart rate to return to normal, but I discovered that many people senior to me in rank and experience who participated in the operation simply failed to function. After a week or so, I realized that this was something that I could, in fact, do. I reached the conclusion that I could not be killed. Everybody else might be, but I knew that I would live. I got a lot of pats on the back, and a lot of people seemed to be impressed with what I had done. My teenage ego just sucked that up. I am very nearly ashamed to admit that. I wouldn't have admitted it a few years ago, but that was the way I felt at the time. I had seen some of the bodies of 101st soldiers that had been mutilated, and I started to have a purpose in life. I couldn't wait to strap all that back on and go out again.

When I went out on other operations I clearly felt an invisible protective shield come down around me. I was put in for the Silver Star, but was awarded the Bronze Star for the operation. I was later nominated for the Medal of Honor, but didn't get it—perhaps because my team leader, Captain Billy G. Chandler, beat up the guy who later was supposed to endorse the nomination, which somehow got "lost." Chandler beat up the guy again when he found out what happened to the nomination. I got three Silver Stars.

One of the pilots who provided air cover near Hill 875 was awarded the Distinguished Service Cross by the Air Force just for flying over the place! This same guy later got another DSC, one as a lieutenant colonel, the other as a colonel; this guy got five Silver Stars and two DSCs. When I compare that to the kinds of things my Montagnards did, it just about reduces me to tears because of the lack of credit, recognition, and respect those guys received. If an American did the same things those little guys did, he'd have to carry his Medals of Honor around in a wheelbarrow.

Dak Seang was a place where the tussling just never stopped. On September 28, 1966, I was trying to put out some Montagnards one morning and triggered an ambush that turned out to be rather messy for everyone involved.

Aw, Bummer—Wrong Army!

We were trying to get the camp at Dak Seang together, but it was very difficult to get anything done because we were in contact so much. We were outside the artillery fire support fan, and the NVA were so close that they would pin messages to sticks and prop them up inside the camp, listing by name the people they were going to kill. It was a little hairy.

The old Highway 1 ran past the camp. It hadn't been usable for years; it was just a trail with a little macadam on it in places, except for about a half mile on either side of our camp. We had jeeps and trucks in the camp, though, and we could travel a short distance outside the gate on the remains of this road.

We were putting out a river crossing nearby on the Dak Poko River, the large, swift river that was just south of the camp. The bad guys had put in a substantial L-shaped ambush along that little stretch of road. Two truck loads of Montagnards had been taken down to the river. The bad guys knew we didn't have very many people available—only about 250 total—and apparently they

159

decided to try to divide our forces with this ambush. While the two trucks were unloading the troops at the river, the VC ambush team moved into position.

About this time I got a call on the radio that a helicopter was inbound to pick up one of the NCOs who was going off to recon school, and he was one of the guys driving the trucks. I hopped in a jeep and went down to collect him. Five Montagnards hopped in the jeep with me, more for the novelty of riding in the vehicle than anything else.

The NVA were still getting in their holes when I rumbled up at 2 or 3 miles per hour. I saw a couple of people on the road. They looked like Yards to me, so I thought they were ours and drove right past them. But I didn't find the trucks and came back up the same stretch of road. As I came back, they must have assumed that the ambush was compromised. They let me drive up very close to them, and then one of them turned around and fired across the hood of the jeep, hitting me above the left eye.

What followed was something like the shoot-out at the OK Corral. They knew what they were doing, but we didn't figure it all out right away. I got a skull fracture and was blind in my left eye. They shot the jeep to pieces. The guys in the back, who were just along for the ride, took most of the fire. It was really weird. I saw everything in slow motion. Nothing was working right. There was blood on the floor, but I couldn't figure out if it was mine or somebody else's. I watched the gauges as they were shot out. I was stunned and couldn't really figure out what was going on.

Then a guy ran over and chucked a couple of hand grenades in the jeep, one in the front and one in the back. I knew what that was! It was right between my feet. I tried to get it, then discovered that I was paralyzed on one side. But I was finally able to get a hold of it and drop it to my left, where it detonated. I was blown out, over on the passenger side, and lay on the ground for a while with 29 pieces of shrapnel in me. Then the one in back detonated and really messed the Montagnards up badly.

While I was lying there, taking all this in, the guy that shot me came over and tried to shoot me again with his Thompson submachine gun. He was pulling the bolt back, but every time he tried to shoot it just went klunk. My M16 had ended up alongside me. I was able to retrieve it with my right hand and arm, and I was able to get it talking. I wasted him. He was standing right beside me. I don't think he believed I was capable of doing much of anything, a fatal error on his part.

People were dancing around on the road. Then everybody scattered, and I crawled over to the jeep. I got up, but in the process another NVA fired and hit me in the back of the thigh. I turned and—with one round left in my magazine—hit him in the spine as he turned to run. I thought my leg was broken, but it wasn't. It was very wobbly, and I could see where the bullet had exited the front of my leg. So I stood there, hanging on to the jeep, when some fool of an NVA came over and tried to collect the weapon from the guy I had just shot. It was laying right in front of me, and he tried to pick it up. I was out of ammo, so I whopped him with the M16, and then he and I got into one of those "let's roll around on the ground; I'll beat you to death with my rifle" tricks. I broke the stock off my rifle, but that was okay, because I was on my knees at this point, and it was easier to swing. After that I passed out.

When I woke up I was looking at the dirt. I rolled over and looked around. There were dead and dying folks everywhere. The guy I had shot in the spine was being unhappy, and so was the guy I had shot first. So I got out my old K-Bar knife, crawled around, and cut everybody's throats. None of them could take a joke about that, either, so it wasn't all that easy. I passed out again. When I woke up, I was now a member of the 304th North Vietnamese Army Infantry Division; I was being dragged by a guy who was pulling me along by the armpits.

I said to him in Vietnamese, "You've got to stop; I'm bleeding to death." The guy freaked out, but he kept dragging me. I still had the knife in my right hand because they hadn't been able to pry it out. I managed to reach over and get this guy by the belt, and he went nuts. Then he and I got into another wrestling match. I got over on my knees. I wasn't going to let this guy get away; I thought he was one of my Montagnards. It had already been a real bad morning for me, and I didn't want to get left. He started kicking my head completely off my shoulders, and then I finally got a good look at him and realized who he was. Aw, bummer—wrong army! I thought. This thing just keeps going downhill! I tried to stab him with the knife, and I couldn't do it. Finally, he kicked me as I had the butt of the knife against my chest, and he stabbed his leg on the knife. That got him to turn me loose! He grabbed his leg, we rolled around some more, and I killed him.

I crawled around for a while. I couldn't get up, and I couldn't walk. I kept dodging NVA folks, and finally I got back to the road. I was trying to crawl back to camp when the NVA reaction force arrived and (as luck would have it) spotted me on the road. They were really bad shots, because they were within 100 meters of me and they absolutely shot the road away. But I only took one more round, this one across the left side of my head (I now have a kind of permanent part in my hair).

The Yards heard all this, of course, and came running up. They found me there and looked at me. Their expressions seemed to say, These lieutenants will do just about anything to get attention! It was a bad day.

By this time I was having a hard time telling who were the good guys and who were the bad guys, and according to the Medal of Honor statements that were prepared later, I was trying to kill everybody. They wrapped me and the knife in a blanket, strapped me to a litter, put me in a helicopter, and shot me out of there to Dak To. Apparently I tried to carve up the medic when he tried to put in an IV, and I'm a little surprised they didn't just dump me out the door somewhere between Kontum and Pleiku.

RIDING THE SHIT-CAN EXPRESS
TO THE HANOI HILTON
STEPHEN LEOPOLD

*Stephen Leopold is an attorney now, still in the Army serving as
a lieutenant colonel in the reserves. In 1968, while a fresh lieutenant
recently arrived in Vietnam, he was captured and held until 1973,
first in Cambodia, then in North Vietnam, including
a couple of all-expense-paid years at the Hanoi Hilton.*

Captured by the NVA

I was captured near the town of Ben Het, a small town near the
Thai border. Our camp was about ten klicks from where Laos,
Vietnam, and Cambodia intersect. I was just plain lucky to be captured there because if it had been anywhere else they wouldn't
have had any way of getting me out and would have just shot me
right there. After I was captured and wounded, I was held in
northeast Cambodia for about a year and a half and then marched
north and held just outside Hanoi for about a year. After the Son
Tay raid [during which helicopter-borne American commandos
attacked the Son Tay prison in North Vietnam in an attempt to
release American prisoners; unfortunately, the prisoners had
been moved], very near the camp where I was held, we were
moved into Hanoi itself for the last two years of the war. During
the last two months they moved us into the Hanoi "Hilton."
We'd finally hit the big time!

Before I was captured, I had been in country all of a month, at
the camp for all of 10 days. At that time there were three officers on
an SF A-team: the commander, the XO, and the civil affairs/psy-ops

officer. I was assigned to be the civil affairs/psy-ops officer, then was kicked upstairs to be the XO when the number two guy had to go someplace else.

I led a patrol mission to a hilltop about four klicks west of our camp overlooking an old French road that went around a bend, past the remains of an old French fort at the bottom of the hill and into Laos. The Ho Chi Minh Trail was three klicks across the valley. We needed to occupy the hill to keep the NVA from using it to rocket our camp, which they did every time we abandoned the place!

Staff Sergeant Michael McCain and I and 100 Montagnards, plus one or two Vietnamese ARVN special forces, set up on this hilltop. Mac had been in country for four tours, as early as 1962. He really liked it over there.

We were overwhelmed the next morning by about two companies of NVA. It was no contest, really. The Montagnards had old, World War II weapons because the Vietnamese wouldn't let them have anything better. So when the NVA attacked, the Yards ran off. I couldn't blame them; they didn't have anything to fight with. I've never been bitter about it. It was like the Italians attacking the Ethiopians.

Combat happens relatively quickly. I'd been in places where mortar and rifle fire came in; you can accept that pretty dispassionately when it's just a stray round. It's different when you're asleep and wake up to a firefight outside the window.

It was one of those things; we had talked a lot that day, Mac and I. He'd been through a lot. If I had been on the other side of the hooch, he'd have lived through it; I would've been just another of his lieutenants that got killed. But this time, he was in the wrong place at the wrong time. It teaches you some of life's lessons. He'd been over there for four and a half tours, and if he'd wanted to stay back in Nha Trang and run the NCO club they would have let him. But he insisted on being in the combat zone. So two grenades came into the hooch, and Mac caught most of both of them. He was dead very quickly.

I was blown out of the hooch. It was funny, in some respects. It happened very quickly. I was lying there thinking, Am I dead or am

I alive? Well, I'm alive. Where am I hurt? Well, I'm hurt here and here, but nothing in the gut, no massive bleeding. I guess I'm not going to die right away. The NVA stuck AKs in my face when I came to. They bound me and then took me off the hill. I could hobble; this was before they were carrying me. We were just 2 miles from Cambodia and the huge concentration of NVA staging and R&R area, hospitals, and camps, so it wasn't much of a problem for them to haul me around for a week.

Your training kicks in. I was thinking, Well, they didn't kill me up there. There wasn't anything I could have done about it if they had wanted to. So I was wondering if I was going to live there or die there. Well, they collected me and took me off the hill, and I was wondering what they were planning to do. By that time I figured that they had orders to take prisoners, rather than shoot them, so everything started to make some sense.

It's really amazing, looking back on it. I wasn't terrified because I was in a state of shock, but I should have been. After a while I figured that if they had been going to shoot me they would have done it two hours ago, and they didn't. Since I was alive, I was going to stay alive unless my wounds went sour or we got bombed or something.

Within two hours of capture, they had me miles away, talking to some NVA division commander and his intelligence officer. The commander, a general, was actually a very nice guy. But they knew more about that camp than I did! I spent my time trying to give them disinformation, but their map was better than the one I could have drawn! They had been watching it for months, and they had infiltrated it, one way or another, through the Montagnard force.

I spent a lot of time in the jungle and was sick a lot. I got malaria. When they finally took us north, they weighed us. I was 112 pounds. The irony was that I was listed as missing in action for five years. The pilots, who were really very grossly mistreated until about 1969, at least were identified and acknowledged. They received at least one Christmas package and letter, unless they were cooperators, in which case they got more. Those of us captured in the south were also in Hanoi, but as far as anyone knew, we didn't exist! Unless you made tapes, nobody knew you were alive. So I spent five years as missing in action.

We called the food they gave us "Uncle Ho's No-Cal Diet." It couldn't have been more than 400 calories a day: a little bowl of pea soup (two chick peas with some broth), or peanut soup (with literally one or two peanuts in some liquid). We had that, plus two small cups of rice each day. The only meat I had in the first 18 months was from a monkey once, and we had some pork fat once. That was it for a year and a half.

It seemed to be a general rule that the farther you were from the front-line combat troops, the worse the treatment was. Front-line troops respected their adversaries. The NVA guarding me in Cambodia were not bad people. And I wasn't in love with their commander, but he was better than anybody we had up in North Vietnam! He'd been a front-line commander. He could be funny about some things; he got mad at me because I was the ranking officer and I didn't take their indoctrination course too seriously. We had three days of lectures informing us that we were the "running dogs of the odious Nixon clique and the U.S. imperialist war." Then we had a goddamn exam! They handed out these lined blue books, just like in college, and said, "Write for me what you think of the U.S. war." Well, what I wrote him was not what he wanted to hear. He was so upset that I was sent back into solitary confinement. He used to tell me, "You know much more than the others, so you must think more carefully about your crimes!"

As we moved deeper into Cambodia, the NVA I was with seemed fairly happy. They had an easy enough mission, although they had to carry me at times. But they were away from the B-52 strikes; it was like an R&R mission for them. They weren't upset with me and didn't treat me badly at all, but when we got to the camp it was different.

The camp in Cambodia was deep in the jungle, under triple-canopy jungle. They kept us in bamboo cages at night. They saw I was kind of hard-core and not cooperating, so they put me in solitary.

I spent the first six months on a hilltop by myself. I didn't see another American for another four and a half months. Then a guy named Pete Dravic came in. Then Mike Benge, a civilian missionary, then Perecone and Dave Suitor. There were three officers, about 10 enlisted guys, and the civilian.

We had one guy die of malaria, over on the other side of the camp, and another guy died in an escape attempt. You could get sick and die in the camp, in Cambodia, although that wasn't true in the north because they did have medical facilities.

My directive to the guys, as the senior officer in the camp, was, "I don't care what you tell those guys here, but I better not hear anybody on the radio!" You've got to make some effort to make a tape for the NVA. They were good troops. They gave the NVA nothing important, and they survived. But boy, it was boring! The boredom in that camp was incredible! They were trying to bore us to death. We were lucky they decided to move us in 1969 up to North Vietnam, where the physical conditions were a lot better but the psychological conditions were a lot worse.

We were marching north and passed a group of Montagnard laborers on the trail. There were a couple of ancient (maybe 40-year-old) women, with black teeth, all bent over, in the group. Black Jack turned to me and said, "Zorro, it's been two and a half years since I've seen a woman, but that's still ugly!"

Conditions in the north were totally different. The war was strictly us against them, and communism had nothing to do with it. It had nothing to do with capitalism or America or any of that. It was strictly personal. It was that group of guards and their commander versus us—and who's going to retain their sanity. We discovered how alone we were, and we reduced the war down to its simplest terms: us against them.

POW Humor

I found that humor helped get me through. The Vietnamese are a lot of fun. They were awfully xenophobic, but also funny. The camp

167

commander called me up for what we called an "attitude check." They trolled all the time to see if any of us were coming around to their point of view and wanted to start making propaganda tapes.

Funny things happened every day. The Vietnamese just didn't understand American culture. And we learned how to use this to our advantage. For example, the Vietnamese just couldn't understand how we could communicate around the whole camp, between these warehouses that were separated from each other. It was incredibly easy. They happen to be extremely prudish, particularly when it comes to non-Vietnamese. They all refused to come within 100 yards of our latrine, which made it the ideal place to use for a message drop. The whole camp used it. It was easy to leave a little piece of paper there, under a rock or even out in the open. The guards sure weren't going to investigate.

We had a lot of fun in that camp. We were really lucky. I was in with guys from all over. Some are still friends, the best friends anybody could have. We had a motto: You can either laugh or cry, and we are going to laugh! If you start crying, getting into self-pity, that will destroy you in a hurry. So we tried to laugh.

For example, Zigler was a dirty old man, and the Vietnamese are prudish and puritanical. Well, we were only allowed to speak English, to control who we talked to, but there were a number of guards who spoke English and used us to practice. But it wasn't like having a real conversation. You got tired of being somebody's language punching bag. So Zigler would insist on talking about sex. At first, they didn't understand what he was talking about, so he explained it in greater detail. God, he could get rid of the North Vietnamese cadre in a hurry! When they realized what he was talking about, they just disappeared!

Communication Skills

The other guys were real good. After the NVA put me back in solitary, we still had a way of communicating. The nearest prisoner hut was just about 20 yards up the hill. I could hear them talking.

Then we worked out a way for me to participate in the conversation. They'd be chatting away, and one would say, "Ain't that right, Zorro?" If I coughed twice, that was "yes." One cough meant "no."

And I could write notes sometimes, with tobacco ash and any spare paper I could find. I left the notes down by the latrine. So, even though I was supposed to be in solitary, I could still communicate with the other guys.

The compound was laid out in a semicircle, with an inner fence and an outer fence, and 10 huts that could hold up to 10 people each. The latrine was down at the bottom of the little hill, and the guard shack was in the middle. There was always a guard on duty, at least one. Before the escape attempt, they let people wander around and visit, but after that we were pretty much confined to quarters.

The camp doctor was a real nice guy, although I don't know how much of a doctor he was. They gave us quinine for malaria, but that was about it. I got a humungous abscess, and they didn't do anything. They weren't about to waste much of their medicine on the likes of us.

I don't remember it as a time when I was brutalized as much as warehoused. They put me in solitary and tried to break my will through isolation techniques, and it didn't work. It didn't work because the other guys were supportive. I encountered very few guys who had a "me first" attitude.

The latrine was only used to dump and clean the big buckets we kept in our cells for sanitation. They were emptied once a day. Messages were consolidated, written with spit and charcoal on the stuff they gave us for toilet paper, then rolled up tight and tucked between the lid and the rim of this bucket. There was no way any Vietnamese was going to look in there, believe me! It was fairly easy to let the other guys know which bucket they were to retrieve. Once they were all cleaned and back in their cells, with the doors closed, the notes could be removed and read. The guards never caught on because they refused to come close to the latrine.

I started a food fight once (and got decorated for it later, after we got home) so I could be put in solitary so I could communicate with some other guys there who were out of the loop. The guards got furious and beat the shit out of me and tossed me in solitary for 30 days. But communicating with the other guys was real simple. Unfortunately, at first, the other guys didn't know about our message system. At first I left them a message in my shit-can, but it came back. They didn't notice it. So I took some old, stale bread that they gave us, wrote a note, and stuck it into the bread with a little sliver of bamboo. It said, "I am Lieutenant Leopold. Look for message under rim of bucket."

I put this inside an empty bucket where they were sure to see it. And sure enough, my bucket came back, empty. Now these guys were into the loop.

Until the Son Tay raid, Dave Suitor and I were kept in an awful prison outside Hanoi. God, it was bad! The walls were black. We were only let outside for maybe five minutes a day. It was terrible. Suitor could hear the attack on Son Tay in the middle of the night, although I slept through it. We didn't know what happened, but the next morning there were 400 Vietnamese at our camp, in the rain, digging.

The Shit-Can Express

We developed what we called the "shit-can express." I got put in charge of communication for the camp by Colonel Guy. Some new guys showed up in the camp, so we sent them a message in the shit-can express. The first message was along the lines of, "Hi, how are you?" just to make sure that they were getting the message. Then we sent them a message saying, "Pay attention down at the cistern." That's because the bath house, down by the camp cistern, was another place the guards kept far away from. Their prudery kept them as far as they could get from a naked American body!

Well, everybody came to the bath house on a regular basis, and we had a hole through the wall so we could talk to them. The guards stayed outside, smoking and chatting, and the door was closed. While two guys kept an eye on the guards and four guys made a lot of noise yelling and splashing, one guy could use the hole to listen to whatever the current information was. The messages came down from Colonel Guy to us, and we passed it on to all of them.

This way, although we were segregated from the enlisted guys, we could still pass the word to this group. They went back to spread it around the enlisted cells. So, everybody knew everything! Everybody, that is, except the people who were cooperating. Colonel Guy didn't want to expose the communications network to these guys, eight enlisted guys.

The Plantation

Three nights after that they moved us. At two o'clock in the morning, the trucks showed up inside the camp and they told us to get our stuff and get on the trucks. I thought we were going to China. But we went to downtown Hanoi. We called it the Plantation, right in the middle of Hanoi. It's where we think Jane Fonda came to visit in 1971. My cell had "black-washed" walls, and I spent the next year in almost total darkness. Then they moved me to a cell with white walls and a light bulb that was on all the time! But it was a better camp; they fed us better, and there was more of it. There were more people and less room, so they put more of us together. They even gave us a deck of cards. I knew how to play bridge, so I taught the other guys in the cell how to play, and we played bridge for three hours every night! I haven't played bridge since. Three hours a night, every night for months and months—you tend to "bridge" yourself out!

They had a cook Zigler called "Mama Yang," and to us she looked like Mona Lisa and Marilyn Monroe, but, God, she was ugly.

Officers and enlisted men were kept apart, as were the prisoners who were cooperating. We had names for the buildings—the Corn Crib, the Hog House—and we weren't supposed to be able to communicate. But when Colonel Guy took over the camp, he started tap codes, which we used at first to communicate between rooms. We started out by talking through the walls. If one of the

171

guys lay on the floor, he could see under the crack, outside, and watch for the guards. Then, with a blanket over your head to muffle the sound, you could talk through the wall to the guys on the other side. Even though the walls were two bricks thick, if the other guy had his ear to the wall at the point where I was talking, he could hear me. Then we came up with something better.

We took the wire bail off the buckets and used it as a drill. We drilled holes through the walls, two bricks thick.

Life in the Hanoi Hilton

We got half a loaf of old French bread twice a day. For six months we got cabbage soup (which was okay; I still like cabbage), and for another six months we got squash soup. You can't get me near squash! I hate squash! You have to eat it because it has fiber, but their idea of a treat was on Sunday we had sugar squash soup! I ate because I needed what was in it, but God, it was bad! I still like rice too.

We ended up with about 100 people in this camp. It was a good camp, in a way. We were able to communicate with each other. When a new prisoner was brought in, we caught up on what was going on in the outside world. For example, when one guy showed up in the camp, the first thing that made the rounds was that *Playboy* magazine was now showing "muff" shots! That was what was important back in the U.S.! I didn't know about the moon landing until years after it happened, until I was in the north. Once we got to this camp in the north, we were getting caught up on all kinds of things. It was like we had died, in a way; we were completely out of contact with our society, in my case from 1968 to 1971.

I took the opportunity to learn Spanish. One of the guys and I spoke nothing but Spanish in the room for about two months. There were very few books in the north, and none in the south. In Hanoi we got a few Russian novels and the *Pentagon Papers* and that's it.

There were two types of guards, the English-speakers and the others. If any were particularly friendly to us Americans, they had

172

a tendency to disappear in the direction of the front. If they were more than formally correct, they generally disappeared. The guards had a great assignment, right in the middle of Hanoi. The bombing raids avoided the compound, and they were far from combat. They were happy. This was as good as it got for the NVA, and they followed orders.

It was different with the cadre. They had learned English, and we could indoctrinate them. There was one guy—most of us really liked him, he was really nice—who always let us out for extra time in the rec room. He always had a light for your cigarette. You could talk to him. He'd tell you about his family, about what he was interested in. He liked to practice his English. He was a good enough communist to think that the Americans should lose, and if they sent him to fight in the south, he'd pick up his AK and go. But he had no particular interest in the war. His attitude seemed to be, "Life's short enough. We don't have to rush things, do we?"

Most of the cadre, though, were rigid, cautious, and no fun at all. Some, like a guy named Phong, were either exceptionally dumb or actually believed that stuff their government was handing out. When you saw them coming over to practice their English, you knew you were in for a very boring 10 minutes or so. The best way to get rid of them was to turn the conversation around to sex somehow. It worked on all of them except one guy, who was married. If we tried that on him, he didn't care; all he said was something like, "Well, I'm getting some and you're not!"

They dealt with us by keeping the hard-core officers separate from the others as much as possible. Then there were the guys they thought they might convert someday, and they were kept together. Then there was the so-called Peace Committee, the collaborating officers who were recording broadcasts. The newly captured officers were housed next to them. Finally, there were the great unwashed numbers of enlisted men, and the NVA didn't want to have anything to do with them.

We called the collaborators "green socks" guys. They were recording the same kind of drivel that came from Tokyo Rose during

World War II, utter nonsense. Well, the guards handed out socks to these guys during the winter, when it was cold, to wear with their sandals. I figured it was just standard Uncle Ho issue that everybody was supposed to wear, but the stories that went around the camp about this development were incredible! Somebody thought the socks came from the British, who had entered the war on the side of North Vietnam! Other people thought the socks had some relationship to how the peace talks were going; the war was going to be over in two months!

That was the kind of thing that kept people going for a while, kept them revved up for a while. But then, two months later, when the war didn't end, there was a tremendous depression. That's when people needed their friends to keep them going, to keep them on the straight and narrow, because the NVA were trolling all the time for the weakest, then putting them in groups to reinforce each other.

Even the hardest core got attitude checks, including Major Montgeau. The Vietnamese didn't like him, and he liked them even less. Monte decided one time that he wasn't going to bow to them anymore. Well, this was sometime in 1972. He decided that he was a major and this kowtowing to the enlisted NVA guards was bullshit. Well, the guards solved that! They took Monte to a camp outside Hanoi and didn't bother to give him any water. Forget the food, he didn't get any water at all! After six days of this, Montgeau decided he'd bow after all.

So, if you kept your head, you could deal with the situation. We tried to be reasonable about everything, and the guards (we figured) just wanted to survive the war.

I got to that camp outside Hanoi on Christmas day, "Black Christmas," 1969. Until about that time pilots shot down over the north were brutalized—not as punishment, but for propaganda value. They were trying to get them to break, make statements over the radio that would then destroy the morale of the U.S. troops in the field. It was stupid, but that's what they did.

But after that they just pretty much warehoused us. The only times I got brutalized were when I broke their rules. As far as they were concerned, there was no Geneva Convention, no camp commander within the prisoners. We were all treated as individual war criminals who they might or might not let go home after this thing was over. But Colonel Guy put us together and kept us together as a military organization—a half-assed group—but a military organization just the same.

The way some people survived it was through hate. Hate is powerful. Hate works. Montgeau used it every day. The problem with that is that, when the war is over, it still isn't over for you. Then there were the Bible-pounders; it worked for them. But I was in it for my friends. They kept me alive, and I kept them alive. It was us against them. I reduced the war to those of us in the Plantation against these other guys, the guards, in the compound. When you do it that way—us against them—and you keep faith with the "us," you are in fairly good shape.

The other thing I found is that self-pity will destroy you. The opposite of self-pity is the ability to laugh at what is tormenting you. You either laugh about this stuff or you cry about it, and I found that once you start feeling sorry for yourself, you are in real trouble. I've seen it happen, and you can't talk them out of it. It's pretty frightening. What I learned was that, if you wanted to disarm some Vietnamese trying to propagandize you, just start talking to him about eating pussy. We stopped more interrogations this way than you could believe!

My mother believed I was alive, although she had no reason to. My father, with no better reason, believed I was dead. I was missing in action for five years. It was a long time.

HAPPY NEW YEAR,
SPECIAL FORCES STYLE
ANONYMOUS

Our Christmas had been pretty badly interrupted by a group of uninvited guests, an NVA unit that attacked on our holiday. So we spent pretty much all the day in action, without any of the usual festivities.

Life in this camp in the highlands was extremely austere. We certainly never got any USO shows or any other form of entertainment that we didn't manufacture ourselves. Since we hadn't really had a Christmas, I decided that we were definitely going to have a New Year's! So I went into Nha Trang, about 50 miles to the east of our camp, with our deuce-and-a-half truck to collect a band and whatever girls I could find.

We found a band and told them we were having a party on the other side of town. We offered them some money to come along and play for us, and they agreed. They loaded their drums and guitars in the back of the truck, and the musicians and their three dancing girls all piled in. We also bought up most of the beer and booze in Nha Trang, the best stuff we could find (Johnny Walker and Jack Daniels), and that went into the truck with the girls, the band, and the instruments.

Now, the women were "go-go" girls, and they were dressed in little outfits with lots of string and tassels. We decided that three girls just would not go far enough around. We had two MAT teams, an A-team, and a district team, all of whom were going to attend our party. So we started looking around Nha Trang for more girls. We told them we were having a party, and all the ones that wanted to go climbed into the back of the deuce-and-a-half. After we had eight or nine girls and the three musicians in the back, we figured we had enough and started back for camp.

It was starting to get dark as we left town, and the MPs at the exit point looked at us with rather funny expressions as we rolled out the gate. At night every bridge was guarded and had concertina wire across it, and as darkness fell the VC started roaming the countryside. The NVA started coming into the hamlets. The night was completely unlike the daytime in Vietnam, and those MPs must have thought we were out of our minds to be going out into the countryside at night.

But as we left the city, there was a long, blood-curdling scream from the girls as they realized that they were not going to any party within the city of Nha Trang. And they kept screaming for about 15 kilometers! Finally, I stopped the deuce-and-a-half, got out, and walked back to the girls. They were calling me every swear word they knew in Vietnamese and in English. I told them, "I am going to my compound where we are going to have a big party tonight. You have a choice: You can come along and go to the party, or you can walk back to town. If you keep screaming, we will be hit by the NVA, and nobody will get to party."

There was a lot of anguished debate. I said, "Okay, what is it going to be?" I was serious; it was just me and Sergeant "Smith" out there with a band and about nine girls in the back of a deuce-and-a-half, and by now it was fully dark.

They decided to keep going. We drove the rest of the way up into the mountains as fast as that truck would go, right through concertina wire and the occasional shots from the PF guards. At least the guards were bad shots, and since the NVA didn't usually drive up in American trucks, most didn't fire at us. But we didn't have time to mess around and stop to explain to them what we were doing out driving after dark.

Finally, we got to the camp. And did we party! The band set up and started to play. The go-go girls danced, and the other girls partied with our guys, sat on their laps. Everybody was there: the A-team, the

MAT teams, the district team. Even the local Montagnards showed up and joined in. It was just one hell of a party!

We planned to truck them back the next day, but there were some missions that needed to be run, some other things that had to be accomplished, and our vehicles were all unavailable. So we told them that they'd have to stay one more night.

So the festivities began again the next night, with more wine, more song, and more of the same women. A good time was had by all until about 2300 when, over the sound of the music, we all heard a distant sound: Whump! Whump! Whump! Whump! Whump! We all recognized the sound of mortar rounds coming out of the tubes. All of us were suddenly running everywhere, but the band and the girls didn't have a clue that anything was wrong. They kept playing and dancing while the rest of us were scurrying around. The girls kept dancing and the band kept playing, but when I looked over at them, the expression on their faces had changed. They knew something was seriously wrong because we were all suddenly running around like maniacs. That party was over in a heartbeat!

We all recognized the sound of incoming mortar rounds and I knew we all had 10 to 20 seconds before the impacts. We all had a plan for what we would do. This was not the first time this sort of thing had happened, believe me; but we didn't have a plan that accommodated the band and the girls!

It didn't take long for us to be in our bunkers and set up our fighting positions, but the girls were still running around the compound in their cute little micro-mini skirts, with the fringe and the tassels, squealing. Mortar rounds were already impacting. We were busy trying to check our wire to see if there had already been a breach, preparing to fight, while the girls and the band members were running all over the compound. We had to climb out of the bunkers, go out and collect these people, and find a bunker for them.

The attack didn't turn out to be much of a threat and didn't last too long. The next day we decided that the party was over and it was time to get the girls and the band back home. But rather than take them back in the truck, we called up some friendly helicopter pilots to come and get them for us, without telling them the whole story before they arrived.

When the Hueys landed to pick up the girls and the band, one of the pilots asked me, "So, just how do you suggest we explain this mission?"

I told him, "All you have to say is that you were taking out indigenous personnel."

LBJ

ANDY DULINA

Andrew Dulina III spent two tours in Southeast Asia, the
first in 1967–1968 as the executive officer of an A-detachment
in III Corps, north of Tay Ninh. His second tour was split
between training Thai soldiers preparing to go to Vietnam
and as the commander of an A-detachment involved in
long-range recon patrols (the LRRPs, usually called
"Lurps") up north.

We captured a particularly large monkey on one of our patrols and
dragged it along with us, trying to keep the Vietnamese from
killing and eating it. We brought it back to the camp and turned it
into a team mascot, although we certainly didn't need anything
else to keep us busy.

The critter became somewhat friendly, not tame, exactly, but
manageable; and we named him LBJ. This monkey lived with us for a
month or so while we tried to keep the Vietnamese troops in the
camp from absconding with LBJ for dinner. He was taught all sorts of
nasty tricks and was a source of amusement. When we deployed
north to a new camp, the monkey came with us in the helicopter—a
memorable experience!

We were in the new camp for a couple of weeks when the NVA
started firing mortars at the camp occasionally. The rounds mostly
landed outside the perimeter. We didn't think much of it; they were
probably just registering their weapons.

We had a daily "mad minute" at this camp while we were getting everything together and planning some tactical operations.

Every evening, just about dark, we all lined up around the perimeter and fired our weapons into the jungle for about 60 seconds. I don't know that we ever hit anything.

After about a month we received a particularly fierce mortar attack. Usually mortar attacks only lasted 15 or 20 minutes; 25 or 30 shells would be thrown at us every night about 8:30. We got our mortar pits in and started to do some counter-mortar fire missions and threw a few back at them. Then, after at least 100 rounds landed on the camp, a ground attack followed. We estimated that at least a couple of battalions were involved.

But we had just gotten all our wire out, and the Claymores were installed, so we felt pretty strong defensively. We hadn't had a chance to rehearse all our contingency plans, though, and all hell broke loose. We started taking casualties, mostly among the CIDG who were running around, basically out of control. It took a little while, but we finally got our Vietnamese Special Forces counterparts together with us, got a plan together, and called in some air strikes and some artillery support from the fire base a couple of klicks to the south of us. The NVA broke through the wire in a couple of places, but not in strength. Things stabilized. We fought them all night, and about daylight, the attack petered out and the shooting stopped. We counted our casualties and went out and picked the bodies out of the wire and cleaned the place up.

This damned monkey had managed to get loose during the battle and had gotten wounded. The medics patched him up, though, and he was fine.

We got a lot of publicity for the attack, maybe because we were a new camp, or maybe because the command was using us to "bait the hook" for the NVA, to get the bad guys to come after us so they could then put a large American unit on the ground. So the day after the attack, General William Westmoreland came into the camp for an inspection and a pat on the back. He flew in with his normal entourage, five or six helicopters of aides and assorted hangers-on.

The team leader, team sergeant, and I all went out to meet him. Westmoreland noticed the monkey and asked, "I see you've got a team mascot; what's his name?" When the team leader replied, "LBJ, sir," you could see a lot of eyebrows rise. Special Forces were known to be disrespectful of just about anything, and nothing was said about it. But all of his aides looked at us like we were entirely out of control.

We took him back to the team room for a quick, informal briefing on what we were trying to do. While we were giving the briefing, LBJ decided to climb up on Westmoreland's shoulder, and he starts to attack the supreme commander of the whole world! He started beating him on the head, biting his ears, and generally abusing him! At first the general just tried to ignore the attack and stay focused on the briefing, but then the two of them became involved in hand-to-hand combat.

Of course Westmoreland's whole entourage went completely bat-shit. About 14 aides were going for their pistols and were about to shoot our monkey. But we went over and pried LBJ off the general, and the general tried to pretty much ignore the incident. No real damage was done, no blood was shed; but the festivities went downhill from there. Afterwards the team leader, Captain Joe Lucas, turned to the team sergeant and said, "This monkey had better be out of Dodge by sunset!" Within 24 hours the monkey was nowhere to be seen, but the Vietnamese all looked happy and well fed.

THE SPECIAL FORCES A-TEAM

The SF A-team of legend and lore is properly called an A-detachment. It is a unit of 12 men, two officers and ten sergeants. This team can be deployed as a complete unit or as two six-man "split" teams, or even as two- or three-man subdetachments.

The basic team's officers are the commander (a captain) and the executive officer (a first lieutenant). When the team is split, each will command a subdetachment. The classic team includes medics (one senior and one assistant), two engineers, two heavy weapons specialists (mortars, mostly), two light weapons specialists (rifles and machine guns), and two communications specialists. This 12-man unit is designed to train, equip, and lead a 500-man battalion of partisans, guerrillas, or irregulars in operations behind enemy lines.

All team members are supposed to be proficient in the language of the operational area, although real language proficiency has been a problem for SF through the years. But each member of the team is expected to work comfortably with people of very alien cultures; it is an idea that worked in France and Burma half a century ago, it worked in the Vietnamese highlands, and it is still working today in about 50 nations around the globe, some of which you've never heard of.

—Hans Halberstadt

HOOD, RIDING, RED, LITTLE

JIM MORRIS AND *GREEN BERET* MAGAZINE

*Special Forces had its own magazine in Southeast Asia for
five years, a fizzy little journal that contained a lot less of
the "eyewash" that most command-sponsored rags exhibit.
During Captain Jim Morris' tenure as editor,* Green Beret *magazine
was often a solid and entertaining periodical. The following story
is the product of an unknown author, but Morris recognized the
humor in its parody of the writtenformat required for military
reports (then and now).*

Once upon a time there was a female personnel whose nomenclature
was Hood, Riding, Red, Little (one each). She was a girl, little, happy.
Her duty uniform consisted of the following named items: (1) Dress,
red, cotton, shade 76 (one each); (2) Cape, HBT, red w/hood (one
each). Her MOS was 94B4S, food handler.

One day Hood, Riding, Red, Little received a TWX from her
Mother, grand, old, who was billeted off-post in a cottage, brick,
red, Capehart type, w/chimney, w/o TV, initial A/DPEN issue (one
each). The TWX read as follows:

"Dear Hood. This is to advise you that morning report should
read: DY to SK conf to qrts as of 0100 hrs, 1 Jan 68. Went on sick
call yesterday (LD: yes), conf for indef pd. However, I am feeling
somewhat better. Love, related-type Mother, Grand, Your. Added:
Pls see about Sep Rat for me. MGY."

Hood took the TWX to the message center with the following
1st endorsement: "Basic communication complied with. ETA your
station approx 1600 hrs this day."

While en route to the TDY destination, personnel concerned came to a forest, thick, primeval. Suddenly, out of the thicket, briar, emerged a wolf, brown, bad, big (one each). Wolf said, "Halt, who goes there, and what are your last four?"

Hood answered, "Hood, Riding, Red, Little, 4032. I am en route to my TDY point and am looking for the house of my Mother, Grand, Old."

"It is two klicks down the road; turn left at Building 2355," instructed the wolf.

"How do you know where she lives?" questioned Hood.

"I've pulled guard duty in those parts," said Wolf, who then caught a bus to the Granny's. Upon arrival, wolf, bad, swallowed Granny with a gulp, single (one each). Wolf then policed up the area, including butt cans, and jumped into bed, initial A/DPEN issue type, and pulled on Granny's AC 146-92s.

Hood, entering: "Hello, Mother, Grand."

"The fool, little, stupid, does not know that it is really me, the wolf, bad, big," chuckled the wolf.

"My, what big EENT you have," exclaimed Hood, Riding, Red, Little.

"All the better to maintain maximum efficiency at minimum cost with Zero Defects," replied the wolf.

Then, entered the chopper, wood type, handsome. Chopper killed wolf with a blow (one each) and performed necessary surgical procedures to remove Mother, Grand, from stomach of wolf, bad, big, dead. With allowance for quarters and rations, they all lived after, ever, happily.

CHRISTMAS WITH THE CONG
DAN PITZER

Dan Pitzer retired from the Army but still worked with Special
Forces trainees as a civilian instructor in the Survival, Evasion,
Resistance, Escape (SERE) program, passing along some lessons
learned during his years as a prisoner of war.

I was the senior medic on a Special Forces A-team. We were out on
a patrol, got overrun by two battalions of hard-core VC, and I was
captured on October 29, 1963. My first year of captivity was spent
in isolation. They were trying to break us down and trying to
indoctrinate us.

My upbringing had been fairly religious. During that first
year, I kept asking God, "Why are you doing this to me? Why am I
being put through this kind of torture?" It was "fist-shaking" time,
and I was angry.

Then, on December 24, an FAC appeared over the camp and
dropped red smoke in the prison camp. I didn't know it until later,
but it was a rescue attempt. It was frightening and profoundly
exasperating. I was running and hiding from my own country's
aircraft (I was dressed in black pajamas and looked like Viet Cong),
and I looked up through the trees to see a Huey overhead. It was so
close that I could see the gunner, behind his M60, and read the
"U.S. Army" on his jacket—that close! But I was afraid to get out
in the open, to signal them to come and rescue me.

We had been working outside the camp, and when we returned
the place was all shot up. We were told to collect our meager
belongings and were given some cold rice. Then the Viet Cong

started moving us. We marched for several hours, into the night, and moved along a river, toward a new prison camp.

As we came around a bend in the river, we saw a huge ever-green tree—a Christmas tree—30 or 40 feet tall, standing alone by the water. Something on the tree was attracting fireflies, thousands and thousands of them, and they were twinkling like strands of lights. A brilliant light was moving directly over the top of the tree; it was a satellite, but it looked like a very bright star.

As we moved closer, even the Viet Cong guards were impressed. "*Choi-hoi!*" one said (which means "My heavens!"). A peaceful feeling came over me. We were taken to a new prison camp, and while I was there I had a chance to think about the event quite a bit. I decided that God didn't have to use lightning bolts or burning bushes to talk to me; he had chosen to use something we recognize every Christmas.

From then on, when I spoke to God there in my little bamboo cage, all by myself, and the guards would come by to ask who I was talking to, I always replied, "Someone you will never know."

PIGEONS AND TIGERS

CLAY SCOTT

*Clay Scott retired from the Army in 1983 as a lieutenant colonel
with 20 years of service. He is a past president of both the Special
Operations Association and Chapter 23 of the Special Forces
Association. His stories come from the central highlands during the
late 1960s.*

Number One Chop-Chop

I commanded Camp Polei Kleng (Detachment A-241) outside
Kontum. One of our tasks was to patrol out to the Plei Trap Valley
and to the border, a distance of about 40 kilometers. My C-team
commander was always leaning on me to get patrols out, all the
way to the border. But my camp was already at the extreme limit
for artillery supporting fires from the batteries at Kontum, which
meant that any patrol west of Polei Kleng could forget about calling
for help in an emergency.

Well, I wasn't about to send a company out there just to have
them massacred. Nobody would come and support us. We couldn't
even make radio communications from out there. If we sent a
patrol in, and if we ran into a North Vietnamese battalion, we'd be
in deep shit.

To help deal with the communications problem and still get the
kind of information my boss wanted, we came up with an alternative
plan. It was my intel sergeant's idea: carrier pigeons. Now, there
was really something to be said for this idea, so we put in a request
for some. Well, lo and to say nothing of behold, a C-130 showed up

on our runway with a whole shit-pot full of carrier pigeons. We had cages of these things!

My intel sergeant was as happy as a pig in mud. He trained those carrier pigeons for a month. First, he'd take them to the edge of the perimeter, and they came back. Then he took them out to the runway, and they came back from there. Then he started taking them on operations, and they still found their way back to our camp.

We developed a plan to use them to report on NVA activity out at the border. We recruited one old Montagnard guy and prepared him to go way out, 40 klicks to the border, with some of these pigeons. He had a specific area to go to, and if he saw a lot of bad guys, he'd put a red band on the bird. If he saw just a few bad guys, it was a yellow band. If there were no bad guys at all, he was supposed to put a green band on the pigeon.

Sure enough, the fated day arrived. We sent him off to trail-watch for us in the Plei Trap Valley, happy as a clam—just an old guy with a walking stick, a knife, and a bag with a few pigeons inside. All he wore was the usual Montagnard loin cloth, no weapons, nothing to suggest that he was anything but an old Jarai farmer. He looked so innocent that, if they caught him, he could just say, "I'm just an old farmer, checking out a new area to move the village to."

A week went by, with no carrier pigeon—and no Montagnard. Another week went by: nothing! We started to wonder, Did he get captured? Did something terrible happen? Then, about three weeks after he left, we got word. The old guy was back home in the village. The intel sergeant went running down to the guy's house.

"What did you see?" the sergeant had to know.

"Didn't see anything," replied the old man.

"Did you let the pigeon go?"

"No," the old man said.

"Well, what did you do with it?"

"It was number one chop-chop!"

Don't Feed the Animals

While I was with II Corps Mobile Strike Force we had a Montagnard killed by a tiger. It happened at night, in a RON position. A tiger jumped up hill, over a guard, moved two or three paces, and then was on top of one of the Montagnards who was asleep. It evidently attempted to smother the guy with his tongue, covering his mouth and nose. Of course the guy woke up. The tiger then instantly grabbed him by the throat and ripped his throat out. The tiger then grabbed the Montagnard by the leg and dragged him away into the woods, with an entire Montagnard company shooting at him in the dark. Of course, they couldn't hit him. The rest of the night you could hear the tiger chewing on this guy. We recovered the body the next day, most of it, anyway. The lower leg and foot were missing, but the femur was picked clean as a whistle.

MEDALS

The subject of medals is a difficult one for civilians to understand and appreciate. I will try to explain how soldiers think about the subject of awards and decorations.

They are not, as some people claim, meaningless "fruit salad," at least, not for the people in this book. The colored ribbons on a soldier's dress uniform each have a kind of code. If you know the code, you get a pretty good idea of what a guy has done just by reading the ribbons. They are arranged in a strict order of priority, from the top-left on down.

The Medal of Honor is the most precious and rare American decoration. As Jon Caviani emphatically insists, it is awarded, not "won." Seventeen Medals of Honor were awarded to SF soldiers for actions in the Vietnam War. It would have been more but even this process is subject to the most petty brand of politics, and Green Berets are notoriously poor at the kind of game-playing that is sometimes involved in decorations. Otis Ashley Hedges III thinks his recommendation might have gotten farther had his team leader not beaten up the guy who later reviewed and disapproved his nomination. But John Caviani got one, and so did 16 other SF operators—far more, man for man, than any other participating unit.

Other combat decorations are the Distinguished Service Cross, Silver Star, and Bronze Star with "V" (for valor) device. The Air Medal, with "V" device, was sometimes awarded to Special Forces personnel for actions in flight. The Army Commendation Medal was sometimes awarded for heroism.

Many genuinely heroic actions by men from this community produced no decoration or award. There was a feeling within Special Forces at the time that the community was really above all that. As a

191

result, the highest award on the dress uniforms of many of the men whose stories are in this book is a Bronze Star with V, a decoration handed out by some other units in almost wholesale fashion for very minor engagements.

—Hans Halberstadt

Green Berets quickly developed an affectionate, effective relationship with the tribal hill people who inhabited the mountains of South Vietnam. Skilled at hunting animals for subsistence, tough, cheerful, brave, and loyal, they made superb soldiers. This tribesman, probably from the Rhade tribe, waits and watches for North Vietnamese moving down the trail 5 meters or so in front of him. *Don Green*

A large patrol moves out from its base in the central highlands. Such bases were vulnerable to attack but could be resupplied and supported by air. The short dirt landing strip beyond the buildings was sufficient for small cargo aircraft, like the DeHavilland Caribou, as well as helicopters. *Don Green*

Ambushes were often set up at river crossings where an NVA unit would be visible and vulnerable, and this very frightened enemy soldier is the only survivor from his squad. The rest were slaughtered while attempting to cross the stream. Slightly wounded, this man is being secured before being taken back to camp for interrogation. *Don Green*

A patrol checks out a river crossing for a heavily traveled trail. Such locations are classic "danger areas" that are natural sites for ambushes. Well-trained units are extremely careful about movement across places like this and take precautions to protect themselves . . . but not all units were well trained, and one NVA unit was destroyed crossing this shallow river. *Don Green*

Sergeant Dennis Mack inspects his map during a patrol in the jungles of Vietnam. *Dennis Mack*

The standard formation for a trail ambush was in the form of an "L" with the long leg parallel to the trail and a blocking force of two or three men at one end. This ambush was set up with the hope that the enemy would walk into the trap, passing along the hidden soldiers until they get close to the blocking force. The ambush is initiated either by the patrol leader or by the first shot by anybody else, whichever comes first. The blocking force fires down the trail while the others shoot across it, catching the enemy in a crossfire. But sometimes, as Gerry Schumacher describes, the enemy refuses to cooperate and walks up the trail in the wrong direction. *Don Green*

Deep inside the jungle, well away from trails or open terrain, the patrol halts for food, rest, and a conference between the team leader and his assistant. *Don Green*

The team leader conducts a preliminary field interrogation of the VC captive. Without the intervention of the Special Forces troops, the Montagnards would kill the VC. *Don Green*

Captain Roger Donlon returns to the Special Forces Camp at Nam Dang, where he was Officer in Charge when the camp was attacked on July 6, 1964, by a Viet Cong force estimated to be of battalion size. He inspects the mess hall that was blown down two days prior by heavy winds and rain. *Sp5 Gilbert L. Meyers, USA Sp Photo Det, Pacific*

The smiling Montagnard in the center is a converted VC who surrendered and went to work for the opposing team. *Don Green*

(From left) Lieutenant Kenn Kubasik, Captain Stringham, and Master Sergeant Strickmakier. *Kenn Kubasik*

Another captive NVA, closely guarded by two Montagnards. He is understandably apprehensive; the guards will cheerfully shoot him down if he attempts to escape. Once back at the patrol's base, he will begin a long, stressful interrogation period. *Don Green*

Movement through this kind of terrain and vegetation was always a challenge, especially since patrols normally tried to stay off trails and roads, where they were more likely to be discovered. *Don Green*

The result of one successful ambush—a dead NVA. The tribesmen loathed the NVA and were often reluctant to take prisoners. Dead and dying enemy soldiers were carefully searched for documents or other useful information, all of which was collected and brought back to the Intel section. *Don Green*

Don't mess with this small, tough man. Americans who knew them almost always admired and respected these tribal soldiers. This one is about to leave on patrol, and that's a white phosphorus (WP) grenade on the muzzle of his M16. He's got spare magazines in those canteen covers and wears a McGuire rig too. This guy is ready to tear up the town. *Don Green*

One of the Americans pauses for a quick portrait near the ambush site. *Don Green*

This Honduran soldier (photographed at San Pedro Sula) during the "Contra" era of the late 1980s) has good reason to take his training from 7th and 12th Group SF instructors seriously—he will soon be on real world combat patrols, firing real bullets at real enemies.

Sergeant Mike Jacquard, a member of the Weapons Committee at the Special Warfare Center, with an M60 medium machine gun. *Hans Halberstadt*

Sergeant Mike Jacquard with a Remington 870, an optional weapon once popular for short range combat.

Members of 3rd Battalion, 12th Special Forces Group (since inactivated) tell each other lies and await the call for chow at their Mountain Warfare Center. Instead of the usual MREs, the menu on this occasion was a whole pig, fresh salsa, and beer... none of which is on the menu for SF soldiers in Afghanistan or Iraq. *Hans Halberstadt*

Just one of many challenges for Q-Course students, you have to get through here as fast as possible while scurrying along in an uncomfortable crouch. Much worse, however, is to come later on the long course. *Hans Halberstadt*

3rd of the 12th soldiers prepare for a land navigation exercise at the Mountain Warfare Center. *Hans Halberstadt*

You can tell this is the first day in Afghanistan for these guys—they're still pretty clean and their "battle rattle" is still issue. Most SpecOps personnel soon get a bit more casual about blousing their BDUs into their boots, let their hair grow, and start wearing Tajik headgear.

What the well-dressed special operator wears to work in Afghanistan and Iraq – ball cap instead of Kevlar helmet, unbloused BDU pants, Arab "shemag" or scarf, M9 Beretta or personal pistol in drop-leg holster, Benchmade knife in scabbard on holster straps. His M4 has been tricked out with a custom paint job, dual magazines, PEQ-4 laser aiming system, and AimPoint reflex sight. Many soldiers prefer load-bearing vests from BlackHawk and London Bridge companies (about $250) but some prefer the local Pakistani models sold in the village market for $7. The little pouch is worn by every soldier in the field, always on the left shoulder—a pressure bandage for major wounds, commonly called a "blow-out patch").

SpecOps personnel get nothing but the best gear—even if they end up buying it themselves, as some of these guys have with their gloves and commo gear. You'd think the Army could supply all its units with effective squad radios but little Motorolas, about $40 a pair at Radio Shack, are used by just about everybody.

No matter where SF soldiers find themselves, they will find a way to get good chow and somebody in the unit to do a good job cooking it. This is "surf and turf" night at the firebase and those are thick steaks on the barbecue. Only in the U.S. military will you find cooks wearing "Gucci gear" BlackHawk nomex gloves while fixing dinner.

Invisible to the unaided eye, a target is "lased" by an aircraft high in the night sky, marking it for attack by an Air Force A-10 Warthog. The Warthog is big, ugly, and fires huge projectiles at a high rate and great precision.

The M60E3 machine gun has been a standard for SpecOps gunners for years but is now being replaced by the M249 and M240. This unusual photograph catches the bullet, a tracer round, in flight.

An American Special Ops soldier and his Afghan interpreter detain a suspect. Operations in Afghanistan require sensitivity to extremely complex tribal politics and traditions.

Narrow passes like this, natural sites for ambushes, have made Afghanistan a dangerous place for centuries. This one features an ancient guard house or tollbooth on the far side (partially visible) and a more recent fighting position in the foreground.

A small, platoon-sized unit of the new Afghan National Army forms up for a Kodak moment. The effectiveness of such soldiers has been, in many ways, hit or miss. Afghan men from rural areas are familiar with military weapons from childhood but shoot using the "spray-and-pray" technique. Given the opportunity and time, SF detachments have been very successful training up such recruits into tough, loyal, and occasionally disciplined soldiers.

Even more exotic old weapons recovered from another cache. There's a good reason Special Forces Weapons sergeant (designated CMF 18 Bravo) is an expert on many foreign weapons. Under many circumstances, these relics could be serviced and issued to indigenous recruits.

Part of a large supply of old ammunition hidden in a remote village. Much of the work of SF units involves disarming the rural warlords and their units, large and small. This cache includes large rockets, artillery rounds, mortar rounds, and machine gun ammunition.

A mixed bag of captured weapons—a World War II vintage British Enfield, Russian machine guns in several models, a couple of RPG rounds, and a mortar aiming stake (the red and white tube).

Captured Soviet-era mortar rounds prepared for demolition. Huge supplies of old ammunition, most in poor condition, have kept the explosive ordnance disposal technicians and SF engineers busy. C4 "plastic" explosive has been used to prime the top layer of rounds, each charge linked with detonating cord.

Mounts and accessories for heavy machine guns are piled indiscriminately in a dusty corner of a storeroom along with ammunition for larger weapons.

Since the defeat of the Taliban, girls are again allowed to attend school. These have each just received books and other materials and a Jolly bag in which to carry them.

There are some charming women in Afghanistan, especially the little ones the teams meet when distributing school supplies.

Another handsome child at the girl's school.

STYLE POINTS
MIKE WITCOSKY

Mike Witcosky was a medic in Southeast Asia in 1971–1972. It was toward the end of the game, and President Richard Nixon started pulling American ground combat units out shortly after Witcosky arrived and was assigned to 5th Special Forces Group. Since 5th Group had been one of the first in, it was one of the first out. For Mike, that meant being assigned to MACV and a program called Heavy Hook for a while, then to the 46th Special Forces Company and a little camp on the Thai/Laos border at a place called Lam Phong Dam.Heavy Hook was one of the many covert operations that were forced on Special Forces during the war, most under the umbrella of the innocuous-sounding name of Studies and Observation Group (SOG). But anybody who knew anything about SOG thought of it as the kinkiest, weirdest collection of operations and operators. Even today, many of the participants will keep the cover on their role in the game. Heavy Hook involved a lot of reconnaissance operations in Laos and Cambodia, in places where Americans were officially not present. Green Berets, along with a few other operators outside the official SF community, executed trail-mapping missions, prisoner snatches, and air crew recovery missions.

Big Medicine

I flew into the camp for my first assignment aboard an old C-7 Caribou. The team sergeant was waiting for me with a jeep. I threw my stuff in back and climbed aboard, and he drove me up to the dispensary. He stopped and said, "There are people hurt in there." That was my welcome to my first assignment as a Green Beret.

The old medic had left about a week before. Since then there had been a firefight, and there was a Thai soldier inside who'd caught a load of shrapnel. His knee was all laid open with a bunch of steel stuck in it. That was my very first case. I whipped out my orthopedic surgery textbook to get a refresher on the anatomy of the area I was going to work on. I started digging all the steel out of the wound, extending it and cleaning it out, flushing it, and then sewing it up. Then I held my breath! But it healed perfectly. It was amazing, my first major success.

People showed up at the camp nonstop, day in and day out. It could be war wounds or accidents. One of the village elders fell out of a tree and showed up with cerebral spinal fluid running out of both ears, basal skull fractures on both sides. They showed up in the middle of the night with this man, and I was supposed to take care of him.

About the third week I was in camp, a large group of people showed up with the most senior elder for the entire valley on a wooden stretcher. The old chief was extremely sick: very dehydrated, coughing, a temperature of 105 degrees. He looked like he was about to "buy it." He had a very bad case of pneumonia.

I took him into the dispensary. Then I warned the people that the chief was very near death, that I was sure he was going to die, and that there wasn't much I could do but that I would try. I got a sample of the junk he was coughing up and looked at it under the microscope. In it was the bacterium that causes bacterial pneumonia. Penicillin is the drug of choice for this stuff, and I thought, "Great, I know what the bug is!"

So I started an IV and administered some penicillin, and he turned the corner, big time! He made a dramatic recovery. We were able to feed him, and about five days later I got to send him home. After that I was "big medicine." The chief presented me with a medal, and they all made a big deal out of the event. It had a tremendous effect on the way I was treated in the whole valley.

I wore that medal the whole time I was over there, and I guess it protected me, because I had nothing but good luck the whole time I was over there.

First Combat

My first combat operation was a recon, and I was assigned to a team headed by a guy named Leving. He had been a logger from Oregon, about 6-foot-8, and he carried an M60 around like it was a pistol. I was the new guy, and they were all career SF types. I felt like the weak link on the operation.

While we were out on that operation, I got sniped at. We were moving along a trail, thinking nobody's around, and a bullet went right past my ear, boom! I will never forget the sound of that bullet; I could feel it. I just froze in my tracks. I didn't know what it was. Leving grabbed me, jerked me off my feet, and threw me to the ground. Then all the shooting started. Everybody opened up, even though it was just one sniper. It didn't last long, and by the time I got my face out of the dirt and looked around, it was all over.

Firefights and Rescues

There wasn't a strict routine to the missions we got in camp. During Operation Rolling Thunder, a lot of B-52s were being lost. The crews would bail out over Laos or Cambodia, and we'd go after them. Often the team would be split up into small groups. Two or three guys would hop on a Jolly Green Giant with the Air Force "PJs" [parachute jumpers; rescue specialists] to go out looking for these guys. We went after fighter pilots, too, but with disappointing results. Yet we managed to pick up a number of B-52 crews. Those missions were always a spur-of-the-moment deal. You just grabbed all your stuff and ran down to the tarmac, piled aboard, and took off. That was some of the most gratifying work I did over there.

A lot of the work that I did was long-range recon. We'd go in for about a week, usually, get inserted some distance from our AO, then travel overland to the objective. We did a lot of mapping of roads and investigating Pathet Lao training bases.

Once we got into a firefight with a group of Pathet Lao troops, and one of the guys on the team killed a Chinese major. He had a satchel full of papers and maps, so we dragged his body back, along with the papers, and the CIA guys just went nuts, they were so excited!

We had our share of firefights, but a successful mission really involved getting in, accomplishing our mission, and getting back out again—undetected. If the enemy figured out we were in their area about a half hour after we left, that was a successful mission. When we got into trouble, it was maybe half a dozen of us versus maybe a regiment of them. We considered ourselves lucky if we just brushed the flank of an enemy unit instead of the point, if we saw them before they saw us. But we had a couple of lucky encounters where we bumped into enemy units and managed to get away. The worst of these was the NVA, because they were well-disciplined troops. It only happened a couple of times, and we were lucky enough to see them before they saw us.

I found it interesting how easy it was for a small group of people to bed down for the night and, if they did it right, just disappear into the bushes. On some occasions we thought we were in the middle of nowhere and bedded down for the night, only to discover later that there was a major road nearby, with heavy traffic and lots of people coming by. Suddenly there would be trucks and people, conversation and activity. We had to wait, and wait, and wait until they left.

"Well, I Think They're Going to Shoot You."

I was initially assigned to Heavy Hook, and then, when Heavy Hook was phased out, I went to the 46th Special Forces Company. I was the junior medic on the team, but since the senior medic was also an engineer and spent all his time on engineering projects, I was effectively the only medic in the camp.

We trained all sorts of people: Thai Special Forces, border police, and lots of tribesmen brought in by the CIA. These were Lao and Cambodian troops flown in by the CIA. That operation was run by an interesting guy whose first name was Jack but who was known as Three Fingers because he had two fingers missing from one hand. He used to drop in to check up on his troops. At graduation time he would bring a couple of John Wayne war movies; we'd project the movies against the side of one of the buildings, and everybody would get drunk and whoop it up. Three Fingers financed just about everything that went on in our camp—all the food, a lot of the equipment.

The dispensary where I worked was right next to the main gate in this camp. One day I heard a lot of yelling and commotion and went out to investigate. There was a taxi at the gate—a very unusual event since the camp was quite secure, and most taxi drivers had more sense than to bring people there. The taxi driver paced back and forth nervously while his passenger was lying prone on the ground. The Thai guard had one boot on the guy's head and the muzzle of his M16 in the guy's ear. The guard was extremely angry, and there was a lot of yelling.

The guy on the ground was obviously an American journalist; there were cameras everywhere. He was, as I recall, from *Time* magazine. He had been trying to chase down this CIA operative that we called Three Fingers all over Southeast Asia. He was trying to document what we were doing and had somehow discovered our camp. He saw my face and said, "My God, an American! Help me! Help me!"

"This isn't my camp," I told him. "I'm a visitor here. It's their camp, and they can do with you whatever they want. What the hell did you come out here for? You made a big mistake!"

"What are they going to do with me?" he begged.

"Well, I think they're going to shoot you."

He was really scared and pleading for help. So I had a little conversation with the guard in Thai and told him that he really couldn't kill the reporter. He was, after all, an American, and it just

197

wouldn't do. So then I told the reporter that I made a deal with the guard and he was going to let him go, but he had to leave immediately! And he threw his stuff in the cab and disappeared quickly from view.

Fishing, Green Beret Style

We decided, after the camp was set up, that we would start putting on "feeds" for the village. The first time we scraped together some money and bought a cow and had it butchered and then had a huge barbecue. The village people just loved that! We had great rapport with these people, partly as a result of things like this. So we decided the next time to have a fish fry.

The camp was on a lake, and we had a little aluminum skiff that leaked. One day a couple of us decided to go fishing. We dumped a box of hand grenades in the skiff and paddled out into the lake. Now, the village people were used to catching fish with hand nets by beating the water; the result was normally a small catch of tiny little minnows.

So we paddled out in the middle of the lake and tossed a few grenades over the side. After a *thwomp*, all manner of fish started floating to the surface—huge fish, little alligators, turtles, all kinds of fish. We piled this stuff into the boat and paddled back to the shore.

A crowd of village kids had been attracted by the noise and had collected on the shoreline, watching us. When we started pulling these big fish out of the water, the kids just went nuts, they were so excited. We collected at least 200 pounds of fish, including some very large carp, and went back to the shore. The kids were beside themselves. They had never seen such big fish, apparently, and didn't know they existed. So we gave one big fish to each kid, and some of the fish were as big as the child. They all went running back home with their fish, yelling and screaming with delight.

We ended up eating some interesting things with these people— locusts, for instance. Once in a while huge locusts would fly around in the area, and the local people would catch them. Then, they would roll them in a banana leaf, cook them, and eat them. I tried that once and didn't find it particularly tasty. One thing I really did like, though, was ant larva, a real delicacy. They were very sweet; I was surprised.

Target Practice, NVA Style

The NVA and Pathet Lao would mortar the camp occasionally. They always seemed to aim for the team house. It seemed to be a never-ending desire on their part to put a mortar round on the roof of our team house, but whoever they were using for a mortar team sure didn't know their business because they never hit it. There were far more important targets within the camp for them to shoot at, but the team house had some special appeal for them. They got close a few times, but they never hit it. The team house and the helicopters both seemed to be a special invitation to the enemy mortar crews, but they never scored on either target or significantly damaged anything in the camp. They dug some holes and threw some dust in the air, but that was about it.

When the camp was built, the trees inside the perimeter were left, while those outside were cleared for better fields of observation and fire. The camp must have been kind of pretty when it was built, but the enemy mortar rounds went off when they hit the tops of the trees, so now they were in pretty bad shape.

Always Something on the Stove

We had a Thai woman and her husband working for us in the camp. She did the cooking, and he ran the errands and did the shopping. She was a spectacular cook! They bought fruit and vegetables on the local economy, and we got our milk and meat through a barter system with an Air Force sergeant who worked in the officer's mess at the U.S. base nearby. We got fresh milk and steaks from him and traded for various bits of NVA uniform items and weapons, which he then turned around and sold to American Air Force personnel. All these steaks and supplies were sent out on an Air Force helicopter twice a week or so, and the pilots must have known where it was coming from, but nobody ever said anything about it.

There was always something waiting for you on the stove, no matter what time you got in. She'd sit you down and start jabbering, and then she'd bring all kinds of food! We really appreciated her, and she really enjoyed being appreciated.

The people around the camp were all Meo tribesmen, and I don't think they'd ever seen an American until the camp was built, about six months before I arrived. They were very, very primitive. A lot of the things we did just amazed them. The helicopters in particular were very exciting for them.

Body Count

Once a month an administrative helicopter would fly up to our camp with a pay officer from the finance company, along with other officers dropping in for visits or inspections. One month a new "candy-striper" second lieutenant appeared. After pay was dispersed, we all adjourned to the team house for a cold beer.

After a while, the team leader noticed that the lieutenant had disappeared. He sent me out to look for him with the guidance that I should make sure he didn't get into any trouble.

After some searching, I found him down behind the motor pool. He had gathered some of the security team and had them laying on the ground, around the wire, and on top of the bunkers, playing dead while he took photographs. I yelled at the guards to get back to their positions and told the now-indignant young officer that the commander wanted to talk to him.

We went back to the team room, and I explained to the commander what had been happening. The CO was so mad that he read the lieutenant the riot act, and sent him to wait in the helicopter [the most dangerous place in the camp, an obvious target] until it left, with the guidance that he was never to set foot in that camp again. And he didn't.

"They Paid."

I never felt really bad about anything until an incident in the village outside the camp. I had been working with some of the young men in the village, teaching them some basic medical techniques for treating injuries and improving the health of the other people. The enemy came into the village one night and shot up a bunch of the people, including the ones I had been training. They came through the village, and anyone who showed any evidence of contact with the Americans was used as an example. There were a couple of people dead and a number who had been cut up. I felt bad that I had brought that on them.

But we burned the enemy's ass for that. The next morning, when we found out, we tracked them down. They paid. We mobilized some of the foreign special forces that were in our camp, some of our best students, and one particular platoon that had been exemplary. Then we tracked them down through the woods.

They moved about 15 klicks through the woods before we caught up with them. They were loud and obvious and easy to follow. Undisciplined. We caught up with them, flanked them, and ambushed them. That was the end of that. There were about 20 of them. It was probably the best-executed ambush we had ever done; they made it easy for us. We had a lot of people, two M60s, one at each end of a well set-up ambush. It was extremely effective.

In 30 seconds the whole thing was over.

What I Remember Most

I enjoyed the time. I enjoyed the camaraderie. When I first went into the Army, I was worried about the war, worried about the kind of people I was going to be around. I didn't like the idea that I might be "greased" because somebody else screwed up. But in Special Forces everybody was really tight, dependent on each other, and you could always rely on these guys. If something was supposed to happen, a rendezvous, an extraction, it always happened!

It made me feel extremely confident. I always felt like I was in good shape. I was around good people who knew what they were doing, even if I didn't know what I was doing, since I was so new at it.

And I felt very good about all the things we did. We did a lot of "civic action" work that improved the lives of the people around the camp. We helped the young people do things to avoid contracting TB; improved their water supply; and treated broken bones, infections, and cuts. I never felt very comfortable about the military operations where you're fighting and shooting people, killing people, although I was able to rationalize it.

It was a very emotional experience for me. When I start thinking about it now, it still has a weird effect. I don't mind, necessarily; I just get reflective.

The small group and the close-knit nature of the team had a lot to do with my ability to tolerate things like that. My team sergeant was a crusty old guy, a veteran of World War II and Korea before Vietnam. His decorations filled up all the available space on his dress greens. I went out and ran operations that would sound just about impossible. But I did them with people I was so close to, that I had so much confidence in, and thought nothing of them. They weren't that hard! If you planned it right, used your brain, you could find a way to get it done. I had so much confidence in my team that I never really worried. I really enjoyed my time in SF. When it was time to go, it was a very hard decision for me to get out of the Army.

I found SF people to always be very truthful. If somebody made a mistake, they took responsibility for it rather than trying to shift the blame. Of all my time in the military, I never encountered that high level of integrity or the level of intelligence and insight, except in SF. Everywhere else in the Army was completely different.

MARTHA RAYE—GREEN BERET
JACK ABRAHAM

Jack Abraham retired from the Army as a colonel and started
a new career as a project manager for a large civilian firm.

Putt-Putt and Martha Raye

This happened at Boun Ea Yang. We had a little Montagnard we called "Putt-Putt." Putt-Putt was not "all there"; his elevator just didn't go all the way to the roof. Whatever he saw you do, he would duplicate. If you walked up to a tree and kicked it, Putt-Putt would do the same. The problem with that was that Putt-Putt was barefooted. He was funny as hell. If you took your finger and drew an imaginary line around your head, he would do the same thing. I will never forget Putt-Putt!

When we lost the camp at Boun Eano and moved to Boun Ea Yang, we lived in extremely primitive conditions for a while. Our mess tent was no more than a regular tent with some mosquito netting hanging down the sides. There was no way you could control the flies. So it became a habit that you ate with one hand and waved the flies away with the other. It also became a habit, while shooing away these pests, to say, "Fucking flies!" Putt-Putt picked up this habit, and all you had to do was to move your hand, and he would say, "Fluckin' flies!" We thought this was mildly amusing, but not a big deal, until Martha Raye came to the camp.

We were very honored when she decided to visit us. I told the team sergeant, though, "Now, no matter what happens, Ferrell, you make sure that Putt-Putt is not around Martha Raye!"

"Yes, sir," he said. "No problem."

Martha Raye arrived, and we were sitting in the mess tent drinking hot Cokes or hot beers, I don't remember. Like the rest of us, Maggie was shooing the flies off with one hand. From out of a cluster of Montagnards looking on came Putt-Putt's voice: "Flucking flies!"

I thought Martha Raye was going to shit. She was about to die laughing. She thought that was so funny! Of course I was profusely apologetic; I was very embarrassed. "I'm so sorry, Maggie. I don't know what to say."

"He's right!" she said. "The fucking flies are terrible!"

Martha Raye

Martha Raye is one of Special Forces' living legends. She served during World War II as a nurse, maintained a reserve affiliation, and was a lieutenant colonel in the reserves despite her entertainment career. She took a special interest in SF, visited many camps, was wounded during visits to two of them, and drank many of the troopers right under the table. They all fell in love with her, and she with them. They still consider her part of their community. Her house has always been open to any SF soldier. If you ask the SF community, Martha Raye had more balls than most of the rest of the men in the Army.

Martha Raye was a big deal with Special Forces. She was our gal! We were standing at the bar in the club at Ban Me Thuot, drinking with the "leg" colonel who was the district senior advisor. This colonel was trying to impress Maggie with his accomplishments. Maggie put me on the spot. She said to him, "Colonel, when you start soldiering like Captain Abraham here, then you'll be winning the war."

"ALOHA," AND MORE FUN
WITH MARTHA RAYE
Clyde Sincere

*Clyde Sincere retired from the Army as a colonel after 22
years of service, but he didn't get completely away from
the profession of arms. He works today as a project manager
for a company that provides training assistance under
contract to the Department of Defense. He is highly
active in the Special Forces Association and the
Special Operations Association.*

"Oops, Wrong Uniform!"

It was November 1966. I was a "strap hanger" [just along for the
ride—not part of the tactical unit] on a Mike Force operation
commanded by Captain Bob Jacobelly, 3rd Company of the II
Corps Mike Force.

We were moving along a trail when the point element came
back to report that six NVA were moving down the trail toward us.
We set up a hasty ambush. When the six NVA entered the kill
zone, we opened fire. All of them were hit. Four seemed to be killed
immediately, and two took off but left blood trails. We started
searching the bodies.

While I was working on one of the NVA, I noticed out of the
corner of my eye that one of the "dead" enemy soldiers started to
get up, then lay down again. "Playing possum" is an old trick that
can get you killed when the "dead" guy rolls a grenade at you. I
called over to one of the guys: "Hey, he ain't dead!"

205

One of our guys (I won't mention his name) moved over to the NVA soldier and kicked him, to get him to react. But the guy was a good actor; he didn't move! So then our guy shot the NVA in the leg. He was still good! Then our guy took a machete and ran it right through the guy.

"I think you got him now," I told him, "but God will get you!"

We started to follow the blood trails, with Bob Jacobelly and me out in front of the troops. We spotted one of the NVA at the base of a tree. I ran up to the guy; he was covered with blood, from head to toe. He was just sitting there. He handed me something, but I was paying more attention to the blood.

Bob yelled, "Sir! Grenade!" The NVA had handed me a "potato masher" grenade. He'd pulled the string they used for a safety, but he hadn't hit it against his helmet or the ground to activate it. I didn't know that at the time! All I knew at that moment was that I was about to accept a hand grenade offering from this guy. I was kneeling on the ground in front of the wounded NVA soldier, so I took off running, on my knees! I wore the fabric right off the knees of those pants, getting away. As soon as I was out of the way, all 400-plus guys opened up on the man, and then there was nothing left of him.

Those six NVA were part of a larger unit, and we captured parts of six heavy machine guns from them. From the parts we were able to assemble three functional machine guns, one of which is still on display today at the Special Forces museum at Fort Bragg.

Those guns were really heavy to carry, but we brought them out. We speculated on how many lives of the U.S. Army 4th Division we saved by the capture of those guns, because there was a joint operation in progress with the 4th, and their helicopters were extremely vulnerable to the 12.7-millimeter antiaircraft machine guns.

Although we wiped out that squad of NVA, we nearly were wiped out ourselves later on the same operation. The NVA discovered that an American unit was coming into their area of operations, and Charlie [slang for Viet Cong, from the phonetics Victor Charlie] left us alone. When we made contact with these enemy units, they didn't engage but pulled back and disappeared. Instead, they waited for the 4th Division. They hit Colonel Bob Lee's battalion and killed nearly all of his company commanders.

The NVA mauled the 4th Division, even though the 4th was well dug in, behind sandbags and in bunkers. The NVA sent two regiments against that one 4th Division battalion. After they had engaged Colonel Lee's battalion, they sent a single battalion after Captain Bob Jacobelly's company of Mike Force strikers, and Bob was just about shot in half by a machine gun. He lived and spent the next year in a hospital.

I took two prisoners back to Pleiku, and I was still there when we got word that the Mike Force was under attack. I loaded a chopper up with ammunition and supplies, all bagged in sandbags, and we flew them out there to resupply the company. The crew chief, a guy named Leonard, was supposed to have been packing to go home, but because of the emergency he flew the mission. A supply lieutenant, a guy named Hess, had been in country three weeks. The lieutenant jumped up beside the door gunner.

When it was time to land, the pilot called up the unit on the ground. They popped smoke. The VC and NVA knew our SOP, and they often popped smoke, too, trying to lure the helicopter into an ambush. We tried to counter this by having the unit on the ground authenticate the color, in this case, yellow.

Well, the NVA popped smoke, and it was yellow too. We didn't see the first smoke from the friendly unit. We had already passed them when we saw the yellow smoke that was supposed to mark our LZ.

As the pilot came in to a hover above the LZ, the NVA opened up on us and shot the chopper to pieces. Hess and Leonard were killed immediately; a heavy machine gun virtually took their heads off. The copilot was severely wounded. The door gunner on the other side was also wounded. Major Cartright, the pilot, turned to me and said on the intercom, "Hey, Clyde, somebody's got to get off."

I was the only one who could still move, so I jumped out. As I jumped, Lieutenant Hess' weapon hit the ground beside me, an M16 with magazines taped together, "cowboy style."

I started running to the tree line, still thinking our guys were in there. Then the NVA came out. I thought, "Oops, wrong uniform!" I hit the ground and got off a few rounds. Then they threw a grenade that got me, and I had to stop. There was enough blood on me that they just came over, collected my weapon and my boots, and left me to die.

I lay there for a couple of hours before Frank Quinn, my sergeant major with the Mike Force (and who was also a "strap hanger" on the operation, but with one of the other companies), Sergeant Danny Panfil, and a couple of Montagnards came down and started looking around the area for me. They got me back to the lines.

Although I was covered with blood and looked terrible, I wasn't really hurt so bad that I couldn't function. The Mike Force had fought bravely and had lost their commander and had about 50 percent casualties. They were running low on ammunition. I took over, got on the radio and called Pleiku and said, "Hey, we need a resupply."

I forget the little redheaded major's name, but he was an asshole. He came out and, at 1,500 feet, he threw out the resupplies! You can imagine where it landed—in Cambodia! So Frank Quinn and some Montagnards and I ran across the dry lake bed to the Cambodian side. We picked up all the ammunition we could, then we ran back and distributed it to the troops.

During the battle, a little Montagnard M79 gunner ended up laying beside me in a shallow depression. He was shivering and crying from fright. I took the M79 from him and pointed it toward the enemy and pulled the trigger. It fired. The projectile hit a tree and bounced right back at us! I handed it back to the guy and said, "Here. It's yours; you know how to use this thing!" It scared the hell out of me. I didn't know that the projectile didn't arm for about 25 meters, and it hit the tree at about 10 feet.

The battle lasted 10 hours. Finally, they sent in a 4th Division relief force to help. When it was over, we policed up 58 NVA bodies from our immediate perimeter. We were picking up the bodies to bury in a big pit the 4th Division engineers had blasted for us, when we came across a body that had been cut in half by the effects of a cluster bomb strike.

"I never knew what the inside of a human body looked like," I said to one of the sergeants with me. He just about turned green. It was just strange at the time to see a half of a man, from the waist up.

When it came time to go and we were loading bodies on the choppers, I discovered that, as I was loading Montagnard bodies on one side of the helicopter, the crew chief was pulling them off on the other. I "braced" the pilot with a weapon, threatening to kill him. I told him that if I ever caught any crews doing that again, I wouldn't be responsible for my own actions. I told him to tell the other chopper pilots the same thing.

I thought they would report me, but at that moment my mind snapped. They said that they were only there to pick up wounded. My thought was, I've got to get the dead back home too. You don't leave Montagnards lying on the battlefield if you can help it!

During the operation, NVA documents were captured that showed they knew who we were and where we were, all the time. They were just waiting for something bigger to come along. We didn't even carry entrenching tools. We slept in the open, and if the NVA had wanted to, they could have killed all of us easily. We took more than 50 percent casualties as it was. That was the last time the II Corps Mike Force went out without entrenching tools. We learned our lesson from that.

Bob Jacobelly and Frank Quinn got the Silver Star for that, and everybody got the Purple Heart. I got a Distinguished Flying Cross for getting off the helicopter. We didn't usually get medals; we figured that this was part of our jobs. We often went on long operations with a lot of action, and nobody got anything except Purple Hearts.

They Fell for It Every Time!

Black Jack missions got their name from Colonel Francis Kelly's call sign, "Black Jack." The senior officers all had call signs; mine

209

was "Thunderbolt." We trained to operate in a particular AO, for 30 days or more at a time. Every seven days we got a resupply. The way I did that was with A-1E Skyraiders and empty napalm containers.

I went to Nha Trang and worked out the system with Bob Barris, the assistant S-4 at that time. We sawed off the ends of these napalm containers, added a cargo parachute, and filled them up with food and ammunition. Sixteen of these things would provide enough resupply for a whole Mike Force for a week.

A flight of four Skyraiders could deliver these to us out in the field. They dropped them from 300 feet. The chute would open, and the container would just hit the ground. Then the guys would unbolt the ends, and inside were sandbags filled with food and ammo, each one tagged for distribution, with color codes for the contents. It was an excellent way to bring in mortar ammunition and almost anything else.

Each Skyraider carried four of these containers plus another four with real napalm in them. They flew cover for us while we policed up these containers, and that took quite a while.

One thing we always did, and it always worked, was to pile all these containers and parachutes up in the drop zone, then booby-trap them. We got them with this every time. You would have thought they would learn, but they fell for it every time!

"Somebody Stop Them!"

I was extremely proud of how well the Montagnards fought on the Cambodian border, and when I took the third Black Jack operation out for a 30-day mobile guerrilla mission (Black Jack 23), I took the Montagnards with us.

We were bombed on March 9, 1967, by the U.S. Air Force. I asked for a "combat proof/sky spot" to verify our position and coordinate with our air cover. The two pilots dived on me and bombed my unit. They thought we were enemy in the open. One of my American guys was killed, along with several Montagnards, and we had 27 wounded. I was screaming on the radio, "Somebody stop them!" But we didn't have direct radio communications; they were on UHF and VHF, and we only had FM. A buddy of mine, Ralph Miller, was an FAC or Covey and came up on the radio to say hello to me. He was the one who got them to stop bombing us any further.

The troops were so shell-shocked afterward that they were useless as a unit from then on. I relieved everyone when we got home and reconstituted the unit. They had fought so hard on the first battle on the Cambodian border, only to be bombed on this one. It just ruined them. So we broke them up and put the individuals in other units.

There was a big investigation. It turned out the same two F-100 pilots, flying out of Phan Rang, had killed a substantial number of civilians at Lang Vei the day before in another indiscriminate bombing. Both were kicked out of the Air Force.

Opcon to the 1st Air Cav

Colonel Kelly put Black Jack 23 and me, as commander, under the operational control (OpCon) of the 1st Air Cavalry, operating out of Bong Son at the time. We were supposed to work on the western side of the Cav's AO.

Major General John Norton, the Cav commander, said, "Clyde, if you get in serious trouble, I'll send you a company to reinforce you. Two hours later, if you still need help, I'll send you a battalion. Two hours after that, a regiment. If that doesn't do it, I'll give you the whole division!"

Well, on a single day we got ambushed between 25 and 30 times. My poor combat recon platoon was taking the brunt of this, so as a considerate commander and to give them a break, I put them at the tail of the march and let them bring up the rear. The next time we got ambushed, we got hit from the rear, and they got nailed again. During all this time we didn't get so much as a squad from the 1st Air Cav!

We were on Hill 709 and surrounded. I was lying on the ground with Andy, in the middle of the perimeter, about four or five in the afternoon. Suddenly I heard a blood curdling scream; it was Andy. He said, "Sir, somebody's squeezing my balls!"

Everybody was looking at Andy. I said to him, "Andy, I'm the only one here, and I'm not that kind of guy."

He was passing a kidney stone, which is supposed to be as painful as anything. The troops were looking at me, and I said, "Hey, not me. I'm not touching him!" Anyway, we got a chopper in to evacuate him. They lowered a stokes litter on a cable, we put him in, and up he went.

I had called for help, and Major General Norton sent Captain Vern Gillespie out to see what was going on. Vern was talking to me over the radio from the chopper, from about 15 feet in the air, when Charlie opened up and shot that chopper right out of the sky. Well, Vern fell into my arms! The shock of the hits on the helicopter had knocked him out. Then the chopper crashed at the foot of the mountain. Within less than an hour, Major General Norton had two companies surrounding that chopper!

That was my cue to take my force and depart. We headed down the mountain, to where those two companies were. Gillespie was the only one in a regular American uniform. We put him in front to help identify us to the Cav, since the rest of us were in black pajamas. We got down in a dry creek bed and received some more fire. The casualties weren't bad (cuts and bruises from the flying gravel), but it sure shook up the troops again.

Aloha

As the commander at My Loc (which became FOB-3 following the closing of Khe Sanh on June 30, 1968), a field-grade officer, I wasn't allowed across the border into Laos, Cambodia, or North Vietnam on insertion missions. However, it was okay for me to go along on extractions following a "prairie fire," which usually meant that the team was compromised and in serious trouble!

On November 30, 1968, Major Sam Toomey came up from MACV SOG headquarters in Saigon and asked for a recon team that could be used for an Elder Son/Italian Green mission (substituting sabotaged mortar rounds and ammunition that would explode when fired) at a recently located enemy arms cache. Lieutenant Raymond Stack was the recon team leader, and Major Toomey and five enlisted men—Art Bader, Rich Fitts, Gary LaBohn, Mike Mein, and Klaus Scholz—went on the mission. I was in the chase ship and could only go as far as Khe Sanh, where I had to get off. They went on.

As I understand it, they never made it to the cache site. I don't know for sure, because nobody made it out alive. The team got picked up and were coming out when the chase ship picked up a transmission from somebody for helicopters to stay clear of a set of grid coordinates because an FAC had reported a heavy-caliber antiaircraft weapon, a 37-millimeter, on the ground. The chase ship crew assumed that the lead chopper, carrying the team, copied the broadcast, but apparently they missed it. The lead ship got shot down at 4,000 feet!

The gunship escorts reported that the chopper exploded on impact and that there couldn't be survivors. Even so, there was a lot of pressure for us to go in there to retrieve the bodies. But 5th Group said emphatically, "Don't you dare! There will be two regiments of NVA surrounding that crash site, just waiting for you. Unless you've got something bigger than that, forget it!"

Well, I wasn't going to go in there with my little Hatchet force against two regiments. We'd just add to the body count, so we didn't.

We could hear the NVA talking about all this on the radio. They reported that it was a helicopter full of Vietnamese. The explosion and fire and the fact that nobody was wearing American uniforms—the recon team was wearing tiger-stripe fatigues— made everybody unrecognizable. So we didn't make an issue of it at the time.

But, many years later, the bodies were recovered, and they were finally buried in Arlington Cemetery. Unknown to any of us, the media had secretly wired the chairs of the families at the graveside service. All the remains from the seven guys were put in one

213

casket, and I had the privilege to put seven MIA bracelets (one for each man) on top of the casket to be buried with them. All seven names were on the same stone. I spoke to all the families, told them about the circumstances, and told them why I was sure that everybody on the chopper was dead. One of the families, though, the LaBohn family, sued the government to have that name removed. They just couldn't accept the idea that their guy had died.

Sam Toomey's father was a retired colonel, and his wife was Hawaiian. They brought a little ukulele, and at the end of the service they sang "Aloha," which can mean hello or goodbye. It was very beautiful.

Going Native

I loved the Yards. I was very lucky. When I had an A-camp at An Loc, I had a little Hmong captain who had been made an officer by the French; he was my counterpart. I had a Vietnamese XO, but he was as worthless as tits on a boar hog. The majority of the LLDB in our camp were Montagnard. We had only two Vietnamese, the XO and a sergeant. The sergeant was brilliant! He worked like a horse. The Yards loved him, and he loved the Yards. He got along fabulously with the Hmong captain, but I had to watch the XO like a hawk.

I had to send one sergeant home because he was getting too "native." He was always taking the side of the Montagnards over that of the American NCOs, regardless of who was right or wrong. I had to take him aside many times and counsel him on his actions.

I sent him home. When I got back myself, I picked up a copy of *National Geographic*, and sure enough, there he was, back at my old A camp, as the team sergeant.

When he finally went home, after 14 years, he walked up to the door of his mother's house and knocked. An old lady came to the door. "Get away," she said to this disreputable character.

"Hey, Mom, it's me!" That's what happens when you stay away from home for 14 years.

Martha Raye

Maggie came to visit the Mike Force a couple of times. One evening she said, "How about some coffee in the morning?" In the morning we gave her a cup of coffee, and she said, "What the hell is this? I wanted vodka! I was just being nice!" So we got some vodka for her.

I gave Maggie an AK-47. Now, she wasn't authorized to take that AK home any more than the rest of us, so she took it apart and taped the pieces to her body. She walked off the plane with a crutch and a limp, and that's how she got it in the country.

When I gave her the AK, she noticed the sign I had over my door that said, "Fuck Communism!" She loved it! She saw it and said, "Can I have that? I want to put it in my 'team house' back in Bel Air." (She kept a room in her home set up as a Special Forces refuge, her "team room." A Green Beret was always welcome to spend the night at Martha Raye's.)

So I said, "Sure!" We took it down, and I gave it to her, and she hung it up in her team house.

She called me one time and said, "Clyde, I had a woman reporter show up here, and I took her in the team house to show her how things were. She saw that sign. She said, 'Isn't that sign utterly disgusting!' I told her, 'Get your fucking ass out of my house!'" That's the way she talked.

Another time we invited Maggie out to our camp, and there was a big battle at Bong Son. She immediately left us and went to Bong Son to help out. She worked there until she was exhausted.

She loved the enlisted men. She said she liked taking the officers' money in poker games, and she loved being around "her men," the sergeants.

THE AGENCY

If you get to know any Vietnam-era Green Beret and start swapping stories about the big war, sooner or later you will find yourself at the edge of an informational "black hole." You'll know this because your friend will say, "I had two official tours over there" or "I went over in 1969 as a 'person,'" or some other evasive answer. That's because your friend did a tour in the employ of the U.S. Central Intelligence Agency and was sworn to eternal secrecy about the experience.

The agency used SF personnel for many worthwhile programs in Laos, Cambodia, and Thailand, all at the same time that the U.S. government was saying, in effect, "Nope, we certainly wouldn't do a thing like that!"

It is still going on, too; I once asked about a friend who hadn't been visible for a few months. "Bill just retired," I was told. "He's flying the 'black flag' down in the Caribbean." It's nice to know the CIA still needs a few good men.

—Hans Halberstadt

MORE WALT SHUMATE,
EVEN MORE MARTHA RAYE
Conrad "Ben" Baker, CISO

Ben Baker is one of those old, legendary "China hands." He lived in Asia for 28 years. Much of that time was spent in the deep, dark world of covert operations. As deputy director of the U.S. Army Counter Insurgency Support Office (CISO) from 1963 to 1974, he was responsible for keeping the camps supplied with all the essentials of uncivilized life. During that time, he made more than 50 TDY trips to Vietnam, Thailand, and Laos, visiting more than 100 special ops locations. His many years (1947–1975) in the Far East, Corps of Engineers, logistics background, and those field trips served him well. He designed knives, rucksacks, air drop containers, and other items for the indigenous forces. Most important, he developed the indigenous patrol ration. Although he wasn't an official Green Beret, Ben was as hardcore and was as much of an operator as anybody in the theater.

Walt Shumate

I was out at Bon Sar Pa, checking up on the camps to make sure they were getting what they really needed, when I met the legendary Walt Shumate for the first time. He approached me one day and looked me over with a jaundiced eye. "What do you need, sergeant?" I asked him. He gave me a long list of stuff.

I said to him, "Sergeant, you had better not tell me you need 10 of something when you only need 1. Because, if you do, you will rue the day you lie to CISO. If you tell me you need 10, you're gonna get 10. But don't tell me you need 20 in order to get 10!"

217

"Okay, yessir, yessir," Walt said, and reduced the quantities on his list. I got on the radio and called back to CISO Okinawa and ordered his stuff. About three or four days later, an airplane arrived from Nha Trang, loaded with everything he had ordered. After that, we became close friends. Walt Shumate was just about the only Special Forces sergeant who would even give me the time of day. I was a "leg" at the time, a "dirty, rotten, carpetbaggin' civilian leg!" Six months later I was given a short course, and I parachuted with the 5th Group into Thailand and Laos. Colonel Mike Healy later appointed me an honorary life member of the 5th Special Forces Group (Airborne). Walt and his wife, Helen, corresponded with me and my wife, Shirley, until he passed away on March 1, 1993. We sure miss Walt.

Ho Chi Shumate

Walt Shumate asked Shirley to take care of a small, furry, bug-eyed lemur he had brought back to Okinawa. He was making a quick trip to Vietnam; then he was reassigned to Fort Bragg. Walt had named the lemur Ho Chi because "he moved slowly, only came out at night, and only ate bananas."

Anyway, Walt returned, picked up Ho Chi, and smuggled him on the plane home in his jacket. He was sitting in the rear by a fuse panel and fell asleep. Ho Chi decided to investigate the panel. The lights flickered, and all hell broke loose on the plane. Walt woke up and snatched a singed Ho Chi back, trying to look nonchalant, as crew members ran up and down the aisles.

Martha Raye's Happy Hour

I was up at Pleiku one time, when 30-plus wounded were flown in. Everyone not otherwise occupied pitched in to help. I was working at the beginning of the line, helping to pull surface shrapnel out of wounded Yards. Martha Raye was down at the other end of the line in surgery and worked there for about a day and a half straight. After it was all over, Martha went down to the sergeants' hooch to drink with them. She never wanted to have much to do with the officers; she preferred to socialize with the NCOs. Since I was a civilian, I was permitted to join the group. We sat down at a big table, and each of us had our own bottle. Let me tell you, she could hold more than any of us guys.

Snoopy

Back on Okinawa I kept a pair of purebred AKC beagles that had an occasional litter. Realizing that the Logistic Support Center at Nha Trang was in dire need of a mascot, I gave Sergeant First Class Bill Coombs a pup. Named "Snoopy," she was probably the only dog in Vietnam to eat steak and live in a bomb-proof, air-conditioned dog house.

When Martha Raye was in town, Snoopy was in dog heaven. Seems that the one thing you couldn't get in Nha Trang was a beef bone, since meat was shipped in boneless. Martha would invariably bring Snoopy a huge beef bone and get a wet kiss in return.

Liz

The Tactical Operations Center was located in an old French villa in Saigon. In the garden was a large cage that was home to "Liz," a 12-foot python. Numerous troops pulled Liz out and took photos of each other holding her, and Liz generally tolerated it. But then she started striking out and biting people. Liz was about to be terminated with prejudice when it was learned that the Vietnamese cook was stealing Liz's live duck ration. The cook was sent off to the Army for training, and Liz went back on her duck-a-week schedule.

The Barfly at Can Tho

We had a problem getting enough parts for the Lycoming airplane engines installed on 5th Group's airboats. While awaiting transportation to the airboat company at Cao Lanh, I went into the club at Det

C4, Can Tho, for a drink. No sooner did my brandy arrive than their mascot, a small honey bear, jumped up on the stool next to mine.

The bartender said, "She likes brandy."

Too late. That bear bit my thumb, and I bled like a stuck pig for about an hour. How did I know the lady wanted her drink first?

Crocodiles

"Requisition Order Form

"From: Plei Djerang, Engineer, Det A-214

"To: 5th SF Group (Airborne) S4

"1. Crocodile, 10–12 year old, minimum length 8 feet, 20 each.

"Crocodiles are needed to stock the local swamp as protective devices. Air land at Chu Dron. Greenwood."

"Action: Disapproved, for the following reasons:

"1. Not available from local or CONUS sources. CONUS only has alligators.

"2. Local sentry dog school commander refuses to train crocodiles to not eat tender Montagnard babies unless we supply him with fresh live VC to use as bait.

"3. Air Force won't fly the damn things anyhow."

Ears

Special Forces became notorious for stories about the taking of ears from dead VC and NVA, but the real story is more complicated than what appears to be the mutilation of enemy dead (a war crime). In fact, it was a Montagnard tradition.

I was out in the boonies at a camp close to Ban Don that nearly got overrun. One of the SF guys got wounded, so I went out and took over his machine gun. We shot the shit out of them on the wire. We repelled the enemy, they managed to get in the wire, but they didn't overrun us.

220

When it was over we had a big sacrifice for the dead Montagnards, in traditional tribal style. The Americans all got their bracelets, except me—I'm not supposed to be involved in that kind of stuff, I'm supposed to be a yellow-bellied carpetbagger!

When it was finally time to go on to other things, I got on a helicopter. They gave me an elephant scrotum bag to take with me, and I put it in my rucksack without looking inside. You get pretty tired after being up for three days and nights, pumped full of adrenaline, so I went to sleep in the chopper. When I woke up, I remembered the bag they'd given me, the one I had stuffed in my rucksack. I pulled it out, opened it up, and damn if it wasn't full of ears!

The witch doctor had cut the ears off the enemies so that their souls would wander forever, searching for the missing part, and couldn't be reincarnated! It wasn't a war-crime sort of thing; it was to keep the enemy from coming back again. And they really believed that kind of superstition.

Anyway, I started throwing the ears out of the helicopter, one at a time. I was sitting on the right side of the chopper, by the door in front of the door gunner. While I was shucking these things out into the air, the door gunner reached over and pounded on my shoulder. "What's that, man?" he yelled.

"It's an ear, man!" I yelled back. And I took one of the ears, put it between my teeth, and spit it out into the slipstream, right past his head. If he had not had a safety belt on, he would have sailed right out of there. He passed out and turned gray!

Here's a guy who shot people from the air, but when he saw a body part up close, he couldn't take it. When he landed at Pleiku, he was still slumped over. The copilot asked, "What happened to him? Did he get hit?"

"No, I think he's just a little sick," I said and walked away.

SHELL-SHOCK
JON CAVIANI

Jon Caviani spent 23 months and 11 days as a POW in North Vietnam. He received the Medal of Honor on his return to the United States for his actions at Hickory on June 4 and 5, 1971. He stayed in the Army and served as sergeant major of the operational squadron of Delta (the U.S. Army counterterrorist unit). He retired from the Army in 1990 and now lives on a ranch in California.

SF Veterinarian

When I first went to Vietnam, I had visions of going off to an A-team. But they noticed I was a medic, and a farm boy, and they told me, "You are now a veterinarian." And that's what I did for about six months. I don't know who was more terrified, the water buffalo or me! After a while it became like anything else: You just smacked them, shoved in the needle, and gave them their shot.

The war pretty much passed me by during that first six months. I liked it. I lived in the villages, did my medcaps during the day, and took my rifle out into the woods at night. The VC pretty much left me alone, and I treated VC water buffalo and NVA sympathizers along with the rest.

Where's the Beef?

One of my jobs was to take a high-quality bull around to the different camps for breeding, trying to improve the quality of the herd. We hauled this bull around from camp to camp; it had cost us about $65,000. We flew the bull around in a C-123 and dropped him off at an A-camp; then two weeks later, we came back and picked him up and took him to another camp.

I dropped this bull at one camp (it might have been Gia Vuc) and then went back to my unit to work on my chicken and pig project. When two weeks had passed, it was time to go back and pick up the bull. I flew back to the camp, and I didn't see the bull anywhere. I asked the Yards, "Where's the bull?"

They said, "Well, we had this real big celebration. . . ."

Since the bull was the biggest and the baddest, they figured that if they sacrificed him they would have the most good luck possible, so they ate him! And I had to go back and tell the "old man" about it; I thought I was going to be a private! God, he was mad!

Ruff-Puff to the Rescue

Another sergeant and I had gone out of the camp at Ba To, across the river. We were talking to the Bru village chief when we noticed some beautiful urns up on the hillside. We asked the chief if we could take them, and he said, "Sure, take them."

So the two of us went up the side of this hill in our jeep. It was a gentle slope, with a nice view of the Ruff-Puff company down below. We got out of the vehicle, and like damn fools, we left our rifles in the jeep. We were checking these things out, and the other sergeant had one of the jars up on his shoulder, when a bullet went right through it! The jar shattered, and we hit the dirt. There was a little depression in the ground, and we dove into it. A few more rounds popped our direction; we knew we weren't going to make it back to the jeep!

We used our pistols to provide a little return fire, exchanging shots with whoever it was in the bushes. Then I heard a blood-curdling scream, and I looked around. There was a guy who must be 50 years old, with his old, old rifle, complete with bayonet, and this old guy was charging! While we were watching this interesting performance, we heard another scream, this time from up the hill!

An NVA, complete with an AK, jumped out of the bushes, and he had his bayonet out too! The two guys charged each other, the Ruff-Puff guy doing the high-step just the way the French used to teach.

The two of them converged, and the old guy did the most beautiful parry and horizontal butt stroke I ever saw in my life! He put the younger guy down on the ground! Naturally, we came running, and we tied the NVA guy up, patted the Ruff-Puff guy on the back, and loaded him and the NVA in the back of the jeep for the trip back down the hill. The Ruff-Puff guy was the hero of this one. We weren't taking any credit at all!

We got down to the village and then discovered something quite sad: The NVA was in reality the village chief's son! The village chief had banished him years before. The villagers insisted on taking the man, and they talked to him that night. He had left his unit to come home.

The next day the village chief sent somebody over to report, "The execution will be tomorrow."

We tried to talk them out of it, but they were adamant. If nothing else, we could have gotten some more information from the man, but they wouldn't stand for it. They really didn't like the North Vietnamese! The next day, the Bru who had soldiered for the NVA was executed, by his father.

"Jon, Use the Knife."

The most terrifying thing I ever did in my life was to kill a guy by throwing a knife at him. We had moved up to an area and encountered a sentry. We didn't have a silenced .22 pistol, and we had to take this guard out. Nobody felt comfortable moving across the road before we got to him. It was gravel, and the noise would have given us away for sure.

I had always practiced throwing my knives, and I carried one over my left shoulder, in my ruck. We were contemplating this situation when my partner—I forget who it was—turned to me and whispered, "Jon, use the knife."

224

I shook my head no.

He nodded his head yes!

Ordinarily I would just reach up, grab, and throw, but not this time! I carefully considered and calculated the throw. When I finally let go, my adrenaline must have been way up, because the knife went in up to the hilt. The sentry gurgled a little and collapsed. That was scary! I had this vision that the knife would fly right on by the guy, and then he would turn around and nail us. I didn't like that.

C&C North Recons

I started running with Staff Sergeant Keith Kincaid. Keith, bless his heart, was the most unlucky son of a bitch I'd ever been around in my life! We'd go out, and within seconds of getting on the ground, it seemed like the whole world was there to greet us! We even tried inserting "dummy teams," and, no matter, the whole world would break loose on us! God!

I told him, "Keith, I don't know about this!"

We went in on one LZ on the other side of the fence where they were waiting for us. We had been unable to go in and do our own visual recon of the area before the mission, and the "zoomies" [U.S. Air Force fighter planes] did it for us. We figured that the Air Force had swooped down to take a closer look at the spot, a sure way of giving away the plan!

My first mission with Keith was just like that. About 20 minutes after we got on the ground, Charlie showed up. Keith put his head up to look at something, and a round came by so close it just slammed Keith's head into the ground. A couple of grenades got thrown, and I still hadn't seen anything! I was looking, but I wasn't seeing anybody. A couple of my Montagnards got hurt by the grenades.

I got the Yards over beside me; one had been hit through the artery in his arm. I opened him up, put a hemostat on both sides, set up an IV with Ringer's lactate through his ankle, ace-bandaged him up, and went to work on the other guy. The second had taken some shrapnel between the scrotum and the anus. There wasn't a lot to do for him; he wasn't in trouble, other than just beginning to go into shock.

Suddenly Keith decided to pull back. There I was, working on the Yards, and when I looked up, there he was; and he was pissed, because I hadn't fired a round, and because I was blocking his egress! I grabbed up the Yards, and the helicopters started coming in. I raced over, threw the first guy in the chopper, raced back, got the other guy on my back, raced back to the helicopter and tossed him on, then climbed on myself. Because we had the wounded, we went into the med-evac hospital at Quang Tri.

When I got back to my unit, one of the sergeant majors started talking to me as if I'd been a coward on the mission. I thought I'd been doing my job!

"How much ammo did you fire?" he said.

"None," I told him. "I didn't see anything to shoot at!" I really didn't like the feeling of that.

So we were going to go back into that area again, about a week and a half later. The G-model Huey had just come out, the one with the 40-millimeter grenade launcher on one side and the mini-gun on the other, but otherwise it looked just like a slick.

We had gone into isolation to prepare for the mission, then went up to LT-1, up around Quang Tri; then we went out on the mission. It was the same area where I'd gone on my first mission with Keith. I started by doing a map reconnaissance with the aerial photographs from the Air Force. I noticed all kinds of stuff that nobody had mentioned in the briefings; I spotted a goat trail that looked very promising. I told Keith, "We have got to go in here!"

On the way in, from the helicopters, we could see that the NVA was building an all-weather road, with timbers and drainage. It was not a good feeling. There were a lot of people on the ground!

Keith was the team leader, and he was in the lead ship. His ship landed and unloaded first. I was in the next ship. Even before we landed, I could see 70 to 100 people in pith helmets and NVA uniforms running with weapons at port arms toward the LZ. The door gunner wasn't even firing on them! I grabbed his helmet from him and used the intercommunications system [ICS] to report the targets on the ground to the gunship. That G-model came in and opened up on the NVA formation along its long axis and worked them over with the mini-guns.

Our helicopter flared over the LZ, and it was time to go. We were at about 10 feet, but the pilot wasn't going lower, so we had to jump. We all jumped out. At the same time, Keith was trying to call the whole thing off, but we were having communication problems and couldn't hear him.

Once on the ground, there wasn't a hell of a lot to be done, and the helicopters got the hell out of there. Keith's group had run into a platoon of enemy as soon as they landed, and his element got shot up pretty badly. He was trying to get the next ship to come in and get them out. We weren't going to be running any recons out of this LZ!

Fortunately, we all were loaded for bear, so we had a lot of ammunition. We set up a perimeter. I got the open area; Keith got the trees. I was getting all my people into position when a .51-caliber heavy machine gun opened up on us and plowed a furrow in the ground right next to me.

Every time that gun fired, you could see where the rounds were hitting, and it was obvious that his traverse was limited; the barrel must have been up against a tree. I could tell that he was going to have to move the whole gun if he was going to get any closer to us. I took one of my Yards, one with an M203 [which replaced the M79 grenade launcher; it serves the same function but is attached to an M16].

I told him, "You watch right up there, and if you see where he's shooting from, hit him with a grenade." Every once in a while my Yard would chunk a 40-millimeter up there.

There was sudden movement to my front. I had already put down my RPD [a Russian machine gun similar to the U.S. M60, very popular with Special Forces and considered by many superior to the M60]. I reached for the shotgun that I always carried, a sawed-off shotgun loaded with 00 buckshot. We were firing at each other through the brush, 20 yards apart. Up jumped three or four

227

NVA. I took them: Boom! Boom! Boom! Boom! The guys used to give me shit for carrying the shotgun, but nobody was giving me any shit about it this time.

Finally, we were able to get some helicopters to come in and get us. My guys and I got on our chopper, and off we went. As we were lifting off and climbing out, one NVA guy stood up below us, with his AK on "rock and roll" [full auto], firing straight at us! And he didn't hit us with one round! Next thing I knew, somebody shot the NVA in the head, and he went down.

We swung out, and I told the pilot, "We've got to cover the exfiltration of the other guys." As we maneuvered, I could see a large number of NVA racing toward the position of the other part of the team.

I was beating on the door gunner: "See that? Those are people down there, and they are headed for my team! Fire them up!" We all started firing. We shot the hell out of them! Keith's helicopter got in and collected him and his guys. We turned around and started to leave . . . *Blam!* the helicopter took a hit, and down we went.

Fortunately, we didn't lose anybody when we went down. We got on the ground. The pilot, the copilot, and the door gunners, they didn't like this development at all. We got out, and I told them, "Okay, you've got a thermite grenade; destroy the KY-6 [a scrambler used to help provide secure radio communications]. Take the M60s out of the chopper and flip the bipod legs down. Let's go!" I told them.

We moved to an area where we could set up a defensive position and still see the helicopter. "Don't shoot until they fire at you!" I told them. "If they are running at you, let them come. If they see you, they'll shoot. You can take them then."

I got on the horn with Sergeant Donald Chaney, my Covey, and asked if there was an exfiltration LZ in the area.

He called back, "I've got a nice one at about 150 meters from your position," and he gave me an azimuth to it.

"Okay," I told him. "Do you have another?"

"I have another LZ at 100 meters," he said, and he gave me another azimuth.

"Okay, send the helicopters in to beat up the first LZ. Shoot the hell out of it! Then you have them race over to the other one to pick us up!"

So the helos started shooting the LZ up big time, with guns and rockets. And we could see Charlie just racing past us, over to catch us where they thought we were going to try to get out. The helicopters finished shooting, then started to land. Then they picked up, slid over to where we were, and got us. The crews had eyeballs as big as saucers! We all piled aboard, and we pulled pitch. The crews still had extremely stoic expressions, but by the time we passed 2,500 or 3,000 feet, you could see the faces start to crack into smiles.

We lucked out on that one and didn't lose anybody, and Keith didn't lose anybody out of his group. And that, basically, was what it was like to run recons in that area at that time. Occasionally you got to stay longer, to RON, and maybe spent two days and didn't see a damn thing!

The Yards

I was told that I was supposed to run with some Americans who despised the Yards, and they let the Yards know it. The result of that would have been that if that American got hit, I'd be the one who'd have to carry him out; the Yards certainly wouldn't. These guys called them all the derogatory names: "slant-eye," "gook." I did that once, and one of my Yards turned around to me and said, "Is that what I am?" I never did that again. I had Yards who died for me.

I had a deal with my Yards: "If you get shot, I won't leave you on the ground. I will come back and get you." And I did that! I was very, very close to them. I lived with them in the highlands when I was a vet.

Special Forces was successful in Vietnam because we understood the people, because we knew basic tactics. We were misunderstood by a lot of Americans who thought of us as sneaky Petes. But we conducted conventional tactical operations; we knew basic first aid, basic engineering, and basic communications. Other units didn't. Even when we were closing down the camps and handing the operations over to the Vietnamese Rangers, I remember the Yards saying, "Can you take us out on one more operation?"

229

I remember ARVN troops sitting down on the helipad, saying, "We aren't going out on this operation until we get paid." I never had that problem with the Yards. The Yards knew that, if it was humanly possible, we would recover their bodies if they were killed on an operation. Most of us disliked the ARVN immensely.

The Vietnamese thought of the Montagnards as savages, the same as Americans did of the Indians during our western expansion, because we didn't want to understand them. The Indians weren't up to our standards. That's the same way the Vietnamese looked at the Yards, and it was a real tragedy.

In other ways the Montagnards were similar to the American Indians. Many tribes didn't get along with each other. If you put Rhade, Steng, and Jarai all in one camp, you were just asking for a battle right in your own compound. We succeeded with these people by understanding them. The tribes were all different, and they had to be treated differently.

We were able to operate effectively because we were very sensitive about our security. We knew we were heavily infiltrated, and we learned to work around it. Even the Yards didn't know where we were going. I'd come back sometimes from isolation and planning a mission into Area Oscar, and they'd look at me and say, "That bad?" But they always had confidence in me, and I had equal confidence in them.

Sometimes, we'd be walking along and I would have a Yard on either side of me, one holding each hand. I didn't have a hand on my weapon; I put my life totally in their trust. They knew that. The hand-holding was brotherly, and I thought nothing of it, although other Americans would sometimes say, "Look at the fucking faggots!" But that was the Yard custom, and they were great! They made you feel a part of their community.

Recon Tools of the Trade
RPD—the Soviet-Designed Light Machine Gun

I normally carried a captured and modified machine gun the Russians called the RPD. I did not like the AK, and I'm glad Charlie had it. It was too powerful a rifle for the little VC and NVA, and they couldn't manage the recoil. After the first shot, everything else was going to be over your head! That was kind of a blessing. If they had had the M16, that would have been a different story.

I liked the RPD because it probably had the best buffer group of any automatic weapon anywhere. It fired 7.62x39-millimeter ammunition from a drum under the weapon. Unlike the M60 used by most American units, the RPD was balanced. Charlie recognized the sound of the RPD when it fired, and he usually stopped to think when he heard it: Is that our guys? If that slowed him down for just a second, you could get out of his ambush kill zone, get up to the side, and then flank the ambush.

We took off the bipod, cut off the barrel, and put a sling on it. Then you had a very good weapon. The only thing I didn't like about it was that it used 25 round, nondisintegrating link belts. In combat, you found yourself reaching down to retrieve those segments from the ground because they were hard to come by. It was a fantastic weapon, accurate, powerful, easy to use. I carried one, and some of the other guys were believers too. But other weapons were also powerful, and one of our guys carried a little Swedish K.

M79

I also carried a sawed-off 40-millimeter M79 grenade launcher, with most of the stock cut off and the barrel chopped down to look just like a pistol. The range was unchanged, and it was really useful. We could shoot accurately with it to 200 meters, normally with the HE [high-explosive] round.

Shotgun

I also carried a cut-down pump shotgun loaded with 00 buckshot. There is no question that a guy knew he'd been shot when you hit him with a load of buckshot, unlike the "dart" rounds that would

231

go right through the guy but would leave him shooting at you because he didn't know he was dead yet!

The stock was cut off at the pistol grip, and a loop of "dummy cord" was tied to it. I carried the shotgun in my rucksack, muzzle down, with the grip sticking up over my left shoulder. I could pull it out without taking off the ruck.

Rucksack

We all mined our rucksacks. If we had to jettison them, we had a Claymore inside, primed and fused to a striker taped to the rucksack quick-release. If you had to drop your ruck in an emergency, it would drop and fire the fuse-lighter. [The fuse allowed time enough to get a safe distance away before the Claymore exploded. The hope was that the NVA or VC who were pursuing us would pause to pick up or search the ruck about the time the Claymore would detonate. At very least, the explosion would slow down the pursuing enemy force.]

Medal of Honor at Hickory

My commander said, "I've got a place I want you to command."

I didn't like the idea; I liked doing what I knew. He said, "You're gonna do it anyway." He sent me to the radio retransmission site called Hickory, across the river and northeast of Khe Sanh.

I went out there, and the place was a mess: concertina wire hanging down on the ground, old French mines poking out of the dirt. The first order of business was to get the defenses repaired. We got the Navy's Seabees to bring up a little bulldozer. We used that to get rid of the old mines and dig new fighting positions. We fixed the wire and made a lot of progress.

But we were also seeing a lot of enemy activity outside the wire. We reported it, and the intel community reported back, "Bull-shit!" This was typical. We were seeing a thousand NVA guys a day, sending helicopters out to shoot them up; and the intel weenies still refused to believe me. They had been setting up a network of electronic sensors all across the northern part of the country, and these sensors weren't indicating the level of enemy activity that we were seeing. So our reports were dismissed. They said, "Our assets don't show anything out there."

I sent them a message in the clear in response: "Then you don't have any fucking assets out here!"

There was a hill overlooking our camp, Hill 1051. The 101st Airborne tried to land on top, but it didn't work. Some helicopters came in to get a couple of teams out, and one of the gunships made a straight run in from about 3 miles out. When he was about a mile out, I saw a single NVA kid stand up with a rocket-propelled grenade, put it on his shoulder, and take careful aim. The ground around this kid was getting all torn up from the fire from the gunship, but he just stood there, preparing to fire.

I grabbed for my rifle, because the kid was right at the range I like to snipe at, about a thousand meters. But before I could do anything, he put that RPG right through the cockpit, and the "bird" went right in. Then I had to call the gunship flight leader to report what had happened.

The buildup around us continued, and we were obviously in a bad tactical location.

The night of June 4 was rainy and miserable. I checked on the Yards and the perimeter defenses a couple of times. Under cover of the rain, the NVA had emplaced Chinese Claymore mines around the camp. Some of the Yards noticed these things. We put everybody in the camp on the wall.

There were some concrete half-culverts down the hill, by the helipad. Sergeant Hill and some of the Yards moved down there. I took over the .50-caliber machine gun. I had it set up with a special ammunition mix, four "ball" to one HEI [high-explosive incendiary] round that I'd gotten from the Air Force.

While I was setting up the position, I noticed one of these Chinese Claymore mines off to the side. I called, "Claymore! Hit it!" I was whipping the gun around on it when the NVA fired it. Sergeant Hill caught a piece just above the knee.

We started firing about that time. Charlie came up out of his holes, and we had a merry little firefight going for a while. They were using some old RPG-2s that were so slow you could see them coming and roll out of the way. They kept shooting, trying to knock out my 50. I finally put a few rounds on the guys who were firing on me. A couple of the HEs must have killed them, because there wasn't any more fire from their position.

A sniper started working from the southwest of my position. Every once in a while that son of a bitch would put one really close to me! The guy was close, not more than 75 or 80 meters away. I couldn't spot him, though, and I got really pissed off. I called one of the Yards over and told him, "Watch right over there."

About this time a young kid—a slovenly, overweight kid with glasses (Walton was his name)—came running over. He was a sensor reader, a technician. He said, "Sarge, I think you better come back and check on your people. Everybody is just standing around. They don't know what to do."

He was pointing out to me my duties as the commander; he was right, and I had been wrong. "I'll take over the .50,'" he said.

"What do you know about a .50-caliber machine gun?" I asked him.

"Nothing. I thought that, since you are Special Forces, you could teach me in one or two minutes."

Just then another shot went past my head. The Montagnard came running over, and he pointed to a spot where the sniper was. I could see where the mat was moving over the guy's hole. I reached down and grabbed my rifle. I lined up on the spot and waited. Then his rifle started to come up out of the hole . . . and as soon as he came up and began to level on me, *blam*, that was the end of that son of a bitch!

I moved back into the compound and made sure everybody knew what to do, which I should have done in the first place. Then I went back to work on those Claymores, because nobody would want to stick their head up over the berm as long as those things were out there.

I grabbed an M60, peeked over the edge, then hosed one as soon as I could spot it. I went down the line blowing these things, one at a time. I got to the last one, flipped the gun over the berm, and started to move; and they blew it on me. That took care of the Claymores.

Then Charlie started laying on indirect fire. Those sons of a bitch could shoot! They're probably the best damn mortar men in the world! They dropped over 100 rounds on my camp, a space maybe 60 meters by 100 meters, and not one of them was outside the berm. Those shots had to have been made at a range of more than 1,500 meters—almost a mile.

They were firing a lot of rockets at us, but because of where the NVA were firing from, the rockets were mostly going over the top of the camp, chopping my antennas all to hell in the process. Then everything calmed down, and it got pretty quiet. So I started evacuating guys.

I decided it was time to destroy all the electronic equipment. So I went down to the vans to throw in the thermite grenades [magnesium-filled, incendiary grenades that burn with extreme heat, often used to melt critical equipment, including gun tubes]. I turned on the oxygen bottles (so much for several million dollars worth of government equipment). I came walking down the stairs to talk to my commo man just as a B-40 rocket came zooming in, right between the vans, and blew up about 6 feet away. It blew me on my ass.

"Man," I told the commo guy, "that was close!" The fins on the spinner ripped the back of my pants leg as it went by.

When I picked myself up and discovered that I hadn't picked up any shrapnel, I told the commo guy, Sergeant Jones, "We're going to have to evacuate the camp; I want to get you out of here. You have more experience on the ground, but you know too much about this equipment. We can't risk getting you captured. I don't know how long we can hold them off, or if we can hold them off."

Meanwhile, Walton—the fat, slovenly electronics technician— had been manning the .50-caliber and had knocked out about four machine guns! Then there was a big explosion down at that end of the camp. I went over there. A bunch of Yards had been wounded, and I started hauling them down to my Vietnamese medic.

I came around a corner, and there was Walton, dragging that big .50-caliber back to the camp. The NVA had finally managed to collapse the position, and Walton was trying to get it back where he could use it again. People were shooting at him; there were AK rounds whipping past him.

I knocked the gun on the ground and asked him, "What the hell do you think you're doing?"

I looked at him. His glasses had been frosted by a near miss that had hit a sandbag in front of him. "Sergeant," he said, "I think I'm blind."

I reached over and moved his glasses up. "Does that help any?"

"I can see again!"

"Have you got another pair of glasses?" I asked him.

"As a matter of fact, I do," he said. "Down in my bunker."

I told him to lie down there, at the berm, with the .50-caliber, and I raced down there to get them for him while people shot at me. I got the glasses, raced back, and put them on him.

"It's a miracle!" he cried. "I can see!"

About that time, I heard one of the other guys moaning; he had taken a piece of a rocket that had hit nearby.

"I'm going to take him down to the medic," I told Walton, "but you are going to have to cover me!"

I tossed him a CAR-15. "Do you know how it works?"

"Yeah," he said, "like an M16, only faster!"

"You're catching on, Walton!" I told him.

I loaded the guy up on my back and took off across the helipad. From behind me I could hear Walton firing; he was putting short bursts into the bushes on either side of our route. I turned around and there he was, zigzagging, returning fire from anybody nearby—not a bad performance, especially from somebody who isn't supposed to be a combatant and is about 40 pounds overweight.

We raced for the other side of the camp. I deposited the wounded guy and Walton on a helicopter and told him to get the hell out of there. I had already written Walton up for the Medal of Honor for what he'd done with the .50, and I gave the paper to my wounded team member to take back. When everybody seemed to be aboard, the helicopter took off . . . and there stood Walton.

"I fell out," he said.

I used a common military expression of respect and admiration. "You lying sack of shit!" I tossed him a weapon and grabbed my RPD. "Get over there and take that position," I told him, indicating a spot on the berm.

About 4:00 p.m. some more helicopters were inbound, and I got the word: These were the last helicopters of the day. I got Walton, my commo man, some of the other guys, and some Yards, and I loaded them all on the choppers. I instructed one of the Yards to point his CAR-15 at Walton.

"Walton," I told him, "this guy has orders to shoot you if you try to get off this helicopter. Get your damn ass out of here!" A 37-millimeter opened up on them on the way out, but they made it.

My Covey appeared overhead about 5:00 p.m., along with a fast-mover. It was Chaney again. "Jon, I got an Air Force general up here for you. He's got eight 250-pound 'drags' [bombs with drag brakes]."

"Have him put them just to the south of the camp, on the helipad," I told him.

Chaney called back; the general had declined. "Too close," he said.

"It doesn't make any difference now," I said. "Besides, that's where the bad guys are."

The general still refused the drop. "He'll stay on station until the helicopters come in to get you," Chaney called.

"You tell him there won't be any more helicopters!"

"Okay, I'll drop them," the general called.

I pulled all my people back and we got down. He came rolling in and unloaded on the target. It was close, and we were bouncing all over the ground, but none of my guys got hurt. It really did a job on Charlie.

I called Chaney, "Tell him thanks!"

When the last helicopter left, there was just Jones, me, and 17 little people left. Later I discovered that a team from Operation Heavy Hook in Thailand was en route to us about then, and they made it to just 11 klicks to the west of us when they were ordered to turn around. They were in a "Jolly Green" [a version of the Sikorski H-53, a large U.S. Air Force rescue helicopter]. They could have picked up the whole team. My award says we were left on the ground because of inclement weather; it was inclement inter-service politics.

We could only defend half the camp, so I shrank the perimeter. We fought them off, over and over again. A half-hour went by without them doing anything. I knew then that we were about to get knocked over. I told the Yards, "Get the fuck out of here!"

I set myself up on top of the ammo bunker. I figured that if I had to die, I'd die in style, and that when it blew I would never know what hit me. I was up there when I noticed a couple of Yards who had pulled back. When I looked back, I saw huge numbers of people coming toward the camp. I started firing them up. I had an attack of sanity and started thinking, Just what do you think you're doing up here? I turned and started down, and took a round in the back that threw me asshole over tea kettle. I landed at the foot of the bunker, and my Yards came running back to get me. I told them to take off. They went over the wall.

One of the last things I did was to call in a Stinger air strike on our position, told them there were about 7,500 bad guys in the open.

I managed to run over to the bunker where Jones was. "Get out of here!" I told him. But when I turned around, there were people everywhere, so I dove into the bunker with him. While we were talking, two NVA came in, the first without a weapon, the guy behind with an AK. As far as I was concerned, the number two guy was the real threat. I stepped behind him and brought the knife arm around his head. Then I brought the point up under his jaw, up into the skull, turned his head away, and let him fall.

I was moving on the number one NVA when Jones unloaded about 20 rounds into him. Until then, Charlie didn't know we were around, but that gave us away. A little while later, Charlie threw a grenade in and wounded Jones pretty bad. He decided to surrender. When he got to the door, they shot him down.

I played dead. One guy poked me in the chest three or four times, but I didn't move. I had hemorrhaged real bad and had a lot of blood on me, so he assumed I was dead. They tried to cremate our bodies. The bunker was lined with tarpaper, and they lit it on fire. After a while I decided I wasn't going to burn to death. I got up and made a break for the door, and they'd walked off! As I was walking out the door, I got hit with a round on my helmet. It was the only time I'd worn a helmet in Vietnam. The hit knocked me out. When I came to, the soles of my boots were all melted, and my hands and arms were all burned.

I crawled into another bunker and was trying to dispose of all my stuff except my ID card. I was hiding behind some cardboard in a corner of the bunker when an NVA came in. I heard him, and I held the cardboard with one hand and my Gerber knife in the other. He came over and lifted up the cardboard. My adrenaline must have been up, because I put that knife all the way through his sternum, all the way into his spine. He got a shocked, glazed look on his face, and expelled a load of tremendously bad breath as he realized that he was dead and there wasn't a damn thing he could do about it. And then I couldn't get the damn knife out of him.

I crawled under the cot, exhausted. When I came to, two guys were sitting on the cot, and one of them had ahold of my foot. He was checking to see if my boots would fit him. I guess he figured they were too big, because he just dropped the foot, clunk. I had already disowned the leg; he could have done anything with it, but they got up and walked out.

This bunker didn't seem to be a good place to stay, so I crawled out and around the side. Two NVA came wandering along and stopped beside me. Finally they walked off, and then I crawled down to the side of the hill and started my escape and evasion.

I lasted for 11 1/2 days before being captured, right outside of Fire Base Fuller. The guy who got me was a little old man, about 65 or 70 years old, with an ancient Russian rifle. He was shaking just like a leaf. I thought that if I even blinked wrong he was going to shoot me.

Medal of Honor Hassles

There are a lot of disadvantages to wearing a Medal of Honor if you want to stay in the Army. There is a lot of petty jealousy. When you get a promotion, it isn't because you're a good soldier; it's because you're a Medal of Honor recipient. There are commanders who don't like having a Medal of Honor in the unit because they feel it will bring undue attention to them.

Getting into Delta wasn't easy because of the Medal of Honor, particularly when I had the covert squadron. It was not easy at all. I had units turn me down, not because of a lack of expertise in operations (which was never questioned), but because they wanted to know, "How do you conceal a Medal of Honor recipient in the unit?"

Well, that was easy for me. I didn't go to the conventions. I didn't do speaking engagements. I stayed out of the public view. It wasn't a problem. When I dropped out of sight, or when anybody in these units disappears, you don't question where they are and what they're doing.

Post-Traumatic Stress Disorder

I don't agree with the people who dismiss "post-traumatic stress disorder" [PTSD] as coming from fakes and phonies. I did my thesis on PTSD and have done a lot of research on it. Most people know that about 58,000 guys got killed on the battlefield during the war. What people don't know is that more than 200,000 have died in car wrecks, from alcoholism, from drug overdoses, and from suicide since then.

The reason, I think, is that a guy could be on the battlefield one day, and he could be home on the street the next day, 24 hours later. During World War II and before, it might have taken you a year to get home in the belly of a troop ship. During all this time you were communicating. You had a chance to say, I feel really shitty about what I did. Your buddies could talk you through the feelings over a gradual period of adjustment. When you went to Vietnam you went with a two-way ticket, by yourself. The guys who went off to World War II went for the duration, and they went as units.

I don't think you see the same problem with PTSD in Special Forces that you find with the straight infantry units, but we had much different standards and experiences. For example, in Special Forces, dope smoking wasn't a problem. We only had one dope smoker in my team, and he got a buddy of mine killed. If you saw somebody smoking dope, the guy was gone. We had enough things to worry about.

The average mission in C&C North was what we called the "70/30." You had a 70 percent chance of not coming back, a 30 percent chance that you would return. The attitude in my unit, though, was, "They ain't made the bullet that has my name on it. If they did, they shot it off during a training exercise." Our attitude was that you had a job to do and you did it. When you came back, you were treated well. We had cooks who took care of us, who made steak and lobster for us on Sundays, with wine on the table. But when you went into "isolation" and started working on a mission, it was a totally businesslike attitude. Then, you would never see a guy go to the club.

The one thing that really bothered me about our unit was that the guy that went in, ran his recon, "snooped and pooped," and got back out without a shot being fired, that guy came home with no awards! As a result, I knew guys who would go in, do the mission, and then—just before it was time for the helicopters to come get them—they would do something to really piss off Charlie just so they could have a firefight when they came out, so they would get an award!

THE AIRBORNE MYSTIQUE

The holy trinity of the U.S. Army is called Airborne, Ranger, and Green Beret. Of the three, the Airborne (a.k.a., paratroopers, an archaic term today) is by far the most inclusive. It is the gateway to the elite little enclaves in the Army. All SF soldiers must be Airborne qualified, but that isn't too much of a challenge. Jump school is a three-week program, open to virtually every man and woman in the Army, and about one in five of all soldiers wears jump wings. The current program, as one instructor recently said, is three weeks of low-impact aerobics. Students make five jumps during week three, with three "Hollywood" jumps (no combat equipment), one jump with rucksack and weapons container, and one "night" jump (seldom actually done after dark).

Anyone in the Army who isn't a super-duper-paratrooper is a "leg," normally pronounced "gawddam laay-g," and is an object of profound contempt, regardless of rank. This is more important than you might think; any officer who expects genuine personal respect from the troops in any of the combat arms better wear jump wings—at least.

Part of the SF battle plan involves jumping behind the lines, but there wasn't much of that during Vietnam or since. The Navy's SEALs tried it during the Grenada operation and got a few of their guys killed. On the other hand, the Army's Rangers jumped onto the airport at Point Salines from 800 feet, and although it was a tougher problem than anticipated, the drop worked as advertised. But as soon as those first Rangers got the runway cleaned up, everybody else air-landed.

All SF units continue to train in airborne operations, and all SF personnel must maintain current jump qualifications to remain on a team. That means at least one military static-line jump (1,250 feet above ground level) per quarter, normally with rucksack and weapon.

—Hans Halberstadt

242

BRIMFROST 1989
GERRY SCHUMACHER

A captain in Vietnam in the 1960s, Schumacher went on to command a variety of post-Vietnam missions before his 1997 retirement at the rank of colonel. One of the projects under his command in the late 1980s was the use of SF units to test the security of defense installations such as Ballistic Missile Early Warning sites (BMEWs), radio relay sites, radar posts, ammunition storage facilities, and power plants.
SF teams train with host nation forces around the world—now even with former adversaries from the former Soviet Union—but the relationship between Canadian and American military units is na old and affectionate one, especially when Special Forces units are involved. The Canadians are our "first cousins" next door, with their own resources, skills, and traditions. Some of them even speak English. So it has long been a tradition for SF units to deploy to the Great White North for exercises like Brimfrost, where military operations are conducted under conditions of extreme cold. The lessons of such arctic training can quickly cross the line to the real world, as Schumacher here describes.

As I drove along Fort Wainwright's airfield frontage road, Major Sarhad and I peered through the darkness and ice fog. It was 7:15 p.m. and the few hours of daily sunshine had long since disappeared into the January Arctic sky. Moments earlier a Canadian Air Force C-130 Cargo plane, on final landing approach, clipped the strobe lights, dipped its right wing into a deuce-and-a-half truck, and dived into the runway apron. The giant aircraft began to cartwheel

243

through the air, breaking into three major sections. Some of the dark pieces flying through the night sky were the bodies of Canadian Paratroopers being ejected from the fuselage. It was minus 55 degrees Fahrenheit and my Special Forces battalion now had an unplanned rescue mission.

This was operation Brimfrost, 1989. My SF unit was sent to test the security of critical installations throughout Alaska and the Arctic Circle. These installations included Ballistic Missile Early Warning Sites (BMEWS), submarine radio relay facilities, early warning radar locations, Eielson and Elmendorf air force bases, Kodiak Island Power Generation station, and about 25 other first-line-of-defense nodes. Our mission would include training and operating with the Yupik Indians on the islands throughout the Bering Strait.

Earlier in the day we had planned a parachute jump. The Russians were covertly watching this exercise, as they always had, and we needed for them to know that we could conduct military operations in minus 65 to minus 75 degree temperatures. The parachute jump, in addition to our own training challenge, was an attempt at thumbing our nose at the Soviets. Some higher ups in the chain of command thought it would be useful to demonstrate that we were impervious to severe weather. I'd like to have seen those generals standing on the outside jump platform of an airplane flying at 1,100 feet and 130 knots when the ambient ground level temperature is minus 65 degrees.

We were rewriting the book on cold weather operations. The barometric pressure had only exceeded this level once before in the known history of the planet. After the plane crash it would dawn on the crash investigators that aircraft altimeters use barometric pressure in their calibrations. This was just one of hundreds of lessons learned that would emerge from this arctic venture.

The annual Brimfrost exercise was routine for us; however, this particular year it was far larger than ever before. Active, Guard, and Reserve units were being sent into Alaska to simulate the actual deployment levels that a "real" conflict would require.

My SF unit was briefed a year earlier that when this exercise was executed SF was not to use any method or insight that would not have been available to Soviet Special Operations Forces. In contrast to previous Brimfrost exercises, this was the real deal. Even the exercise control headquarters commanded by the forces command deputy commanding general had more than 1,100 controller/observers to ascertain the outcomes of my battalion's attempted penetrations of key sites.

The weather was the "real deal" too. That year, in the two months that we operated in the bowl of Alaska the temperature never got warmer than minus 45 degrees and in places like McGrath, Alaska, it was typically around minus 75. Engines had to run 24 hours a day. Moisture in the air of tires would crystallize and flatten them. Back ramps of Cargo aircraft would lower to pick up my SF teams, and the hydraulics to lift the ramps would freeze. Plastic fuel bladders cracked. Fifty-five-gallon drums of fuel proved useless because the fuel coagulated and would not pump into our helicopters. Coax cable for our radios cracked in half. We found sled dogs chained to a tree and eerily frozen to death standing upright.

Even the Ford and GM rental cars, which we acquired from the Fairbanks airport, were inadvertently tested. It so happened that if you rented a Ford you were in trouble because the power steering unit was too far from the engine block and didn't get enough of the heat. The fluid coagulated. If you didn't turn a corner every couple of blocks, you were only going to go straight whether you wanted to or not. Hell, the old-timers in Alaska even blew it. They would leave their diesel 4x4s running in the parking lot and go drinking with the boys at the local strip joint. Hours later, and somewhat inebriated, they'd get back into their trucks, reach under the seat for their bottle of unfrozen vodka and take a swig. That was the end of their esophagus and stomach lining.

It was so cold that you could throw a cup of hot coffee in the air and watch as little brown ice balls bounced on the ground. Ice fog is a manmade anomaly generated by any heat source under these frigid and windless conditions. If two men stood talking for 10

245

minutes outside, one could return to that spot five hours later and still see evidence of the fog cloud suspended in midair above the location where they had been. A single aircraft landing or taking off would generate so much ice fog that the runways were often closed for the remainder of the day. It was under these condition that we were about to execute an impromptu rescue mission of the Canadian Paratroopers.

On this day the Canadians had scheduled a parachute jump that was subsequently scrubbed because after circling the area of the intended jump, they couldn't see the drop zone due to ice fog. The ice fog at the drop zone was generated from the drop zone party vehicles that had arrived earlier to mark the location; clearly a self-defeating endeavor. We had the same problem on several occasions that week. The Canadian C-130 was coming back to Wainwright on instrument landing conditions. They didn't know that the extreme barometric pressure had skewed their altimeter readings as they made their fog-laden, and deadly, final approach to Wainwright.

At the time of the crash, I was a few hundred yards away. Eye-witnesses said it was an eerie, seemingly slow-moving plane, 30 feet above and in front of them. As it pierced the dark fog it looked like a black, noiseless, monster tumbling through the night. Their minds could not immediately comprehend what they had seen. I got on my radio and issued an alert order to my operations center to assemble all medical personnel. I raced to the post headquarters just a few blocks away. This was the 6th Infantry Division Forward headquarters. Its primary headquarters was in Anchorage. Up here at Fort Wainwright in Fairbanks, the division's deputy commanding general (DCG) ran the show. I was just a guest on his installation. He called the shots there.

When I entered his headquarters it was quite chaotic. Their one-star deputy, Brigadier General Ebbeson, was also just arriving and was issuing orders to everyone in sight. I quickly gave him my estimate of the situation from what I saw at the crash site. He thanked me and asked that all my medical personnel meet his people at the site. "They're assembled and ready to go, I'll have them there in minutes."

"Good, thanks," was all he had time for. I understood.

I grabbed the mike on my radio and began issuing emergency orders to my battalion headquarters' tactical operations center (TOC). "Suspend all training activities, move all battalion medics and ambulances to the airfield immediately. We have a downed aircraft, I repeat, a downed aircraft, over."

My TOC operations sergeant responded, "Roger, copy, downed aircraft, identify location, over."

"Everywhere on the airfield. Initial ground contact on approach apron and spread all the way across the airstrip. Tell Captain Christianson (our Battalion Surgeon) to meet me in front of TOC and have our other vehicles follow me to the crash site."

"Roger, copy, the surgeon is standing by. Medics loading vehicles now. Medic vehicles will follow you in." That was a fast scramble. From the time of the crash until this moment had consumed all of 5 to 8 minutes.

Captain Christiansen, Major Ron Sarhad, my executive officer, and I were among the first to arrive on the airfield. Through the ice fog we couldn't see anything. There had been no explosion because in the frigid air the fuel did not vaporize for ignition. Parts of our convoy had to crash through the chain link fencing to get onto the airstrip. Driving onto the airfield was out of the question. The danger of running over a rescuer or a victim was too high. Captain Christensen ran into the dark abyss, surgical bag in hand, toward a large chunk of wing and fuselage.

By now rescue vehicles were appearing from every direction. They had generated so much ice fog that you could barely see your hand in front of your face. In our arctic parkas, using our hoods as air-warming chambers, we would have to tap one another and stare inches from each others' faces to figure out who we were talking with. The "warming chamber" was necessary prior to deep breathing, or you could freeze your lungs. I was afraid that we would soon have our own casualties among the rescue personnel.

At a major chunk of the fuselage men were frozen to parts of an engine cowling and others to the fuselage itself. Wherever they had bled extensively they froze to that location. The irony was that had it not been for the extreme cold they would have bled to death. Now they were dying of the cold, but perhaps they were also *living* because of it.

During the night a man was observed wandering aimlessly amongst the wreckage. The dark figure was wearing only a flimsy black flight suit. Our SF medics on the scene realized he was the pilot of the Canadian Aircraft. He was in some kind of shock. He had survived the break up and was now just walking in circles. He had to be firmly removed to a waiting ambulance over his vehement objections.

Captain Christiansen worked feverishly on any and every victim that showed a sign of life. He found one man dead under an engine and another two on top of each other in a wheel well. "The uppermost was face up, thrashing his head and left arm incoherently. The subjacent victim was motionless, unreachable, and later determined to be dead," read Christiansen's after-action report.

Eventually, Captain Christiansen rode with the last living victim to Memorial Hospital in Fairbanks. His report stated: "There (in the hallway) I met Canadian Sergeant Lowery. We had worked side by side for hours in the wreckage and had not seen each other. He informed me that he was on the DZ party for the cancelled airborne operation. Sergeant Lowery knew my patient, Corporal Paul McGinnis. They were regulars in the Canadian Airborne Commando unit and had served together on the UN Peacekeeping Force in Cyprus and the Sinai. Sergeant Lowery had lost five of his comrades in an auto accident three nights before." And now he'd lost at least six more that we knew of at that time.

Despite super-human efforts by the medical team, Corporal McGinnis' core temperature drop, combined with internal hemorrhaging, led to fibrillating and death. Lowery never left his buddy's side. It was a very long night.

We found we had to hack the victims out of the ice and couldn't use any flame or we would risk ignition of slushy jet fuel that was everywhere. We used a fork lift to gingerly raise the engine off of one victim. With the engine partially raised our men slid underneath the forks looking for additional body parts belonging to the man they had just recovered.

The rescue team formed a horizontal, human chain and swept on hands and knees the expanse of the airfield looking for bodies that may have been thrown from the wreckage. In the darkness and ice fog it was challenging to account for all of the passengers and crew that had been on board. The temperature was now minus 62 degrees and falling as the night wore on. We saved many that night, but we lost quite a few too. One of my men became a victim of the cold with frostbite of the cornea. Imagine that, a frozen eyeball!

My medics, as well as several from 5th Special Forces Group that were on Brimfrost with us, set up a triage in one of the hangars. Still others helped the extractions at the crash site while others were offered up to the hospital commander. The hospital commander asked if I had French speakers in my battalion. I replied in the affirmative. "The medical staff can't talk with the survivors that they're operating on. We need fluent French speakers to translate for our doctors," he said. As it turned out, even though the French Canadian paratroopers nearly all spoke English, when they were in excruciating pain, they expressed themselves only in their native tongue.

Sergeant First Class Steve Douesnard was one of the translators from 3/12th SF as was Staff Sergeant Thibodeau from 3/5th SF. Both men translated for the medical staff at Bassett Hospital. The first patient he translated for was the Canadian regimental operations officer, Captain Jorgensen. In addition to a fractured right foot, Jorgensen had a 6-inch gash in his skull, a 4-inch cut across his right eye, and blood coming from his left ear. He was moaning something in French. Sergeant Dousenard listened to the injured man carefully. Douesnard complied. He arranged to get a message to Jorgensen's wife. There were others, and Douesnard stayed through the night until there were no more translations to make.

249

The next morning I had a message from USCINCSOC, which read in part, "The actions of 3rd Battalion, 12th Special Forces were superb. They underscore why Special Forces can always be counted on when demands are high. Upon return of 3/12 to a more hospitable climate, request a detailed report. Congratulations! Extremely well done! General Lindsay." I still have that TWX message in my warm-and-fuzzy file.

Months later, in a gesture of appreciation, the Canadian Government extended an invitation for my battalion to participate in the Canadian Airborne School in Edmonton, Alberta, and to also attend their Cold Weather Survival Course. We accepted both invites, not that we hadn't had our fill of cold weather. My Special Forces battalion had developed a special bond with the Canadian Parachute Regiment, and none of us will ever forget the evening of January 29, 1989.

THE GREEN BERET COOKING ACADEMY
J. R.

One of the major fights of the campaign against the Taliban began
on March 1, 2002, in the Zhawar mountains of Afghanistan,
Operation Anaconda. Enemy forces in fairly large numbers
assembled in the vicinity of a village called Shahi Khot, south of the
city of Gardez. Although not well organized, about 500 enemy had
regrouped in the area. Using caves and the terrain, they had some
strong defensive positions and were well armed with individual and
crew-served weapons, including mortars and anti-aircraft machine
guns and missiles.
Typical of recent combat operations, SOF units from the Army, Navy,
and Air Force were integrated into a force that combined
conventional and unconventional assets—the sort of "joint"
organization that has been a feature of American tactical doctrine
since Grenada and similar ops beginning in the 1980s.
These forces were quite a mixed bag: elements of the 101st Airborne
(Airmobile), 10th Mountain, U.S. Army Special Forces from 3rd
Group and 10th Group, plus some U.S. Navy SEALs far from their
normal element comprised the American part of the show, about a
thousand men. In addition, forces from seven Coalition nations
provided about another thousand soldiers, nearly all Afghan. About
200 of the total, or about 10 percent, were Special Operations Forces.
All were tasked with destroying al-Qaeda and Taliban forces in the
area. They were designated Objective Remington. Terrain in the
objective varied from flat valley bottom to rugged mountains.
During the next week, all the participating units tested the doctrine
of "jointness," generally with great success. USAF aircraft supported

251

ground units with (generally) accurate and timely bomb and missile strikes. Despite the high altitude, MH-47E Chinook helicopters were able to deliver and extract SOF units to key terrain on the battlefield, although two were brought down by enemy fire. Eight Americans were officially listed as KIA in the operation, with an estimated 500 enemy killed. Here is what it looked like for one SF sergeant working with members of the Northern Alliance on a key piece of terrain, a ridge Americans called "the Whale."

Operation Anaconda

My team was part of the big mission called Operation Anaconda. During the initial phase, the 101st and Rangers were the main effort, with 5th Special Forces tasked with occupying observation positions (OPs) to the west of a terrain feature called "the Whale" for its shape on the map. The valley itself turned out to be heavily fortified, so my team was called in to support 5th Group.

We worked with Afghan militia units known as the Anti-Taliban Force (ATF). There were lots of these factions, some part of the Northern Alliance, others associated with various warlords operating in the country. A decision was made to clear the mountain. At the same time, the Northern Alliance was called in to help with the fight on the valley floor since they operated some Russian T-55 tanks and could provide heavy firepower should it be needed to deal with fortified positions.

This was my team's first experience with the Northern Alliance. We were comfortable with our ATF soldiers who were well trained, trustworthy, and super soldiers. They would literally die for you, if it came to that.

The Northern Alliance commander tells us that he wants us to get on line and clear the mountain, using his troops. We put them on line, and right away, all of them take off running toward a village. These guys turn out to be thieves and thugs, and the first thing they intend to do is to steal stuff! We ran around trying to get them back on line. The team leader was telling the NA units, "We aren't here to steal things, and we are here to make sure there is no al-Qaeda on the mountain!"

The Northern Alliance company commander replied, "I have no control over my men. I don't know what they are doing." Not really what we wanted to hear, but then our interpreter told us that he is actually maneuvering the NA units by radio, telling them to go left or right, and saying to the soldiers looting the village, "take whatever you can find, especially if it is valuable!" So he was lying to us, but he doesn't know that we can understand what he is saying to his men.

While this is going on, tension is growing between our ATF and the NA men, the result of a blood feud. Insults are traded back and forth, and at the same time, we notice movement down on the western side of the Whale. Nobody is supposed to be down there. We are getting ready to "light up" the people down there, when the NA commander says, "No, don't shoot them. They are my men! They went down there to get water."

My team leader was suspicious of this claim, so he decides to call the NA commander's bluff. "We've got SF guys in the village. If they see your men, they will shoot them," he says.

"Oh, those other guys over by the village? I don't care if they get shot; they don't work for me," the NA commander said.

The tension between the two factions continued to build. It was pretty obvious that they didn't really care what we wanted them to do, they had their own concept of the operation and intended to execute it their way, not ours, if at all possible. Without a word, the NA factions were checking their weapons, moving safeties from SAFE to FIRE.

But the search of the village apparently didn't turn up much worth looting, and the two factions were prevented from engaging each other. Apparently the sweep of the mountain wasn't going fast enough, so we heard that the 101st would be assigned to clear the Whale instead of the NA. We pulled back to our checkpoint. My team leader sent the NA unit over to the north side of the mountain. He didn't want these clowns anywhere near us!

253

We knew these guys were thieves, but we didn't realize how bad they were until now. While getting things sorted out and preparing the NA unit to head over to the northern side of the Whale, one of the guys on my team, Sergeant Bobby, noticed an NA soldier walking off with what looked like a sound suppressor in his hand. Some of us had suppressors on our M4s, but we are all either holding our weapons or had them within arm's reach. "Hey, you!" Bobby said. "Come here! What's that in your hand?" It was the suppressor from the weapon of one of the guys on my team. The NA soldier had managed to unscrew it without being observed. He had no use for this thing at all since it wouldn't fit on his weapon or any weapons used by the NA. After that, we could not get that group of NA soldiers far enough away from us.

Some of them might have been thieves, but nearly all of them were brave. They would run out into a minefield without fear even if mortars were dropping 50 meters away. They didn't seem to be concerned, as long as the threat was a familiar one, but one night we were in defensive positions with the possibility that Taliban forces might try to infiltrate us. I went out and set up a "flash-bang" attached to a trip wire on a path down the hill from our position. If anybody tried to move up that path in the night, the device would go off and let us know before we could be attacked.

I told the interpreter about the flash-bang, and he passed the word to the militiamen. They became extremely worried about the device. "No, no, it won't hurt you if it goes off. It just makes a lot of noise and a bright flash!" Even so, they wouldn't go anywhere near it, no matter how we tried to reassure them. It was unfamiliar, and that really upset them. The next morning, we prepared to move out and head down to the village of Shahi Khot. None of the NA troops would head down the trail until I retrieved the flash-bang, and they would not move in front of me until we had physically gone past the place where it had been emplaced.

[Most SF soldiers were deployed to Afghanistan and Iraq several times, sometimes as members of an ODA that had been recycled or as an individual replacement. Sergeant J. R. served on three deployments to the area. The stories below are from his last trip to Iraq.]

President Bush's Biggest Iraqi Fan

We were sent into Iraq and then up to Kirkuk where the oil fields were. There was great concern that these oil fields would be sabotaged by the fleeing enemy, and we raced up there to see what could be done to safeguard them. The roads were jammed with people fleeing in the other direction. In the middle of the night, we arrived at a Kurdish checkpoint where the Kurds were making sure none of the fleeing refugees were enemy soldiers.

I was riding on the back of an LMTV, a truck converted to a resupply vehicle. This was ordinarily a truck with 2.5-ton cargo capacity, usually with canvas cover, that looked nothing like its conventional counterpart. We removed the hood and cover, added roll bars, and installed two M240 7.62-millimeter machine guns up front and in back, where I was, and a .50-caliber M2 heavy machine gun for rear security. The truck was loaded down with 5-gallon water and gas cans, plus plenty of ammo cans for the weapons. In addition to all this, we had a big spotlight attached to the .50-caliber for checking out anything suspicious at night.

We slowed to go through a Kurdish checkpoint and heard the kind of noise coming down the road toward us that creates dread in the heart of almost every soldier—the squeak and squeal of tracks and the roar of a big diesel engine, the sound made by tanks! We had no tanks up in this area, and if the Iraqis had one around here, we were dead meat!

I swung the spotlight and .50-caliber around toward the sound, and there was a guy trying to steal a bulldozer! He saw the light and the machine gun, put his hands in the air, yelling as loud as possible, "America! George Bush! George Bush!"

255

Run for Your Life!

SF has always had its share of funny guys, and our ODA was no exception. When we finally got to Kirkuk, we secured one of the refinery production sites. We set teams up at critical locations, but there wasn't anything going on. Everything that could be stolen had already been taken. We had been sitting there for about 24 hours and everybody was getting really bored.

One guy from another ODA, Jeff, was a big, blond, lanky kind of guy with a goofy sense of humor. Jeff went exploring in the abandoned buildings and disappeared for a little while. Then, suddenly, the door slammed open and Jeff came running out in one of those big silver suits firefighters sometimes use. He found the suit, put it on, and did his usual clown act. "Run!" Jeff yelled, "Run for your lives! It's gonna blow!" We didn't run. We just howled with laughter.

The Green Beret Cooking Academy

On my first trip to Afghanistan, we had all kinds of guys in our compound—Navy SEALs, OGA [an acronym for "Other Governmental Activity," otherwise known as . . . well, you aren't supposed to know], and SF. We found a local guy and hired him and his two sons to cook for us all. We paid him $100 a month to cover himself and his helpers. The problem with the guy, though, was that he just kept cooking the same thing: beans and rice, more beans, more rice, and that got real boring, real fast.

Well, I am something of a cook myself, and when we weren't busy, I used the ingredients from T-rations to produce chow that had more variety. Guys from around the camp preferred my meals to the ones prepared by our hired cook. We weren't doing much around this time, and for a week or so, I was cooking every day. People were eating the meals I prepared and avoiding the beans and rice.

The hired cooks were getting far more money than was usual for Iraqis, even considering that they had to buy the rice and beans on the local economy. With rice selling for about 10 cents per pound, these guys were well paid. But, even so, they wanted more and came to the team leader asking for a raise. Considering that nobody really liked their cooking, and considering that I was doing their job for them, the timing for this suggestion was not good.

My team leader walks over and asks, "Do you think you could cook for the whole camp?"

"Every night?" I replied.

"No, just one night," he said.

I had been doing this off and on for a while anyway, so I said, "Sure!" He walks off, talks to the Iraqi cooks, and then comes back over to me. "What about breakfast? Could you do breakfast, too? Just for one day?"

"Yes, sure, I can cook breakfast," I told him, and he walks back over to chat with our hired help. After a few minutes, he walks back over to me again, and says, "Congratulations! You are now the new camp cook!"

"What? How the hell did that happen?"

"I just fired them," he said. "They wanted $20 more a month, so I got rid of them. You get to do it now." So that's how I became camp cook, and I didn't get the $100, either.

AFGHANI T AND A
John Anderson

*Captain John Anderson served in Special Forces as an enlisted
soldier for several years in 3rd Group, most of them on ODA
356, then went to college, earned a degree, and returned to the
Army as a commissioned officer. After serving in the infantry,
he signed back into 3rd Group in April 2002 and was immediately
deployed to Afghanistan.*

Operation WILDCAT

I really wanted to go to Afghanistan with 2nd Battalion, 3rd Group.
It had been my unit when I was enlisted and I still had a lot of
friends from the old days still serving there. I figured that if I was
going to go to war, there would be no finer company of men I would
rather be with. In the end, it was the best place for me. After going
through the Q Course again, this time as an officer, I signed into 3rd
Group and was in Afghanistan two weeks later.

For the first month and a half in Afghanistan, I served as the
Charlie Company executive officer (XO) and was very busy from
the start. When I landed and linked up with the company at Kandahar
airfield, they were in isolation and planning to launch an operation
called WILDCAT down in the southeast sector of the country, near
the border with Pakistan. This region was full of ancient trade
routes that were being used by Taliban forces to infiltrate back into
Afghanistan. Our mission as a "company-minus" (since we didn't
have all our people for this mission) was to move into the area,
establish a base camp, and conduct interdiction operations.

258

Three teams were sent to the area, a B-team that was actually the headquarters element from our Charlie Company, plus ODA 365 and ODA 345. We went into an area with a fearsome history; the British lost an entire regiment in these same mountains, a thousand people, including soldiers and their families. The Russians lost an entire infantry battalion in these same mountains. We were going in with 40 guys at the most. We were apprehensive at the very least.

The drive was the worst and hardest part. The terrain was hellacious—mountain peaks up to 8,000 feet on one side, dropping down to very narrow, dry riverbeds, with steep cliffs all around. You could call the entire region Ambush Alley.

After traveling for nine days through the mountains, we arrived in our area of operations (AO) on the Pakistan border and began patrolling. We spent three weeks in the area getting to know the people and their customs. As we got acquainted with them, we gathered information about the area and set up patrols to interdict the routes suspected as being used by the Taliban. After being in the area for more than a month, we were ordered to move back to Kandahar airfield. We did not have significant contact with the enemy, but by just being in the area we had successfully disrupted all enemy activity along that part of the border.

<u>True Story of the "Wedding Party Massacre"</u>

The "wedding party massacre" refers to the widely reported incident when U.S. fighters were directed to bomb a compound full of civilians at a wedding on July 1, 2002. According to news reports, the attack was partly the result of the celebrants' ritual firing of weapons into the air, the shooting being mistaken for anti-aircraft fire by an AWACS crew overhead, followed by the order to bomb the site. According to the story, dozens of civilians were killed and many more injured. The story made headlines around the world, but as Captain Anderson explains, it turned out to be much more complicated than reported, with much different conclusions in the resulting investigation report—the facts of which were largely ignored by the same media that pushed the inaccurate press accounts in the first place.

My second operation was a direct-action mission that would begin with our forces surrounding the whole community of Deh Rawud. The mission was supposed to be conducted with complete secrecy, and nobody in the area was supposed to know a thing about it.

We had four vehicle-transported ODAs, a detachment of Navy SEALs, and another ODA that would be flown in by helicopter to take up blocking positions, with a B team providing command and control support. The helicopters dropped the blocking teams to the northwest, and the rest of us moved toward the objective in our vehicles. Along the way was a checkpoint manned by the local militia, and as we were moving in, we intended to confiscate any radios or cell phones of the local guards to make sure they weren't alerting the bad guys in Deh Rawud.

We secured the checkpoint, disarmed the guards, and found about 10 guys in this compound. "We knew you were coming; we got briefed this afternoon. John Mohammad [the province governor] told us you were coming, and he already took the radios or cell phones! Now, would you like to sit down and have chai with us?" It was obvious that the mission had been compromised, but we continued on. The company commander took two ODAs to the east and north, and I took two to the west and north of the village.

Right away we started taking small arms fire from the area, then a lot of anti-aircraft guns opened up on the helicopters and the AC-130 overhead. Despite being compromised, it turned out to be a pretty successful mission. We took out 17 ADA (air defense artillery) sites and about 60 enemy soldiers. The next morning we learned there were civilian casualties too. This incident was soon referred to as the "wedding party massacre." We were all surprised because the next day the *New York Times* ran a critical article about the raid.

Two days later we were pulled back to a secure location, and then the Army sent in an investigating team that was on the ground for a week. We knew immediately that something was fishy. The people in Deh Rawud knew we were coming prior to the op; then it turned out that many international media representatives were all around the town during the fight. Then we started asking around the villages about the "wedding." Well, nobody seemed to know about the wedding. The community was very close, a place where everybody knows everything about all his or her neighbors, but nobody could tell us who was getting married at this alleged wedding. The bodies were supposed to be in the local morgue, but when the investigating team looked, they found no bodies. The hospital was locked up tight and looked as if it hadn't been opened for weeks. We found a few bomb craters but no body parts. The whole thing was extremely suspicious.

At the end of three months of investigation, the unit was exonerated and got a pat on the back from the theater commander, but nobody really corrected the story in the *New York Times*. I know we took aimed small arms fire during the operation, and we saw aimed air defense artillery (ADA). The day after the initial operation, the media ran the story as if we had recklessly killed innocent civilians when actually it appeared that the Taliban had used these people as pawns to win international sympathy for their cause and to put us in a bad light. There wasn't a wedding party, but there were media and Taliban waiting for us to arrive. When the report from the investigation came out three months later that cleared us, it was buried deep in the *Times* and not covered at all by some of the other media.

<u>Operational Detachment Alpha 361—Orgun Firebase</u>

After the Deh Rawud operation and the investigation that followed, I was sent to take over ODA 361 and the Orgun firebase, and that was the beginning of the real adventure. When I was an enlisted soldier on a team, we didn't have a captain. Most of the time it was just the team sergeant and the rest of the team. We had a great time, everybody did their job, and it worked well. But taking command of a team like this was something for which I had worked my entire Army career.

Before I went to take over 361, though, we had a weird Fourth of July at the firebase. The sergeant major decided to play Jimi Hendrix's version of the *Star Spangled Banner* over the PA system while we were in formation, and that was pretty unreal. Then we barbecued steaks and hamburgers flown in by our FOB to celebrate the occasion, even though we were deep in Afghanistan.

I'd been involved in the transition of a new company command for a while when I was told, "You've gotta get down to Kandahar, hitch a ride with ODA 364, then you're going to take over 361 at Orgun." So for the next 48 hours, I got one hour of sleep, and that was on the helicopter. About two in the morning, I finally get to Orgun and am unloading my gear from the helicopter. A tall red-headed guy is there and he is tossing his stuff on the bird as I am taking mine off. I help the guy get his stuff on the helicopter and he turns to me with a huge grin, shakes my hand, and says, "Glad to meet you! Have a good time with the team!"

"Same to you, buddy," I say, and off this guy goes.

Some of the guys on the team came out with "gators" [small ATVs] to get me and my gear. "Who was that?" I asked.

"Oh, that was the old team leader," one of them said.

"You guys must really have been hell on him, then," I told him, "because he looked damn happy to be out of here!" They all laughed and brought me inside the team room. So much for a formal transition from one commander to the next.

The team was awake and introduced themselves. I explained who I was, then I found a place to get some sleep. In the morning the first guy I see is Mark, the team sergeant. He has this huge beard, his hair is really long and standing out all over his head. If he had a swastika between his eyebrows, he would have looked exactly like Charles Manson! Mark was talking a mile a minute, sounded and looked like a wild man (and I found out later he was known as The Wild Man of Orgun), and I started wondering, What have I gotten myself into? But Mark turned out to be the best team sergeant I could possibly ever have. I am not really a black-and-white, by-the-book kind of guy; Mark and I turned out to be similar that way, and we sort of fed off each other. I expected a team sergeant who would want to try to keep me in line, but he turned out to be as mission-oriented as I was. We both recognized that to operate in this environment, you have to be very aggressive.

One day, Luke and Jeff [two sergeants on the team] went downtown and were fired upon by guys who really weren't Taliban, just criminals associated with the local warlord. We had run this warlord, Zakem Kahn, out of Orgun, and when we got the call about the encounter, we activated the QRF [quick reaction force]. We zoomed downtown with 100 men from the AMF and a platoon of 82nd Airborne, put the company on line, and swept the town. My philosophy was that anytime somebody shot at us, we would drop the hammer on them. That was the only thing these people understand, based on their own traditions, the law of the gun and the law of the money. And the two have always been connected in this part of the world. Every time somebody tried to compromise or negotiate with these people, they lost respect from the locals who would then try to go around them or blow them off completely. The only way to work with the locals was to show them that you were in charge.

At the time the shots were fired, I was lifting weights in our little gym before Jeff and Luke radioed their report. Right away, I called in a SITREP to the battalion and told them what we were going to do. Then I went off to battle wearing running shoes, PT shorts, a tee-shirt, body armor, and a helmet, carrying my M4 carbine—not like in training. I didn't look anything like a conventional commander, but we got the job done! We had an ABC news crew with us at the time, and they were taping us. "Only show me from the waist up," I told the cameraman.

We actually got one of the shooters, brought him back, put him in the prisoner cage, and interrogated him. He produced some good information, too, and then we sent him off to Bagram for further interrogation.

Clothes Make the Man

When we first showed up in Afghanistan, the command had a "hands-off" approach to the way we conducted ourselves. They understood that we needed to blend in with the local culture, grow beards, and wear a mix of uniforms and civilian attire. That helped us blend into the mix of westerners on the ground—aid workers, journalists—the whole country was full of people from NGOs [non-governmental organizations]. Without wearing Afghani garb, you could fit into the people on the street and be far less conspicuous. When we went to meetings dressed and groomed in a way that fit in with local culture, in a local vehicle, we were almost always successful. Every time we had to go out in a Humvee, in BDUs and Kevlars, the people we were trying to catch were long gone. They or their friends could see us coming from miles away, and it was easy to see where we were headed, giving the bad guys lots of warning and time to get away. Dressing in civilian attire reduced the reaction time of the enemy to set up ambushes against us; they couldn't recognize us as American units until we were right on top of them, and by then it was too late for the execution of a proper ambush. Besides those considerations, the people we had contact with were not comfortable talking to us if we were obviously American soldiers because they were likely to be in trouble with the local warlord or Taliban as soon as we left. We were much more successful when we fit into the culture.

361 Rocks!

After I took over the team, I told them that I was going to let them do pretty much whatever they'd been doing and watch them for a few weeks, just to see how they operated. They were rocking! Mark was a terrific team sergeant, and the ODA was tremendously effective. They hadn't been working out of Orgun long and were just getting themselves established. Our doctrine says that one ODA with just 12 men is supposed to be able to go out and recruit, train, equip, and lead a 500-man battalion. That's exactly what SF was doing in Afghanistan. First the 5th Group teams working with the Northern Alliance moved from north to south and took control of the country from the Taliban.

When the 5th Group teams left and the 3rd Group teams took over the mission, there were still pockets of resistance, especially along the border with Pakistan. ODA 361 was ordered to go into the area around Orgun, get itself established, then recruit local militia, train them, and lead them on combat operations. As I arrived, the firebase was just being completed. The ODA recruited 300 men and organized them into three companies of 100 men each, with two American NCOs in charge of each indigenous militia company. Those NCOs ran these rifle companies just like they were company commanders in the conventional army. These sergeants were responsible for the training, welfare, and leadership of entire companies. My role was just like that of a conventional battalion commander.

In the unconventional warfare role at Orgun, those two sergeants do almost everything a commissioned officer normally does. Instead of being in charge of a dozen men, these young E-6s or E-7s are now in charge of 100—for all their training, discipline, weapons issue, pay, everything! The sergeants on 361 were great at this! Mark and I didn't have to be all over the battlefield, we'd just call over the two NCOs, give them a quick "op order," and tell them to "punch out," to get going with little more guidance. Then they could get going and operate on their own. The NCOs ran the companies while I maneuvered the whole 300-man force on the battlefield; SF hasn't done this since Vietnam, at least on this scale.

BEASTMASTER 4

We had a huge AMF force thanks to the successful recruiting efforts of Mark and the team. Other ODAs might have a few squads or platoons of local fighters, but we had 300. For example, we went out on one operation, I think it was BEASTMASTER 4, and loaded up all three of our companies into what we called "jingle trucks." These were the large, Russian-built Kamaz cargo trucks used locally, normally heavily decorated and loaded with more bells than you would find on a herd of camels. It took seven or eight of these big trucks to carry our AMF guys, with about 50 in each, we had so many. We rolled into the assembly area with 300 soldiers. The other ODAs had maybe 35 or 40 each.

Having all those people allowed us to operate much more effectively than other ODAs, and here's how it worked: We'd load up, then drive perhaps all night to a remote village, then un-ass the vehicles and quickly put a cordon around the whole place. Once the village was bottled up, we went through it methodically and conducted a thorough search. We captured many weapons and lots of ammunition this way. The technique was awesome when you have enough people. The greatest thing about it was that it was done by the Afghans themselves, with the help of just a small American force. We needed very little support, and few American lives were in danger. This is what the Army calls "force multiplication," and it works!

Battle for the Checkpoint

The border between Afghanistan and Pakistan was very porous everywhere, but especially in our area. The Pakistanis maintain their checkpoints every 1,500 meters or so, and each of their checkpoints can observe the adjoining checkpoints and the terrain in between. Nobody crosses into Pakistan without being seen. The Afghan checkpoints are much more isolated, up to 5 kilometers apart, with big gaps in their ability to monitor people moving into the country. So Taliban forces could move back and forth in and out of Afghanistan easily—until one day when we showed up.

During this operation, ODA 361's basic mission was to slow down the influence of these hostile forces infiltrating into Afghanistan. We were to help the AMF secure the area, give the residents of the area a sense of greater security, and pacify the region.

People are always in the equation during military operations, but especially with SF. Conventional units think of taking ground, we think about what people think and how they act. One of the things that makes us successful is relationships with people from foreign cultures: Will they give us the information we need to find the bad guys? Will they tell us where the weapons caches are? When is an enemy unit going to attack, or where are they hiding?

Our op area was starting to get pacified about the time I showed up, and we were able to start doing much, much more. We continued doing combat operations, but seldom the big "muscle" ops with all 300 guys. Instead, we did ops like the one Hector and Jim proposed.

"We want to do a camel patrol," they said, "right up to the border," and it sounded like a great idea to me. So they hired camels and pack mules, loaded them up, and took their 100-man company on a week-long sweep of the border up in the mountains. In the process, they discovered routes the enemy was using to sneak in and out of Afghanistan. They visited villages where no westerner may ever have been before, collected intelligence, and made contacts with the local elder.

We started using the AMF for gathering intel better too. When they went home for a few days, as many were allowed to do sometimes, we told them to collect information from their family and friends. We taught our AMF to be on their best behavior downtown, and when they went home to let the population know we were on their side. Pretty soon, civilians would show up at the compound asking to talk to Commander John or Commander Mark, telling us about problems they thought we should know about. We found out about caches of weapons, munitions, and similar contraband that way. The most significant information was in the pockets of their clothing; we found very good stuff that way with the result that many enemy operations were closed down. We didn't pick somebody up unless we really had good evidence on him, but in the end ODA 361 was responsible for sending five or six enemy personnel to Guantanamo Bay.

Orgun had been ravished and pillaged by years of neglect by the Taliban. Taxes were collected but none were reinvested for the community, so we started doing things to rebuild the place. Instead of rebuilding it ourselves, though, we got involved with the local Shira or town council. Mark started talking to people around town, finding out who could do what. Well, the roads were full of potholes and were dusty, so he found a local guy who owned a dump truck, went up to the guy and said, "You own the only dump truck in town. We're making you the official minister of roads for Orgun!"

"Oh, no," the guy complained, "the insurgents will target me if I cooperate."

"Don't worry about a thing," Mark said. "Once everybody sees that the roads are being fixed, nobody will bother you! They will think you are a hero!"

"Okay," the truck owner said, not entirely convinced.

Mark went to the only doctor in town, a man who had just returned from exile in Pakistan. "You are now the official Orgun minister of health," he said. "We're having a Shira meeting next Wednesday. Be there and bring a list of what you need to build a proper clinic."

Mark found a man who was a ditch-digger. "You, sir, are now the minister of sanitation. You are going to help get rid of the sewage in the streets."

By the time Mark was done, he had appointed 14 "ministers." These new officials started working together with each other and with us. They had a town meeting every Wednesday and started working on a new school (two schools, actually, one for boys, one for girls), a new clinic, and the roads started getting paved.

"But how are we going to pay for all this?" they asked.

Instead of giving them the money from American funds, we took over the custom house that collected tolls for use of the main road. Up until the time we got there, this money went either to the Taliban or to the local warlord, and none was reinvested in the community or the highway. All of a sudden, we had a cash flow and it all went to the Shira to be spent on public works programs.

Now the guy with the dump truck was getting paid to fill the potholes and pave the streets. Since the road was better, people started using that stretch of highway more, so the income from the tolls increased. There was money for building the schools and for books and supplies too.

Orgun had many abandoned buildings at the time, so we went around, identified some that could be used, and cleaned them out. As the region became pacified, lots of refugees came back from Pakistan. Many set up shops in these buildings and paid the Shira tax and rent. Now there was even more money to improve the community, and the residents were doing it all themselves, with their own money and initiative. Soon Orgun had two schools, paved streets, a clinic appeared, and the mosque that had been previously damaged was rebuilt. All this helped accomplish our military objectives because once the people saw things improving they did not want the Taliban back, and they passed us accurate information on the enemy. We then used that information to target the enemy, and the result was that the area became more secure, all because people began to have hope for the future.

Farewell to Orgun

After some months in Orgun, ODA 361 was ordered to shift to the town of Deh Rawud, up north where I had been originally, where a new firebase was being built. But before we left, the local population gathered to say goodbye. At least 500 people showed up; there was a parade, and Mark and I were presented with a sort of wreath made with flowers. Mark was given a huge trophy, and I got a sort of plaque and a bouquet. Some of the AMF soldiers we had worked so closely with were crying and did not want to let us go. It was wonderful knowing that we had made a difference in the area. Then we left, and it took more than four days to drive up to Deh Rawud.

Adventures in Agriculture

As soon as we arrived at the new camp, we went out on an operation. We were looking for a guy named Omar Berader. Forty-five AMF had come with us, and there were two other ODAs at this location. We rolled out, secured our objective, then spent the whole day searching the area for this guy.

Luke and I were riding in one of those Toyota Hilux pickup trucks so common over there. We had a Russian machine gun mounted on the roof, got into our position, and were covering the objective when Jim and George were moving to sweep around behind us, each with their own gun trucks. Their trucks got stuck, though, so they walked about 4 miles to the objective, just about sunrise.

They and their AMF soldiers went on line and were moving into position just about sunset, and as they did, they were moving through a huge field of marijuana plants, all about 9 feet tall! It was surreal, like something from a movie. They all moved on and secured the objective. After we were done looking for our bad guy, it was time to go; but none of the AMF guys could be found. "Luke," I said, "what happened to your guys?"

He turned around and yelled, "Hey, 'meat-sticks,' get out of the pot!" Suddenly heads appear from the marijuana. All the AMF were collecting the stuff and cramming it in their packs and pockets. Some of them had sprigs of it stuck in their hats; others used it to decorate their shirts and web gear.

T and A in Afghanistan

Guys always ask me what the women were like in Afghanistan. I like to tell them that we saw lots of "T and A" in Afghanistan—toes and ankles! A lot of the older women were scared to death of us just because we were westerners. Other times, you drive through a village and sometimes, especially in the Shiite areas where they are not quite so conservative, the younger women will pull back their veil and give you a smile—but nothing more!

270

Mysteries in the Desert

Strange things sometimes happened to SF units operating in Afghanistan, and we had our share. Our ODA was back at the fire-base at Deh Rawud and another unit, ODA 365, was out on an armed reconnaissance patrol. ODA 365 calls us and reports they've come upon a compound with radio antennas on the roof, an uncommon and suspicious discovery, and they ask us to provide backup.

Together we secured the place and checked it out. Inside were 47 men and boys of military age, a very suspicious development. There was also a parachute kit bag containing military radios, making the whole place even more suspect. When asked about the radios, the head man of the group said the gear was from the old Mujahideen days, but the dates on the radios were much more recent for that to be true. The strangest thing we found was a model of a Boeing 747 aircraft. The men were detained and brought back to the firebase. Later we heard that many of them were being sought for capture. We never found out exactly what the airplane model was for, but of course, we had our suspicions. The head man of the group was released later, came back to Deh Rawud, and was soon assassinated by presumed Taliban or al-Qaeda operatives in the area, probably because they thought he had provided information to us.

Gorilla Warfare

As all soldiers know, life in the field, and especially life in a combat zone, will warp your sense of humor quite a bit. When you combine that with our SF tradition of doing things in a somewhat different way, and coming up with novel ideas for solving problems, silly things get suggested occasionally to break the tension. For example, we had a little gasoline-powered generator at the firebase, and it put out just enough juice to run a small television and a VCR. The team used it to watch movies occasionally, but it gave me an idea one day.

Our most recently watched film had been an old copy of *Planet of the Apes*, and I told Mark, "We ought to take the generator, VCR, and TV with us to some of the most remote villages where the people have never seen television. They have never seen anything like this, not even electricity, and it would make a big impression!" Mark looked at me like I was insane, at first.

"Look, we could show them *Planet of the Apes*, tell the people that the Earth was being invaded by these creatures, and that the only hope was for all mankind to unite against the common enemy, the apes, and the villagers could help by giving us all the information they had on insurgents in the area, all of whom we could say are working for the apes."

"Great idea," Mark said. "Let's write up a CONOP and send it up to Bagram! We'll get some gorilla costumes too! What are you going to call this new program?"

"Why, 'Gorilla Warfare,' of course," I said.

Mark went so far as to price the suits, and we actually mentioned the idea to the battalion commander, who laughed at it. For some reason, however, we never got that program funded.

Social Studies 101

One of the strangest things we did was to kick the governor out of his province. We'd been busy in our area for a while, got it pretty well pacified, got the city council up and running, the streets were getting fixed, the schools built, and the community was being rebuilt. Then, in April, the Loya Jerga gathered in Kabul, and not long after that, a man named Mohammad Ali Jalali showed up in Orgun with a large entourage. Jalali was claiming to be the new governor for Paktika Province. We thought this was a great development. The community was being rebuilt, but it was a grassroots effort with very limited resources and without direction from the Afghan government. We expected this new governor to complete the connection of the province with the central government and help the total effort; boy, were we wrong about that!

On the first day, Jalali asked to meet with me, and we talked, but I told him that he really needed to work with the town council, the people who had been doing all the rebuilding. So the next day, for four hours, he listened to the Shira members report on each of their areas of responsibility—roads, schools, the clinic, and so forth—nodding and smiling all the while. At the end of the day, we adjourned till the following day. I went back to the firebase, wrote up a report, and fired it off to the FOB asking, "Who is this guy? Where has he been for the past 10 years? Is he an exile, or an ex-Taliban? Was he really appointed to this job, or just claiming it?" Other people had claimed control of the town before, and we had run them out. They were just trying to establish themselves as the local warlords.

Nothing came back on the guy, but the police chief who had been sent previously by the national government told me, "This man is crooked. Last night after you left the Shira meeting, he called the Shira together and told them that he planned to fire them all! Then he said he would collect 100 percent of the tolls and taxes, all of which must be delivered to his headquarters in another town. That money would be distributed to other towns in the province! And he said he would appoint replacement representatives who would *only* report to him. Finally, this new governor told the Shira that he would not permit the girl's school to open."

This was a shocker for us since things had been going so well in the Orgun area. Mark and I met with the guy the next day. It was just Mark, two interpreters, one bodyguard, and me. We gave this guy a lesson in Social Studies 101 about democracy, about the plans for the country, about all the changes that were needed in the province. Basically, we explained how grassroots democracy was working in Orgun and how it should be encouraged to support the national government.

"Yes, yes," he said, "I understand!"

That night we found out that the guy had been trained by the East Germans for the Russians. When the Russians quit Afghanistan, he rolled over to the Mujahideen. Then he signed up with the Taliban

273

and became an official for them in a province to the north. All this information came from local sources, people who had learned to trust us. I wrote up another report, sent it up to higher again, and asked for every bit of information they had on the guy, and still nothing back on this character.

I agreed to meet this new "governor" at 1000 hours the next day. About 0830 we hear from our friend the police chief that this character was meeting behind closed doors with certain members of the Shira, trying to cut deals with them behind the back of the team. He was trying to get support of the Shira for his administration. If he got that support, he would be in total control and would be able to keep everything for himself.

"What are they talking about?" I asked the police chief.

"He's trying to buy them off," the chief said. "If they will agree to his policies, they get to keep their jobs in the new administration, after he disbands the Shira. He is corrupt, and he wishes to steal money from the taxes and tolls."

I was already downtown when I learned this. I called Mark on the radio: "Mark, send down a company of AMF, send down the 82nd Airborne QRF." I told Mark to detain the security force and make a show of it; I wanted the guy to understand that he could not fuck with us. This character never went anywhere without a 35-man security force, and they carried RPGs and PKMs. They were armed to the teeth, but we were going to change that. I had one other guy with me, Sergeant Mike, but Mike is 6-foot-4 and is all muscle, a good guy to have around.

Mark and the guys from the firebase zoomed down to town. Mike and I went to where the meeting was being held, and Mike kicked in the door. We walked in on this private meeting and one of the bodyguards turned toward us with an AK. Mike slapped the AK out of the guy's hands, grabbed the bodyguard by the neck, and slammed him against a wall, his feet off the ground. I followed Mike in and went straight to the center of the room.

"What the hell is going on here?" I ask. They were all wide-eyed. The color drained from one guy's face, another's jaw dropped.

274

"We weren't supposed to meet till 10, but I hear you've been meeting since 8:30."

"Oh, we've just been talking about—"

"Shut up! I know what you've been talking about! You've been trying to undermine what we've been doing here in Orgun! We know you're an opportunist, trying to set yourself up as a warlord here." I poked him in his bony little chest. "Until I'm ordered out of here, I am the commander in this area! You won't be destroying the system these people have here to rebuild their community. They are practicing democracy and building a new Afghanistan. You are not going to destroy that. This country needs a new leader that will serve the people, not demand that they serve him. You're out of here!"

"But I am the governor, " he pleaded.

"Not if I have anything to say about it! We know all about your history. You are part of the old regime. I don't know how you got appointed to this position, but the people around here don't want any part of you. You are out of here!"

Our guys disarmed the security force while we were inside. I marched the guy out the door and into the courtyard, holding his shoulder. As we emerged, he could see his security force disarmed, all of them flex-cuffed with their hands behind their backs, with bags over their heads. All of them were sitting cross-legged in the courtyard. We had AMF on the walls of the compound with their weapons trained on the warlord's security detail. Just outside the gate were our 82nd Airborne guys in full battle kit and looking very serious. This guy sees all this, and I thought he was going to shit himself! He started shaking with fright.

We wanted to make really sure he got the message, so Mark asked a couple of AH-64 Apache helicopters to make a pass over the compound too. George went to work on the weapons taken from the detail, removing bolts and firing pins, throwing them away, then tossing the useless AKs into one of the trucks. "You have five minutes to get out of town," I told him, and he departed in a state of deep shock without any argument with all of his men.

275

He never tried to come back while ODA 361 was there, although I since heard that he wormed his way back and the whole place has gone to hell again.

THE BATTLE OF DEBECKA PASS
FRANK ANTENORI

One of the interesting developments within Special Forces over the past decade or so has been an evolution in tactical doctrine that has profoundly changed the way some SF groups plan and execute missions. Third Group, as an example, now emphasizes vehicle-mounted, rather than the traditional foot patrols, while 10th Group (at this writing) does not. Beginning in late 2002, ODAs in 3rd Group conducted intensive train-ups with heavily modified HMMWVs ("Humvees") that prepared them for deep recon missions inside enemy-held territory. These GMVs (Ground Mobility Vehicles), as they were called, were set up to carry three men, (a driver, TC, and gunner; they actually can carry an additional four men in the back during assaults and transport operations if needed, bringing the total to seven) a very extensive arsenal of weapons, and enough food, ammunition, and fuel to operate unsupported for up to 10 days (or 600 to 700 miles). Although the vehicle itself is modern, this mission is an old and well-proven one that goes back to the British Army's "Desert Rats" of World War II.
This amazing story describes ODA 391's and 392's incredible fight with a stubborn Iraqi mechanized infantry company—29 men in light, unarmored vehicles who took on tanks, APCs, and large numbers of dismounted infantry, along with a few lunatic members of the news media, in a hasty defensive position they named the Alamo. The fight really began with the two ODAs astride Highway 2 and the Kirkuk-Irbil road, a key intersection. Visibility was very limited during the fight by heavy haze and fog, a major factor in the development of the battle.

The Battle of Debecka Pass, as it was called in Special Forces briefings, is one of the most interesting and intense fights to be revealed to the public in many years. It was a test of many changes in SF doctrine and SF technology, especially including the effectiveness of the new Javelin "fire-and-forget" antitank missile, which was a huge success and a battle-winning weapon at the Alamo. It was also a test of air support, which produced a catastrophic friendly-fire incident and was largely ineffective, unable to destroy a single armored vehicle.
Sergeant First Class Frank Antenori was the team sergeant for ODA 391 during the fight, and here is his account of the battle. The names of the team members have all been previously revealed in press accounts and are, therefore, included here.

Part I: The Alamo

ODA 391 was, along with the other 3rd Group teams, attached to 10th Group for an operation in northern Iraq. Tenth Group was supposed to be the main effort, but they were primarily experienced in doing dismounted foot patrols while 3rd Group had been training to patrol with vehicles. Before the battle, the expectation was that those of us from 3rd Group would serve as a Quick Reaction Force, a kind of fire brigade that could respond rapidly to emergencies. And that's what we did for a while at the beginning of the fight, going from one little emergency to another all across northern Iraq before the big push to the south toward Baghdad.

Our battalion commander made a strong pitch to use us in a more offensive role. We had the mobility and the weapons systems to do that while 10th Group didn't. At the time, there was very limited air support—just two carriers in the Med, and most of the air assets were being sent to the south. As the mission kicked off, we had no preplanned air cover at all. If we ran into trouble, we could call for support, but there would be no "on-station air" assigned to our mission.

Those of us from 3rd Group were equipped with GMVs—ground mobility vehicles, souped-up HMMWVs. All have M240B

278

7.62-millimeter machine guns, and two have M2HB .50-caliber heavy machine guns, and the other two have Mk19 mod IIIs [a cross between a machine gun and a 40-millimeter grenade launcher]. We've got the new Javelin antitank missiles, Barrett .50-caliber sniper rifles, SPR sniper rifles, AT4 rocket-launchers, land mines, and explosives for demolitions, plus lots of ammo for everything!

The poor guys from 10th Group only had some white pickup trucks with one pedestal-mounted M240B on the back, a couple of AT4s, and one or two Javelins—that's all! They didn't really have much to engage targets at ranges over 1,000 meters, so their attitude about what happened later was understandably different from ours.

The ODAs were teamed up in pairs: ODA 391 and 392, then 394 with 395, plus half an ODA from 10th Group to keep a Kurdish Peshmerga force with us under some kind of control. ODA 394 and 395 would operate in a coordinated way with us, attacking the ridgeline about 6 or 7 kilometers from our objective. Our role was to provide fire support with our heavy weapons for a dismounted Kurd assault.

The plan involved executing a "company attack" with about 80 Americans and around 200 Kurds against a fortified ridgeline believed occupied by about 500 Iraqis. Because the Kurds had no night vision capability, the attack had to be conducted in daylight, but we were able to get some air support during the night before the attack and drilled this ridgeline with about 22 heavy (2,000-pound) bombs so we didn't have any trouble getting up on top. But once on top and at our objective, we realized that we couldn't defend the position very well because terrain blocked the view of the roads the Iraqis would likely use to reoccupy their positions. So we moved forward down the hill where we saw a main highway, and on the highway were lots of enemy vehicles moving at a good clip up and down the route!

Our friends from 10th Group didn't like this new location. For one thing, we were a full kilometer forward of our objective, and their commander had told them to stay back at Objective Rock. We got the perception that the 10th Group AOB (Company) commander

279

we were working for issued guidance to his teams to keep us on a short leash, and that's what 044's team sergeant, Tom Sandoval, tried to do with us 3rd Group ODAs. As we started to move even more forward, Tom is saying, "Wait, wait, wait! We're already a klick past our objective! We aren't supposed to be going any farther!"

We looked at Tom and said, "Tom, buddy, that's the Iraqi army down there; we're going down the hill to get closer!"

"No, no, no, we need to stay right here!" he said. He was concerned, too, that we didn't have air cover on call.

"They're just trucks and dismounts!" we said. "No problem!" But he wasn't convinced.

Tom was literally caught between a rock (Objective Rock) and a hard place (3rd Group ODAs 391 and 392). He was doing his best to fulfill the directives of his commander. On our side of the mission, our battalion commander had told us that we were only attached to AOB 040 for the operation to get the Kurds on the "Green Line." Once we crossed the "Green Line" we were "detached" and fell back under his direct command for follow-on missions to get us into Kirkuk.

"Okay, fine," I said, "you guys can stay right here. We're going down the hill! We're not going to sit up on this hill watching the Iraqi army drive by all day; it will drive us nuts!"

Marty McKenna (my team's chief warrant officer) and I went over to talk to the 392 guys; their captain, Matt Saunders, agreed. "Yeah, let's go down and shoot them!" he said. We moved farther down the ridgeline.

The road we saw was Highway 2, Iraq's second most important route, connecting Kirkuk and Mosul, and was the MSR (main supply route) for the Iraqi army in the north. So there was a lot of traffic on the road—jeeps, cargo trucks full of troops, others loaded with military supplies, all rushing down this road. We watched them through our scopes and were saying to ourselves, "This is going to be easy pickings; we'll sneak down a bit farther, get to about 900 meters from the intersection, then we can start lighting up target vehicles as they come up to us."

Our team mindset had been set in the rear, long before we ended up in Iraq. Our whole focus during our premission train-up was to fight it out with the enemy for as long as we could and avoid breaking contact. Our major at the time, the company commander, had spent a lot of time at JRTC [Joint Readiness Training Center, where light forces conduct realistic combat scenarios] and was a firm believer in having SOPs [standard operating procedures] in place for any tactical possibility. The ODAs were generally opposed to this because we routinely operate autonomously, especially, as now, when we were "chopped" to another unit and needed a lot of flexibility. He could go along with this generally, but he really wanted an SOP in place to cover a situation where we were attacked by infantry.

"What are you going to do if you're in a defensive position and you get attacked by a couple of companies of Iraqi mech infantry?" he wanted to know.

"We are going to sit there and pile them up," we told him. "We are not pulling off till we are out of bullets; then we will move back."

"No, seriously, what is your SOP going to be in that kind of situation?" he asked again.

The chief and I were laughing, and we said to him, "We are going to pile them up! We are not leaving!"

"Four hundred guys jump out of trucks and come at you, and you're not pulling back?"

"Sir," I told him, "I fought the Iraqi army before in the first Gulf War. If they are dumb enough to send 400 guys at my team, we are going to pile them up. We are not going anywhere." We knew from combat experience in the first Gulf war that you could engage these guys at long range, take out one or two at a time, especially the guys in front, and every time you did, their attack would falter. The Iraqis tried to take on ODA 525, a recon team that got compromised in the first war, sending about 300 men against a few SF, and never got close enough to hurt the team. "That's what we're going to do, too," I told him. "We've got these big-ass trucks with tons of ammo, tons of weapons. If dismounted infantry start

281

coming at me, we are going to eat them up with our .50-calibers and our Mk19s long before they can do anything to us. I'm not moving." We had a big argument about this. The major wanted us to break contact under those conditions. We didn't think we should if we were not under pressure. "I am not going to pull out of an objective because a bunch of guys with AKs are coming at me, guys who can't hit anything at 50 meters, with us 400 meters away. My guys and I have no problem dealing with infantry under those conditions."

In fact, we were very well prepared for dealing with and engaging man-sized targets at ranges beyond the usual 300 meters. All of us were good at pegging targets at 400 and 500 meters just using our regular ACOG sights, and three of the guys could routinely hit targets out to 600 meters with the M4 and ACOG sights!

The major objected, and we had an extended, heated discussion about the issue, but we stuck to our guns and only agreed to pull back if we encountered a large armored force—six tanks or more. "If we can't stop them with the weapons we have, we'll pull back," we told him. Our reasoning was that we had enough Javelin missiles to destroy five tanks. (We had eight missiles total, two per truck, with an expected three out of four hit ratio, and we figured five tanks seemed like a realistic number to handle for what we had.)

"So you're telling me that if you have 400 Iraqis coming at you, you're not going to pull out? And you're telling me that if you have five tanks coming at you, you aren't going to move? You guys are nuts!" he said.

We weren't nuts, though. We mostly had wives and kids and wanted to make it home in one piece. Our team had a good idea of what it could and couldn't do, and if we found ourselves getting seriously threatened, we would pull out then, and not before. The Army today seems to have a fixation on air support (whether it be Apaches or USAF Fast movers). You can't do anything without air cover, and if you get shot at, you're expected to withdraw until you have air support. "Lure the enemy out into the open where they can be killed by air power" seems to be the current attitude, but we were not buying it.

"See all those trucks on the highway over there?" I said. "You guys can stay up here if you want and guard the original objective, but 391 and 392 are going over the hill and we're going to start killing the Iraqis. We did not come all the way over here to watch the war from inside the cab of a truck."

So off we drove down the hill. We set up about 1,000 meters from the highway and began engaging trucks with the .50-caliber. That turned out to be a little more difficult than we expected. Once the drivers noticed they were being engaged, they naturally sped up. Unlike the depiction by Hollywood, it is actually very hard to hit a truck doing 60 miles per hour at that kind of range. We had trained for similar engagements out to 1,400 meters, but the moving vehicle targets on the ranges could only get up to 25 miles per hour. Since our success with targets going 60 miles per hour wasn't working too well, we moved closer, to about 700 meters from Highway 2.

During this time, half of 391, led by the detachment commander, Captain Eric Wright, took two of the GMVs and six guys to go back to make sure the road behind us was clear. It had been mined, and a berm had been built across it by the Iraqis, but the mines had been so badly emplaced that we could just drive around them in the daylight. At night, under pressure, it wouldn't be so easy, so half the team was up on top of the ridge while we got closer to the highway. They finished with that chore just in time to get back for the big show, having been still at the dirt berm when the tank fight started. Staff Sergeant Kenney Wilson didn't have enough explosives in his GMV to push the needed amount of dirt contained in the 10-foot-high, 8-foot-thick berm. So he sent three of the guys, including our only medic, Sergeant First Class Mike Ray, out into the Iraqi minefield to scarf up as many Iraqi antitank mines as they could carry. He had them bring the mines back and place them in the hole he dug at the base of the berm. Unfortunately, the first explosion didn't move enough dirt, so Kenney sent them back out into the minefield a second time. The second explosion was successful in opening the road.

At this time, the other half of ODA 391 and all of 392 were about 700 meters from the highway, with the Kurdish Peshmerga and their 10th Group half team a little farther up the hill.

Right away, we had our first successful engagement. We shot up an SUV command-and-control vehicle with an officer and a soldier in it, and it veered off the highway and crashed. Almost instantly some Kurds who had been staying safely behind us suddenly drove past at high speed in their pickup truck. They disappeared from view on the other side of the highway where the SUV went, but we could hear some small arms fire. For a few minutes, we had no idea what was happening. Then, suddenly, the Kurds popped back up, dragging the SUV out of the ditch, back onto the highway. They decided to "capture" the vehicle and drag it back up the hill behind their pickup on the end of a chain, even though windows were shot out, there were bullet holes in the doors, and one tire was flat. They dragged the worthless carcass of this vehicle back to their original position like a prize trophy, hooting and hollering.

Another truck showed up, and we lit up this one too. It went off the road, and another pickup full of Kurds went screaming down the hill to claim the prize. This happened every time we shot up an Iraqi vehicle; these Kurds would go collect it—motorcycles, trucks, everything. We had the tidiest battlefield you've ever seen!

At this point, an Iraqi troop truck (2 1/2-ton) with about 12 Iraqi soldiers in the back left the town of Debecka to the west of us. It was a good kilometer away from us and putting distance between us every second. Staff Sergeant Jason Brown, my team's senior weapons sergeant, asked if he could take it out with a Javelin. At first I told him no, but Brown insisted he get the chance to use the Javelin. Jason Brown had been a Javelin gunner in the 82nd Airborne for years. He'd trained on the missile numerous times but had never fired a live missile.

When we were getting ready for Iraq it was Brown who insisted that the team learn how to use the Javelin. He set up a week for us on the 82nd's Javelin simulator to familiarize the team on putting the missile into action. Little did we know back then how important

Brown's recommendation to the detachment's leadership would be when we got into Iraq.

Brown continued to insist: "Frank, 3rd ID is just outside of Baghdad, this war will be over in a week or two, and this may be my only chance to shoot this missile. You've got to let me get this one shot." I finally gave in and Brown retrieved the CLU [command launch unit] and a missile from his GMV. After about 30 seconds, he was ready to fire. By now the Iraqi truck was about 3 kilometers from our position and still traveling away. Brown let the missile go and it immediately disappeared into the low cloud cover.

Several seconds go by and the Iraqi truck was still driving away. "You must have missed," I told him. Just as I was about laugh it off and give Brown a hard time for blowing his only chance with the Javelin, the cab of the Iraqi truck exploded into flames! None of us had ever seen a Javelin fired, so we didn't expect the flight time of the missile to be so long. Brown not only got his chance to shoot the Javelin, but he got a vehicle kill in combat. Little did we all know at the time, this wouldn't be the last missile he would fire that day.

We continued to engage vehicles with our machine guns. We were doing this for a while, then Marty said to me, "What do you think about moving all the way down and setting up on the intersection?"

"You mean, shut the road down? Yeah, I'm all for that."

Marty McKenna, our team's warrant officer, and I went to talk to 392's captain. "Sir, we want to go set up on the intersection. We want to shut the highway down." We told him we also wanted to get some prisoners to interrogate, and the captain bought off on it. "Sure," he said, "great!" So we picked up and moved all the way down to the intersection of Highway 2 and the road to Irbil. It didn't take long for more traffic to arrive, and one of them was memorable.

A big black bus came roaring down the highway, and Iraqi soldiers soon started shooting at us with AKs from the windows! We opened up on that bus with every weapon we had—the Mk19, the .50-caliber, everything. I could see the .50-caliber tracers impacting the bus, and we were really slamming it. The Iraqi driver, though, should get a medal for what he did next. With all this fire hitting his vehicle, he executed a perfect three-point turn and drove back the way he had come, with us pounding that poor bus the whole time.

We laughed about it at the moment, but he probably let somebody on the Iraqi side know about us because the picture changed soon after that. It wasn't long till we began taking mortar fire from about 2 1/2 klicks away from the town of Debecka. The 10th Group guys came down and set up alongside us at the intersection. A USAF TAC-P with 392 (each ODA had an attached USAF controller) was actually able to spot the mortar position and see the gunners dropping rounds down the tube, so we knew exactly where it was.

Captain Sanders decided to take his team out to shut the mortar down. He gathered us together and we made a very hasty five-point contingency plan, where the primary and secondary rally points would be. If things really went to shit, we'd meet back at the original objective up on top of the ridge. He took off with four vehicles, bounding forward—two move up while two provide cover, then they swap.

About the time they went off to get the mortar, my warrant officer, Chief McKenna, saw vehicles moving down the other road. It was about 8:30 in the morning now, and visibility was quite limited by fog and haze. These vehicles could barely be made out now at a range of 1,500 to 2,000 meters. We could tell that they were trucks, and when they spotted us they flashed their lights. Tom and the Peshmerga commander came over and said, "They're trying to surrender. Don't fire them up."

We didn't want to shoot them up either because we needed some prisoners. The Iraqi 3rd Division was supposed to be in this valley and it wasn't there, so far as we could tell. But where was it?

Staff Sergeant Andy Pezzella, the junior commo guy, was sitting behind the .50-caliber in one of the trucks, and Staff Sergeant Bobby Farmer, the junior engineer, is manning the Mk19 in my truck, and we are right on top of Highway 2. Chief McKenna's vehicle is over on the other road at the intersection, a bit closer to the enemy vehicles. "Andy," the chief says, "keep a close eye on them. When they get close enough, we'll send the Kurds out to capture them. We'll stay here and cover them till they get to about 500 meters."

ODA 392 was still maneuvering on the mortar position. The enemy was firing about two rounds per minute at us, very inaccurately. They weren't bracketing us and none of the rounds landed closer to us than about 100 meters. While it wasn't exactly funny, we just weren't getting excited about this very ineffective fire, despite our being in plain sight, out in the open. Had the rounds become more accurate, we were ready to move, but until then we were fascinated with the sight of 392 preparing to attack the mortar position.

We were all pretty relaxed about this, considering, and were more interested in 392's movement toward the mortar, when Andy leaned back and yelled, "Chief! Chief! I think they are shooting at us!"

"Who?" Marty asked, still watching 392's little drama.

"The guys by the trucks!" Andy replied. We grabbed our binos and looked over at the trucks where we could see people milling around, but no muzzle flashes or anybody obviously shooting. We could, however, see the drivers still flashing their headlights in what we think is a signal that they want to surrender.

"No, no, Andy," we told him, "they're just flashing their headlights."

"I'm sure I saw muzzle flashes," he insisted. "I'm telling you, they are shooting at us!" But we didn't take him seriously—right then, anyway. Not 30 seconds later, Pezzella yelled, "TANKS! TANKS! TANKS!"

"What?" I said. "Tanks? No way!" Iraqis don't attack, they usually fight in place, then run or surrender. But he was right; the Iraqis had blocked our view of the road with these trucks, then brought up six MTLB armored infantry carriers and four T-55 tanks. Because of the haze and fog, we couldn't see them until they all had advanced to about 1,200 meters. Then the APCs broke out from behind the trucks, deployed on line with three on each side of the road, and that's what Pezzella was seeing.

I couldn't believe it at first. I looked down there and couldn't see them directly, but I did see the exhaust plume shooting up in the air. Now, the wheat in the fields beside the road was tall and green, very lush but not yet ripe. The MTLBs were partly obscured, but I could see the top of these vehicles, recognized what they were, and thought, "Holy cow, we're getting attacked!"

Pezzella and all the rest of us were in awe. We just sat there for maybe 15 seconds, trying to figure out what was happening. Finally, Marty or somebody yelled, "Shoot 'em up!" and we started firing with the Mk19 and .50-caliber.

Staff Sergeant Jason Brown, my senior weapons man, hopped off his vehicle with the components of the new Javelin missile system, the expendable round and the CLU, assembled them, and sat down in the middle of the road, preparing to engage the enemy vehicles.

Marty called 392 on the radio and told them we were being attacked by armor and to get back to where we were at the intersection. It was essential that they get back to where we were because the only way out of this area is back up the road we came in on from the ridge and the original objective.

The team sergeant for 392, Ken Thompson, looked out the window of his GMV over by the village and saw one of the MTLBs. He said to himself (he told me later), "Why is Nine One getting so excited? There's only one of them, and it doesn't seem to even be moving." From that position, he could only see the MTLB on our extreme left, but then, as the enemy vehicle maneuvered, Ken realized something serious was happening. He turned 392 around and they dashed back to where we were on the intersection.

Jeff Adamec, 392's junior weapons sergeant, also hopped out of his vehicle with a Javelin CLU and launch tube, and he promptly started setting up his system as well.

Meanwhile, the .50-caliber and Mk19 gunners were starting to score on the MTLBs. Their fires couldn't really knock out the

288

enemy vehicles at this range, but the Iraqi crews were forced to "button up" and that slowed them down. At the same time, the Iraqis learned that we were not going to just cut and run, that we would stand our ground. When two of them actually stopped, we all thought maybe we had them intimidated; but all they were doing was letting the tanks move up. I still hadn't seen the tanks, but I certainly did see these six MTLBs lined up in front of us, just 1,000 meters away. All the MTLBs were banging away at us with the little 7.62-millimeter machine gun they had installed in a tiny turret. Happily, the gunners were very inaccurate; in our exposed position, we could have been in big trouble if they were any good.

All this happened very fast, probably just a few seconds, but at that moment it felt like we were in a time warp with everything happening in slow motion. One of the things happening in slow motion was Jeff and Jason getting the Javelin CLU ready for the first shot. It takes 30 to 45 seconds to chill the seeker head and that has to happen before the missile can be fired with the infra-red targeting system.

Now the T-55s were on line, and they were beginning to engage us too. The one on the right of our line, on my side, fired at us! It was the strangest thing. I saw the fireball and smoke from the main gun at the same apparent instant that the 100-millimeter round went past! This round hit right behind us, and that's when CWO McKenna started screaming, "Come on, let's go, let's go, let's get out of here!" He yelled to Brown, "Take the shot, take the shot!" Brown replied, "It's not happening, can't do it, the missile's not ready!"

When McKenna saw 392 pull into the intersection behind us he yelled to Brown, "Get in the truck!" Brown scrambled up on the hood of Marty's GMV, his M4 across his back, the Javelin under one arm, and he grabbed the lifting eye sticking up from the hood as a handhold. Brown, now seeing all the armor in front of him, looked back to McKenna and said, "We gotta go!"

"I'm with you, Marty," I yelled, "we're out of here!" Adamec jumped on the rear platform of the GMV, looking like a garbage man making his rounds, but he also had a Javelin under one arm and was holding on for dear life with the other. We pulled out of there as fast as we could go.

The Kurds had been lounging around behind us during this time, enjoying the show. They decided it was time to leave too, but they got to the road first with their six big, overloaded, underpowered, trucks. Each of their trucks had about 20 guys inside and some hanging off the sides. They headed back up the road, up the hill, at about 10 miles per hour, gears grinding. We were all honking our horns and yelling at each other to get out of the way. The road was essentially blocked, and the terrain on each side was far too rough for even our vehicles to move quickly. We could not get by them, so we just crawled up the road behind them while tank main gun rounds ripped past and overhead. Luckily, the gunners were all shooting high, but the impacts were right where we wanted to go.

It seemed to take forever, but at last we got about halfway up the hill, about 900 meters from the highway, without anybody being hit. Here we found a dip in the terrain that put us in defilade, a place we could defend. We ended up calling it the Alamo.

The enemy T-55s moved into position on the far side of Highway 2, behind the berm on which the road was built. They were in "hull-defilade," with just the turret and main gun exposed. That was the bad news, but the good news was that we had a good place to defend.

As soon as we rolled to a stop, Jason hopped off the GMV with his Javelin. Now the CLU was fully chilled and the system was ready to fire. Jason ran up on a part of the terrain where he could see the vehicles around the intersection, flopped down, and quickly found a thermal signature through the haze. The way the CLU works, the heat of an engine shows up bright in the sight. Two brackets in the sight picture are used to designate the target, and when those brackets are tight on the target, the missile knows right where it is supposed to go. Jason locked on to an MTLB and got a good hit. The infantry in the vehicle came tumbling out the back in complete disarray, and those who were able ran to hide behind the tanks.

None of us had fired a Javelin before, although we had seen one fired and had seen a video demonstrating the new weapon. The video, made at Redstone Arsenal, showed what happens when a T-72 full of ammunition and fuel is hit by the warhead. It came completely apart in a ball of fire. Nothing like that happened with the MTLBs, and we were a little disappointed at first. But the target lurched to a stop and was out of the fight, along with the guys inside. Within 15 seconds of the first missile launch, Brown got a second missile locked onto the CLU, got it cooled down, and fired at another APC—excellent "battle drill!"

At the same time, Adamec got his missile set up, and he fired too. All three missiles hit! Within just a few seconds, we had three of the enemy MTLBs knocked out and smoking, their surviving dismounts scurrying like rats for cover. The other three MTLBs stopped advancing on us and started maneuvering in odd ways, driving in circles and zigzagging, apparently trying to confuse the gunners. Those maneuvers might help with Dragon and TOW missiles, since they are command-guided by wires, but not with this new generation of "fire-and-forget" weapons.

The missile gunners now tried to lock on to the primary threat, the tanks, but because of their skillful emplacement, there wasn't enough heat signature for the CLUs to lock on. As long as they're hiding behind the berm, they're safe from us. There are still lots of jeeps, MTLBs, trucks, and troop-transports reinforcing from the south, though, so we turned the event into a Javelin-fest. Brown, Adamec, Eugene Zawojski, Eric Strigotte, and Mike Ray all had CLUs. (Each team had two CLUs and 044 had one, the one Strigotte used, giving us five total. After Brown fired his fourth missile, he handed the CLU off to me to shoot an MTLB. The tank I took out later on with the final shot was shot with the CLU Mike Ray used.) There were two CLUs per team, for a total of four, and 8 missiles each, for a total of 16. (The 044 had 3, giving us 19 total; 16 were fired in the initial engagement, leaving only 3 missiles until our

B-team showed up to resupply us with 8 more missiles and an additional CLU. This is when Sergeant First Class Jimmie Adams, our B-team weapons sergeant, shot one, Adamec shot one, and I fired the last one, bringing the total fired to 19.)

All five systems were put into operation at the same time. Missiles were really flying across this battlefield, and we were rapidly taking out an APC here, a truck over there, another MTLB, a troop transport, one right after the other! Brown got two APCs, then two troop trucks coming down the road. Adamec got the other APC, then a truck. Eugene was scoring, and so was I. All the MTLBs were destroyed; all the troop trucks had been smoked!

The effect of the missiles on these trucks was weird. They are programmed to fire from the top down, into the center of the heat signature, so when fired at a truck, they lock on to the engine. The warheads detonated right in front of the cab, demolishing it and the engine, killing the driver and front seat passenger, but the soldiers in the back were apparently unharmed. All these guys bailed out of the transports and started milling around, and that's when our .50-calibers and Mk19s started tearing into the dismounts. Andy had one of the .50s, and Bobby Farmer had our Mk19, plus the guys from 392 were really cutting the enemy infantry to pieces. Andy was firing accurate eight-round bursts; then he'd stop to evaluate the effectiveness of his fire. He was hitting right on the Iraqi jeeps and the dismounts around them, so I jumped up on the GMV and told him, "Don't stop, Andy, you're right on! Shoot, shoot, shoot!" I started feeding him ammo and helped him go through about three cans. The combination was really deadly, and we had the attack completely stalled.

Each team had a TAC-P assigned. These are Air Force enlisted men who provided dedicated liaison with Army maneuver units. When we first encountered the MTLBs, they reported, "Troops in contact." It took 35 minutes for the first aircraft to show up; they had launched from the Mediterranean and flown at full throttle to get to us all the way over in northern Iraq. That was probably fast for them, but it seemed like an eternity to us.

Part II: Friendly Fire

By the time these aircraft arrived overhead, we were starting to feel pretty cocky. We had completely shut down these Iraqis; all their vehicles were burning. The only thing we hadn't touched were the four T-55 tanks, and they were just lobbing rounds in our general area, not hurting us at all.

At the same time, the two other ODAs from our company, 394 and 395, along with their Peshmerga, were in another big battle about 8 klicks down the ridgeline. They were in contact with an enemy battalion in fortified positions. They needed air cover, too, and were calling for support.

Our company commander had our resupply vehicles, two GSRVs plus two GMVs and the whole B team with him. He started working on getting 94 and 95 resupplied—they'd already gone through half their ammo trying to get up the ridgeline to their objective. He didn't yet know about our situation because we hadn't called him on the SATCOM yet; the only people who knew we were in a fight were the Air Force because the TAC-Ps made the initial "troops in contact" report. Although our commander didn't know it, all of his teams— Charlie Company, 3rd Battalion, 3rd SFGA—were in heavy contact and engaged. Alpha Company was in a fight, too, on the road to Mosul. Also at this time, 10th Group teams were in fights too, and although they were supposed to be the primary effort, they didn't have the systems available to us. April 6 was a hell of a day; our whole battalion was slugging it out all over the northern part of Iraq.

The first aircraft arrived on station. The enemy was essentially pinned down and not moving past Highway 2 at that point, with the surviving dismounts taking cover behind the berm and in the area between the four tanks. These tanks fired one round every minute or so, a total of 72 100-millimeter rounds during the engagement, based on a count of spent shell casings after the battle, but none of them hit anything.

The first Navy F-14 checked in with 392's TAC-P, who explained the situation to the flight leader. He told them where we

293

were, that we had six GMVs and two white 10th Group Land Rovers on line. He told the fighters that we were about 900 meters from the intersection with Highway 2. The pilots flew right over us at about 500 feet AGL; we could see them in the cockpits. The TAC-P called, "Do you see our position?"

"Roger," flight lead called back. "I see six Humvees." The Tomcats turned left and now could see all three positions: ours, the enemy force down on Highway 2, and the 10th Group trucks and Peshmerga behind us, who had now moved all the way back up the hill to the original objective and were gathered around another road intersection up on top of the ridge. There was an abandoned Iraqi tank near this intersection, and the Kurds stopped not far away.

During the description of the target location, there was some confusion. The Tomcat leader looked down out of his cockpit, saw a road intersection, an enemy tank, some thin-skinned vehicles, and a large number of dismounted infantry milling around on the ground, all exactly matching what he had been hearing described. Apparently confirming the target location, this group was about 900 meters from the position of the six GMVs. The TAC-P told him, "Nine hundred meters to our south is a road intersection with armor, trucks, light vehicles, and dismounted infantry."

We on the ground didn't realize that this description matched both pictures, one on either side of us, one to the north and one to the south. "Roger," the pilot called, "I see an intersection with a tank to the side of the road, some trucks, and what looks like a lot of dismounts running around. Is that the target?"

"Roger," the TAC-P replied, "that's the target!" Neither he nor any of us had an idea that there were two matching versions of this picture, and one of them was the enemy and one was the friendly forces of the Kurds and our friends from 10th Group. All we could see was the intersection down the hill. The TAC-P cleared the flight, and it soared up into the clouds to begin the bombing run.

We were all watching down the hill, waiting for the tanks to get hit any moment, when instead we heard a huge explosion behind us. Everybody spins around, saw a cloud of black smoke coming from up on the ridge, and we all realized immediately that something had gone wrong. Captain Wright came back with our other two GMVs and had just passed the Kurds when the bombs hit; he called me on the radio, "Friendlies are hit!"

The TAC-P immediately called, "Abort, abort, abort—friendlies hit, friendlies hit!" Naturally, the Navy pilots went nuts and wanted to know what happened, but the TAC-P told them to return to the IP [initial point] and stand by. We had a lot to sort out. Wright said to me on the radio, "Frank, there are bodies scattered everywhere up here! We need you guys to come up here and help us!"

"I'm sorry, buddy," I told him, "we have a tank fight going on down here. We can't help you right now, you're on your own." He, his two vehicles, and five other guys went back to where the Kurds were hit. Fourteen vehicles were hit, and most were on fire. Body parts were scattered everywhere. A BBC crew was mixed in with this group; their interpreter was killed, their reporter and camera man injured. Two 10th Group guys with the Kurds were injured. Seventeen of the Kurds were killed, including their commander, another 45 wounded. Wright and the guys dove into this chaos and started working on the wounded.

Meanwhile, Jake Chandler, the senior USAF Special Tactics Squadron Air Controller (he gets offended when you call him a TAC-P) took over. Jake called the Navy pilots and reported what happened. Despite the disaster, we still needed air support. Jake told the pilots, "See where your bombs hit? That's the good guys. On the other side of our position, that's where the bad guys are." Now they easily identified the enemy target, and the wingman began delivering ordnance on the Iraqi position.

Part III: Final Resistance

About this time, it seemed that every reporter in northern Iraq began to show up on the ridge behind us—CNN, Reuters, al-Jazera. All of them dashed down from Irbil, 50 miles away. Apparently the Kurds passed the word that we and the Peshmerga were in a big fight with the Iraqis. So every reporter seemed to have heard about us, and they all suddenly set up shop on the hill behind us. I turned around and could see all these tripods and faces of reporters while we are in the middle of this tank fight!

The first pair of Navy fighters went back to their carrier, and for about 15 minutes we were without air cover. We started taking artillery fire, and this time the gunners seemed to know their business a little better than the mortar crew or tank gunners. They started walking their impacts in on our position. These were huge 152-millimeter high-explosive (HE) shells, each impact about 100 meters closer than the last. Finally, one landed only 25 meters to Marty McKenna's right, and it was a smoke round, not HE! The smoke round must have been fired by accident because it was harmless to us. The smoke round shook up Marty pretty good because of how close it landed.

"Ah, Frank," Marty said, "that one was a little close. Maybe we ought to pull back a bit."

"I'm with you, buddy!" I said.

So we pulled back 500 meters to where the reporters had set up. Later, we called this position Press Hill.

As soon as we got there, the reporters mobbed us! Jane Arraf from CNN ran up to me with her cameraman, saying, "Can you tell me what's happening?"

"Get away from me!" I told her. The two of them chased me as I ran around to my guys, getting them into position. She wouldn't give up. I was trying to point out targets to my guys, manage the situation, run over to check with the 92 guys, and she was following me everywhere, trying to get me to stop and talk to her. Finally, I said to her, "If I give you 30 seconds, will you leave me alone?"

"Okay! Okay! Okay!" she said. So I gave her a 30-second overview of what was happening, and she relented and went back to where the rest of the reporters were congregated. She was a tiny little thing, about 5 feet tall, but totally fearless.

Now that we were in a little higher position, we broke out the SOFLAM laser designator to mark the tanks for the fighters. They were not sufficiently exposed, though, and the beams made the bombs land beyond the targets. The smart bomb option wasn't working, so, for the next hour and a half, we had the aircraft dropping cluster bombs, 750-pound bombs, 1,000-pound bombs, everything—and not a single bomb scored! By now the B-team was with us, we had been resupplied with missiles, and everybody was in on the act. Sergeant First Class Jimmie Adams, our B-team weapons sergeant, got in on the fight. He fired a Javelin at one of the remaining APCs and destroyed it.

Finally, one dumb Iraqi tank driver pulled his tank out from behind the berm on the right side of the line, moved down the highway, and at last exposed a target for us. Staff Sergeant Erik Strigotte, one of the 10th Group team, grabbed a Javelin, fired, and smoked the tank! This one exploded just like in the video, flames shooting out of the hatches. The surviving Iraqi infantry behind the berm, seeing their buddies burned to a crisp in the tank, now called "ENDEX" ("end of exercise" during training).

These Iraqis moved out into the open waving anything white they could find, mostly scraps of paper, trying to surrender. We called "cease fire!" The team leaders and team sergeants all gathered back behind the crest to discuss this development, trying to figure out how to accept their surrender without getting sucked into an ambush, as happened to the Marines. Three T-55 tanks were still down there and a big threat. We decided to let the Kurds go down to scarf them up.

While we were having this discussion about the surrendering troops, Sergeant Mike Foss, the "baby" of 392 and just out of the Q Course, yelled, "They're killing them!" While we were talking, Mike tells us that down on the highway two white SUVs pulled up and six guys in long robes hopped out. He could see them through his scope slapping the soldiers around. For about 30 seconds, these six guys beat and kicked the Iraqi troops, then Mike said he saw one of them pull a pistol and shoot one of the soldiers in the face. The other five guys in the long robes pulled out AKs and mowed down all the surrendering troops! By the time I got up there and saw what was happening, these guys were going around with pistols, finishing off the men they had just shot, about 18 soldiers murdered.

Marty McKenna turned to Jake Chandler, the TAC-P, and said, "Laze their ass!" Jake put the laser on one of the white SUVs and called for an LGBU, a laser-guided munition. The bomb hit right in the middle of the intersection, completely erasing everything that had been there. Although the six enforcers were gone, the survivors weren't willing to risk a second surrender attempt, and now we started taking small arms fire again.

This fire was ineffective, but they kept firing for an hour and a half. Meanwhile, our B-team arrived with a resupply for us. They also brought a mortar. Our Charlie Company sergeant major, Joe Ward, was very skilled with this weapon. Joe set up this 60-millimeter mortar and started dropping rounds on the survivors down on the highway. His first round was a little short, the second a little long, the third was right on, and he kept them coming after that, right on top of the enemy behind the berm.

After a short time of this accurate fire, the Iraqis had had enough again, but instead of surrendering, they just picked up their weapons and start to run. As soon as they did, they exposed themselves to our Mk19 and .50-caliber fires, and we opened up on them again. The gunners started cutting them down as they tried to escape.

Just then one of the female reporters, a different one this time, ran up screaming, "Why are you shooting them? You're shooting them in the back!" She was going nuts.

"Ma'am," I said, "they are still combatants! We can shoot them!"

"I can't believe you would shoot them in the back!" she kept yelling.

Finally, I had to sit this woman down. I could see what kind of story she was about to file so I had to stop what I was doing and give her a short course in the Law of Land Warfare. "Lady," I said, "there are only two categories of personnel on the battlefield, *combatants* and *noncombatants*. If they are holding guns, they are combatants and they are legitimate targets! If they put their guns down, we can't shoot them. If they have weapons and are not surrendering, we can kill them. If they retreat and we don't stop them, they can reconsolidate and attack us all over again! Until they surrender, we can shoot them! They have two choices, surrender or die. That's what we are here to make happen! We are *not* going to let them retreat and then come at us again!"

"Oh, I see," she said.

The next day, another six Iraqi APCs and six tanks tried to get at us, but we shut that down with more Javelin shots and more bombs. They came in at us from around a village on the other side of the highway. We spotted them through the haze. Staff Sergeant Lihn Nguyen saw them first. He called out "More tanks!" One tank tried to come around to our right to flank our position, part of another effort to overrun us. Two Iraqi soldiers were riding on the tank. They were sitting on opposite sides of the main gun, just above the treads. I had a lot of trouble getting a lock with the Javelin. The tank was so far away and presented such a small heat signature, I couldn't get a good firing solution with the missile. I finally gave up and just fired the missile. I got up knowing I had missed. After several seconds of flight time, I saw the missile hit near the tank; it looked like a miss.

Bob Farmer was on the spotting scope and yelled back, "Frank, you smoked it."

"No way, Bob," I replied, "there's no way I hit that tank from this far."

Farmer answered back, "You know the guys that were on the tank before? Well, they're gone now!" I couldn't believe it and was skeptical until we rode out there and I saw the hole in the tank from the Javelin. The tank was 3,700 meters from where I was, much farther than the maximum published range for the Javelin system. But Jason Brown had already gotten the longest shot, killing an APC at 4,200 meters, while it was moving!

Then the Navy air showed up and started taking them out from the air. They started dropping cluster bombs, and that finished off the last attempt at resistance. This caused the armor crews to just bail out of their vehicles and run, abandoning the tanks and MTLBs where they were.

We fired 19 Javelins during the engagement and thousands of rounds of .50-caliber ammo plus perhaps 2,000 rounds through the Mk19s.

The total BDA was two T-55s, eight MTLBs, and four 2 1/2-ton troop trucks, all killed with Javelins. An additional eight small jeeps and trucks were destroyed with .50-caliber, Mk19, and small arms, plus three light-skinned vehicles were destroyed by Navy aircraft.

We counted 32 bodies in the intersection. We "conservatively" estimated enemy KIAs at 40 to 50. This is solely based on the bodies we saw and on the charred remains of the two tanks (four guys per tank), plus the drivers/TCs of the APCs. We found several bloody uniforms and other clothing items on the battlefield, leading us to believe many more were wounded or killed but evacuated during the four and a half-hour fight. In my opinion, we probably killed more than half of them, somewhere around 70 to 80, but we didn't want to play the Vietnam game of "estimating" body counts, so we reported only the number of actual bodies we found.

AFTERWORD:
IRAQ AND THE HUNT FOR WMDS
Gerry Schumacher

At the time of the first Gulf War, Schumacher commanded the military side of a joint Department of Defense and Stanford Research Institute project to design and deploy biological detection equipment in the Persian Gulf. As this last story reveals, SF officers— senior officers especially—sometimes become enmeshed with political issues of national and international importance. As Schumacher reminds us, Iraq clearly had WMDs and clearly had used them. As he explains in this different kind of war story, conflict is sometimes with the regular Army and within the chain of command as well as with the enemy.

Considering the elusive nature of Iraq's alleged weapons of mass destruction, it is a difficult time to be writing about our once frantic efforts to counter this threat [at the time of Desert Storm]. Iraq had weapons of mass destruction. They were there. This story really happened. Both before and after the first Gulf War we captured Iraqi weapons of mass destruction. Some of those weapons we never told [the public] about. If, since then, Iraq has destroyed their WMDs, there would surely be DNA in the ashes of their destruction. .

There seems to be nothing to be found, not evidence of construction, not witnesses to destruction, nor tracks to follow to their hiding place. Everything seems to have vanished to the shock, dismay, and embarrassment of many. Finding certain Iraqi weapons of mass destruction could prove to be more embarrassing than

301

never finding them. Perhaps we are the ones covering up some of the tracks.

It was about 5 p.m. on New Year's Day 1991. We met at Mel's Drive-In on Van Ness Avenue, just a few blocks from the main gate of the U.S. Army's Presidio of San Francisco. Sitting and waiting nervously in the front circular booth were three scientists from Stanford Research Institute in Palo Alto, California, and Captain Evan Planto, my team executive officer. They were waiting for the outcome of a briefing that Major Joe Leonelli and I had given to Major General Kent Hillhouse, commander of the 91st Division. His deputy, Brigadier General Tom Murchie, and his chief of staff, Colonel Dan Balough, were also there.

My briefing took place around 2 p.m. that day in a back room of the Presidio Officer's Club while the three officers changed into their dress blues for the occasion of a New Year's Day "Commander's Call" to the 6th Army commanding general's home. The three-star, 6th Army commander was Lieutenant General William Harris. The purpose of my briefing to Hillhouse at the Officer's Club was to ensure that he was up to date on the mission details prior to his meeting with General Harris. Two days earlier Harris' operations center had received a classified message to support the deployment of a specially trained biological detection team to Saudi Arabia. The message had originated at the State Department, was passed to Department of Defense, then to Department of the Army (copy to U.S. Forces command liaison), and then to General Harris' 6th Army Headquarters.

The problem was, Harris immediately balked at supporting the directive since he knew nothing of any such biological detection team. Harris could not imagine how a "by name" list of soldiers could originate from such high levels without his prior knowledge of the existence of such a team. I was the team commander. Harris was angry.

Since September, Major General Hillhouse, my boss, had quietly supported my involvement in a sensitive operation to assess the Iraqi biological weapons threat and develop a "real-time" biological detection system for deployment to the Gulf. We worked at Stanford Research Institute, at Dugway Proving Grounds in Utah, and at Yuma Proving Grounds in Arizona. The project gained momentum, and there were few opportunities to meet with Hillhouse to keep him abreast of developments. With the exception of my hand-picked team, no else in the division and, for that matter, few people in the country were aware of the project. The division personnel officer was directed by Hillhouse to accommodate my request for various travel orders without questioning the purpose. Telephone conversations with Hillhouse were not secure and therefore not an option.

I have no doubt that Hillhouse was planning on briefing the Army commander, General Harris. Unfortunately the State Department message got to Harris before Hillhouse did. Things like this don't go over well in the military. Harris was blindsided, but after that, he never regained his composure long enough to realize that soldiers' lives were at stake and thousands of people may get sick or die if our team was not deployed. Harris was going to teach Hillhouse a lesson.

Harris put on permanent blinders and put up every obstacle to not send my team. He offered up soldiers from Fort Lewis as an alternative, soldiers who were completely clueless as to the nature of the equipment and mission. They would never understand the threat, nor would they be privy to the intelligence reports that I had read during the planning stages. They had no training on how to use, let alone deploy, the sophisticated detection equipment, and particularly significant, they would never know what enemy biological delivery systems looked like.

The Fort Lewis, 9th Infantry Division soldiers did not know of the CIA's computer simulation model, which indicated that just *one* of the sprayer delivery systems, under favorable climatic conditions, could expose as many as 180,000 American soldiers to deadly germ agents. None of the equipment, or any of the deployment training that my team was working on, had ever been included in any chemical or biological military course of instruction elsewhere in the military. We were writing a new chapter in biological warfare defense.

The group at Mel's Drive-In was apprehensive. They had worked very hard on development of the equipment. They had worked seven days a week around the clock. The SRI guys had even gone beyond the prototype detector and built 12 units for deployment to the Gulf. Several of the SRI scientists needed to deploy in-country with my military team because we required their expertise in calibrating the mass spectrometer integral to the detectors. The scientists were going to risk their lives. After knowing what biological delivery systems Iraq had available to deploy, we were scared for our country, for our soldiers' lives, for the outcome of the war.

The scientists knew Harris was attempting to stop the deployment. It was General Hillhouse's job to get a private moment with Harris at the New Year's Day "Commander's Call" and try to convey the complexity and criticality of my team's mission. Given Hillhouse's precarious position with Harris, we knew this would be a challenging conversation. Hillhouse was to get back to me with the "go" signal and we would give final instructions to the SRI guys (at Mel's Drive-In of all places).

Harris was implacable. He consented with Hillhouse to meet with me in a few days for a more thorough review but gave Hillhouse little, if no, hope for changing his position on obstructing the deployment.

It seems that the State Department and the CIA were reluctant to step in and brief Harris as to the gravity and details of the mission. In retrospect, I believe now that it was because too many people would then know about the "biological sprayers." The CIA had not expected the intransigent position that Harris had taken.

"If our team and equipment doesn't get to the Gulf, and Iraq's biological sprayers are used or leak, there will be a lot of court-martials in the U.S. Army following this war. There'll also be a lot of very sick and dying American boys." That was the last comment I heard from one of the SRI guys before a deeply disappointed group left Mel's Drive-In on New Year's Day 1991.

In August 1990, when Iraq had invaded Kuwait, I was a Special Forces lieutenant colonel and had recently transferred from having Commanded 3rd Battalion, 12th Special Forces to the position of brigade executive officer in the Army's 91st Division. My operations officer (S3), was an Army Reservist, Major Joseph Leonelli. In Leonelli's civilian capacity he was the lead scientist at Stanford Research Institute on contract with the U.S. government to develop real-time biological-detection equipment for deployment to the Gulf.

The startling reality was the United States had no *real time* biological detection equipment. The only devices available for use in the pending battle were units that required random collection of air samples followed by an 18-hour incubation period at a naval lab in Ryadh. This would be followed by an announcement as to whether the air sample had contained a lethal agent or not. Of course this battlefield evaluation methodology was nothing short of a bad joke.

We had developed the means to provide immediate warnings for a chemical agent attack, but our technology for discerning the presence of a biological agent was nothing short of prehistoric. The scientists at SRI were frustrated and angry because for many years prior to this they had pushed the U.S. government for a contract that would allow them to develop biological detectors. Evidently we simply did not believe that any country would dare use heinous biological agents against the United States of America.

Now the scientists from SRI were given the mandate to develop, in three months, what had previously been projected to require several years of work.

At first, and in a limited manner, Joe revealed the nature of his civilian government contract work to me. There was only a moderate sense of urgency since, as Joe reflected in those talks, Iraq's suspected biological delivery systems, including missiles, mines, and aircraft, would probably be largely ineffective against our superior forces and technology. This relaxed attitude was about to abruptly change a month later.

In mid-September, Joe returned from a briefing in Washington where he would learn for the first time about Iraq's acquisition of more than 50 agricultural-style sprayers specifically designed to disperse lethal biological agents. The sprayers were intended to disseminate biological agents in an effective droplet size and aerosolized pattern so as to maximize downwind casualties. This threat had not been anticipated by U.S. forces. Few, if any, military officers had ever been briefed on this type of equipment.

While back in Washington, Joe not only proposed the research and development schedule for the detectors, but he also proposed a plan for fielding the equipment in Iraq. Leonelli convinced his audience that the Army resources required to assist in developing, testing, and deploying the detectors into the war zone were available within his military unit. He promoted my background as evidence of the available talent he could tap into. Joe was given the green light to proceed, pending concurrence from the 91st Division commander.

Joe reasoned that if he used members of his own unit in the development and testing of this equipment, these same members would be the best suited for the in-country deployment and application. They had to be very skilled and intelligent soldiers. Joe's primary responsibility was in his civilian capacity as the SRI team chief. My primary responsibility would be to train our team on the equipment utilization, develop the deployment plan, and control and direct the mission deep in enemy territory. A series of two-man teams would have to operate independently and with almost no external support.

The plan would ultimately require the approval of the Central Command (CENTCOM) commander, General Norman Schwarzkopf. Just days before the ground war was executed, I would learn that Schwarzkopf's battle staff knew nothing of the sprayers they might confront.

When Joe brought me up to speed on his return from Washington, I briefed my boss, Major General Hillhouse, and sought permission to execute the mission. There were a number of phone calls between our headquarters and the Chemical Command. Planning for the mission was approved and Hillhouse gave me authority to quietly recruit the best men in the division. I began scouring personnel records looking for soldiers with extensive active-duty experience and special operations, chemical, and biological warfare training. We built a team to take on this unusual mission. At the time, I never queried Hillhouse as to what he may or may not have related to his boss, the 6th Army commander.

Over the next several months, in the fall of 1990, we worked feverishly on designing and testing our detection system. My military team developed deployment plans based on reported sightings and likely locations of the biological sprayers. I specifically recall one very alarming sighting that Leonelli related to me with an air of extreme urgency. On Christmas Eve 1990, Joe called me and related that a sprayer had been identified on the Forward Edge of the Battle Area (in military parlance; the FEBA). This was essentially just forward of the established friendly lines. Particularly troublesome was that the ideal weather existed for maximum damage to U.S. forces.

Our work on the ground detecting platforms was done at Dugway Proving Grounds, while the Airborne platform testing took place at Yuma. Much of our product was created in the bowels of the SRI complex in Palo Alto. Joe made frequent trips to Washington, D.C., and upon each return brought the team up to date on the most recent intelligence relevant to our mission.

After one of Joe's briefings he called me from the airplane on his return flight. He said Colin Powell was visibly upset that U.S. forces were so ill-prepared to deal with such a potentially devastating threat. He wanted our efforts redoubled on the real-time detection system and needed a fielding plan in place sooner than later. Reportedly, the briefing consisted of major players from the CIA, DIA, Chemical Defense Command, and State Department. The threat became more ominous to us after each of Joe's many Washington trips.

During the work at Dugway we were married up with members of the Air Force Geophysical Labs who were working on a pulse laser to fire into biological clouds and track density, direction, and so on. Somewhere along the way we realized that the pulse laser could also be used as an offensive weapons system. But that was a distraction from our primary mission. From what I could tell, the SRI team consisting of five or six scientists, the Air Force team of about eight people, and my team of about twelve personnel were the only people who knew of the project outside of Washington.

We tested three variants of a real-time detector. One was based on a xenon lamp, another a mercury vapor lamp, and the third used a laser. Basically a box with a vacuum on top sucked in and concentrated air and then diagnosed the air through a mass spectrometer. Many false positives had to be logged into the system and the mass spectrometer calibrated to accommodate the regional nuances of nonlethal agents, which might otherwise trigger the biological agent alarm.

We began to have a modicum of success. We acknowledged that our success was not based on the actual Iraqi delivery system and could be flawed when deployed against the real thing. To be sure our detectors would work in the theater of operations we needed to test it against Iraq's actual sprayers if possible. Besides, if we could test the Iraqi sprayers we might uncover additional strengths and weaknesses of their equipment. We started the groundwork to acquire some of their units.

The starting point was apparent to both Joe and me. The manufacturer of the equipment was not Iraq. It was one of our allies. We had the shipping records, dates, and quantities of sprayers sent to Iraq. The great majority of sprayers were shipped into Iraq during the Iraq/Iran conflict. However, notably, the last two of them actually shipped from the factory *after* Iraq had invaded Kuwait. The design of the sprayers could have no agricultural application. They were biological weapons systems. Now it seemed we could simply go to Italy and get a couple. It didn't turn out to be that simple.

The first approach was using a "front company" to attempt to buy sprayers with the same specifications. That was dumb. The Italians got a warning shot and scrambled to cover their tracks. One has to wonder why the State Department didn't just muscle Italy to cough up a couple. That remains one of the elusive questions that still haunt me. I have my suspicions, and I will share them with you shortly.

There was no time to waste. Soon after the failed purchase attempt, an operation was launched to recover two sprayers from Iraq. Two were acquired, complete with Iraqi markings. One of the two was brought to Dugway, and the other was delivered to SRI. I was not there on the day of the SRI delivery but Joe was, and he was livid at the lack of security surrounding its arrival. As he relayed the story to me, when the second sprayer reached SRI in Palo Alto it was uncovered in broad daylight in the parking lot and drew the attention of dozens of people who began turning knobs and nozzles.

Of course, there were no biological agents inside the sprayers, but they had been loaded with a simulated green slime that ended up sprayed on some Porsches and BMWs in the parking lot. Joe and I shared shock and laughter in the absurdity of this occasion. All the subsequent testing of the sprayers confirmed that they exceeded our worst nightmare scenario. This was a poor man's nuclear bomb. In the presence of a meteorological inversion condition, with 7- to 8-knot winds, and in the hours of darkness, this could be an extraordinarily lethal weapon. Coincidentally, these were the exact conditions existing in the Gulf many of the nights in the months proceeding the war.

The sprayers could be truck-mounted, boat-mounted, or trailer drawn. They could be easily concealed in the bed of a pick-up. They could be stationary in a cave. They were ingenious in their simplicity and difficulty of detection. We had intelligence that suggested that the Iraqis would load them with biological cocktails, a mixture of different agents making both detection and treatment extremely complex.

On or about January 4, 1991, I had an audience with General Harris. From the outset he proclaimed: "I know all about this operation and your team's not going anywhere." He knew nothing. At one point during the meeting, he argued that the detectors weren't necessary because "all of our troops are vaccinated." Nothing could have been more incorrect. He believed our own propaganda. We didn't have anywhere near sufficient quantities of the anthrax vaccine, and we had serious doubts as to its effectiveness. I urged him to call certain government and SRI officials to confirm my position. Several times he reached for the telephone and then set it back down. It was clear that his personal vendetta with General Hillhouse was more important than ascertaining the facts. He needed to win, even at the expense of thousands of others that could lose.

The team was not going to the Gulf.

After I accepted that fact, I told Joe that as a minimum we needed to alert CENTCOM to the existence of the sprayers. By now we had concluded that it was highly probable that this information had never reached Schwarzkopf's war planners. I contacted my old Special Forces boss, then Brigadier General Bill Cockerham, now a Special Operations liaison to Central Command. We made arrangements to discuss the project on secure phones from SRI to CENTCOM. On a Sunday afternoon in mid-January, from an office at SRI, Joe Leonelli and I discussed the project and the sprayer threat with Cockerham in Central Command Headquarters at MacDill Air Force Base, Florida.

Cockerham communicated the information to the CENTCOM operations center in Saudi Arabia. No, Schwarzkopf's staff knew nothing about any sprayers or any real-time detection equipment. The essence of their response was, "Frankly, my dear, we can't give a damn at this point." They were up to their eyeballs in the momentum of their planned attack and could not suddenly shift gears to consider this 11th-hour information. In a later conversation I had directly with a CENTCOM chemical officer on Schwarz-kopf's staff, he couldn't fathom why, if this information was accurate, he had not heard of it through his own intelligence channels. At that point, it would have taken the president himself to draw attention to the sprayers. The CENTCOM staff was already awash in information overload.

It would seem all this had a happy ending. The war ended, there were no biological casualties, and my team had cried wolf.

But perhaps not all had ended the way it seemed. Immediately following the war, Joe worked with the Battle Damage Assessment (BDA) teams inside Iraq to search for sprayers. He contacted me and said, "Hey, we actually recovered six of the sprayers. Looks like they were never turned on. Guess we got through war after all." He continued, "I think the local Iraqi commanders were afraid to use the stuff. We severed all their communications, and Saddam's orders would never have been received. Guess we skated on this one."

A few years passed. I had all but forgotten about the ill-fated mission. I was on to other projects and enjoying the challenges. I had completely dismissed reports of Gulf War illness as the imaginations of disgruntled soldiers who wanted be on the government dole. However, increasingly more and more soldiers whom I deeply respected were showing signs of illness, or their families were. Eventually it troubled me enough to call Joe.

"Joe, what did you find in the six sprayers you recovered after the war?" He said he didn't know. That was an odd response. I continued, "Were the sprayers shot up, blown up, burned up, or what? Could they have leaked? Have we ever attempted to correlate if there is a geographical relationship between the recovery locations and reports of sick soldiers?" Joe was essentially mute. "Joe, have we communicated with the Pentagon's Gulf War Syndrome committee the presence of those six sprayers?"

And so it went that Joe and I may as well have never worked together, nor ever been friends. He would only say that he *did not think* that Gulf War Syndrome was attributable to the sprayers. He was not going to accommodate my request for the possibility to be investigated. Joe was now working down the hall from the group investigating Gulf War Syndrome. His firm, Battelle, even had people assisting the Gulf War investigating committee. Why wouldn't he reveal the sprayers?

Over the next several years I tried to surface the issue with both Army and government representatives. I simply wanted to investigate whether there may have been a relationship between sick soldiers and recovered sprayers. I hit a brick wall everywhere. I

311

wrote Congressman Joseph Kennedy Jr. I wrote and called Diane Feinstein and spoke with Colonel Edelsen on the Pentagon's Syndrome Investigation Team and many others.

A congressman from Utah urged President Clinton's Gulf War Investigation Committee, chaired by Joyce Laschoff, to interview me concerning the sprayers. Laschoff was not interested in pursuing questions concerning sprayers. No one would confirm the existence of any sprayers nor the recovery of any sprayers after the war.

I had largely given up pursuing this matter. It was now around 1996 or 1997. One of several active-duty Army officers who worked for me at the time was Major Mark Galdi. One afternoon he wasn't feeling well. Two days later he was dead. The autopsy revealed every major organ disintegrated: pancreas, liver, stomach, kidneys, and so on. Suspected cause: alcoholism. OK, but no one who worked with him had ever known him to be drunk or imbibe on a regular basis. Two of my officers had just recently had dinner at his home and they witnessed no signs of an alcoholic. Nevertheless, I dismissed it until about a week later when I received a very disturbing phone call.

I was a full colonel at the time, and one of our brigade commanders in Salt Lake City called me. "I hear Major Galdi died," said the caller, Colonel David Irvine.

"Yeah, did you know him?"

He responded that Major Galdi had worked for him several years earlier in Utah. Dave asked me what he died of, and I told him it appeared to be a case of a closet alcoholic. Dave said "I don't think so."

"What do you mean?"

At that point, Colonel Irvine related a story to me. Shortly after the Gulf War, Galdi, under Irvine's command, was part of a detail of men and women sent to inventory several large shipping containers of equipment that were returning from the Gulf. Strangely, the equipment was not being returned to the *owning* unit, but rather it was being inventoried and collected at Dugway Proving Grounds, the Army's chemical and biological test center.

Galdi and everyone else who inventoried that equipment, unknown to one another, subsequently became seriously ill. Each had gone on to other military assignments and one by one became disabled. Irvine had tracked the health of several of them.

Irvine had no knowledge or recollection of any alcohol-related issues in Galdi's personal life. Galdi's medical records reflected a recurring history of debilitating bouts of illness following the approximate timeframe in which he participated in that inventory. My recollection is that none of the personnel on the detail had actually served in the Gulf. Galdi's family was in complete disbelief that Mark had died from drinking. They had good reason to be.

A Russian, Vadim Morganouv, a personal friend and a former major in the Soviet Spetznach (Soviet version of Special Forces) now living in the United States, met with me one evening in the spring of 1997. I expressed my dismay over the inability to get any government agency to investigate the possibility that sprayers had contaminated soldiers with some latent acting, possibly contagious agent. Just as Dave Irvine had shocked me, I was about to get a second shock.

Vadim and his wife, Eleena, had been friends of mine for several years. I had come to know the whole family. Eleena, while in the Soviet Union, was a neuro-response analyst for Russian fighter pilots. She worked on their "heads-up" displays and on hand-eye coordination. Her father was a colonel in the Soviet air forces but as a Ph.D., he worked as a scientist on antisatellite missile systems. The Soviets weren't interested in allowing Eleena's mother and father to leave Russia. They knew too much, said Vadim. Eleena and Vadim asked for my assistance. At the time, there were many Russians claiming to have valuable information to give the United States in exchange for assistance in getting out of the Soviet Union. The CIA usually yawned at the prospect of another person wanting special assistance to leave. I told Vadim he'd have to have proof of Eleena's father's work if anyone I knew was going to lift a finger to help. Vadim said, "OK, I bring you proof." And a month later, he did.

One evening Vadim met me at our local watering hole and handed over a briefcase full of documents ostensibly validating the inventions and research that Eleena's dad had worked on with the intent of disabling U.S. satellites. I was no expert at deciphering this kind of information and actually took the gift with a skeptical eye. I considered different agencies to relay this to and concluded Joe, of course. Joe was deeply in bed with the CIA and also had technical contacts at his new position with Battelle to unravel the significance of this 2-pound package. I gave the documents to him. Two months later, Eleena, Vadim, both her parents, and I celebrated a reunion together, here, in the United States. Vadim's credibility had skyrocketed with me. I no longer thought of him as a stereotypical boisterous, vodka-drinking Russian.

So, later on that evening, Vadim and I spoke concerning my frustrations getting visibility on the sprayer issue; I couldn't help but to give some credence to Vadim's muses. My friend said in his heavy Russian accent, "Ah, Colonel, this was the great experiment in genocide. Maybe both sides work on germ agents that would only affect certain gene structures unique to specific races." He continued, "Ah, maybe it work, maybe it doesn't, I don't know. Maybe some of it is very slow working still, and just maybe your country designed those sprayers. Perhaps both your side and mine know of this project."

"You're not serious," I responded with incredulity. He raised his brow and twisted his head as if to suggest the question was rhetorical.

The prospect of such collaboration between the Soviet KGB and the U.S. CIA was nearly unthinkable. I asked Vadim if this was raw speculation or did he have a factual basis to suggest such a scenario. *He said it happened.* I said I needed proof. Vadim responded, "Perhaps I bring you proof. You should not trust me, uh?" That too, was a rhetorical question.

At some point I realized that even if this were true, there would be no one I could go to with such evidence. Hell, if no one was going to give the time of day to the sprayer reports, surely such an outrageous allegation as the development and use of these germs was not going to get attention. It was pointless to push Vadim for validating material. But I began to wonder if there was some substance to Vadim's suggestions.

More and more clues concerning the sprayer design and the structure of the Italian company led me to the conclusion that, at a minimum, we were complicit in furnishing the biological delivery systems. Why else would Leonelli be so reticent to expose the sprayers to the committees studying Gulf War illness? I knew also that we had furnished anthrax and botulism agents to Iraq. These were supplied by two American firms, the American Type Culture Institute in Baltimore and, I believe, another firm in Houston. Significantly, we knew the biological cultures were not intended for medical research.

The international implications of the United States supplying known biological delivery systems, let alone the actual agents, to a Muslim country for use against another Muslim country would have serious ramifications to our image abroad. Still more damaging is the idea that we may have had a hand in furnishing *designer germs* that were selective in who they attacked and difficult to track due to the delay in the onset of symptoms. And this might explain why most military personnel were never briefed on this type of threat. Too many questions could surface. I concluded that for one or more of these reasons, the existence of biological sprayers would never get serious attention. My efforts to expose the sprayers had taken another setback.

At the conclusion of Desert Storm and following the recovery of six of the sprayers, I had several opportunities to dialogue with the United Nations Special Commission, which was running around Iraq searching for and dismantling Iraqi weapons systems. I spoke with the chairman, Rolf Ekeus, and members of his staff. They were only vaguely familiar with stories of sprayers and wanted more guidance as to what to search for. Joe was supposedly going to address that. I wouldn't bet on it.

During a conversation I had with Patrick Eddington, a disillusioned former CIA analyst, I asked if he knew anything about the

315

sprayers. He claimed to have heard bits and pieces with respect to biological sprayers within the interior of Iraq. He said that photo imagery and human intelligence concerning the existence or sighting of sprayers always seemed to disappear into another room behind more closed doors. Pat said that he evidently was not on the "need to know" list when it came to biological sprayers. So it appears that even within the intelligence agency it was highly compartmentalized information. Another dead end.

Hiding the actual germs is a lot easier than hiding the 40-plus sprayers that we believed were still in Iraq. Destroying 40-plus sprayers without a trace is challenging; however, no one is looking for them with the exception of a handful of Joe Leonelli clones. The net is that if they have not yet been found, Leonelli and his peers are going to find them, destroy them, and no one will be the wiser. And worse, we will never know if the ailments of sick and dying Gulf War vets are attributable to U.S. intelligence agencies' forays into the unthinkable.

INDEX

3rd Battalion, 293
3rd Group, 251, 278, 280
4th Division, 206–208
6th Infantry Division Forward, 246
9th Infantry Division, 303
10th Special Forces Group, 118, 119, 251, 278, 279, 284, 293–295
12th Special Forces Group, 250
82nd Airborne Division, 119, 121, 138, 274, 275, 284
101st Airborne Division, 251
A-Detachment, 9, 44, 100, 128, 143, 180, 183
A-team, 9, 127, 128, 130, 140, 186
Abraham, Jack, 203–204
Afghanistan, 251, 256, 258, 262, 264, 266, 267, 270–273, 275, 284
Air Medal, 153, 191
Al-Qaeda, 251, 253, 271
Anderson, John, 258–276
Antenori, Frank, 277–300
Anti-Taliban Force (ATF), 252
Arlington Cemetery, 213
Army Commendation Medal, 191
Army Counter Insurgency Support Office (CISO), 217, 218

Ashley, Otis Hedges "Bane," 145–162
B-team, 260, 292, 293, 297, 298
Baker, Conrad "Ben," 217–221
Ballistic Missile Early Warning (BMEW), 243, 244
Ban Dong So, Ap, 81, 82, 100–108, 220
Ban Me Thuot, 142
Banar tribe, 147
Bank, Aaron, 118, 119
Batman, Sherman, 31
Bering Strait, 244
Becoming a Green Beret, 40, 41
Ben Cat camp, 81, 84, 87, 91, 92, 94, 100, 101, 103, 106
Berg, Charles, 113–117
Biological weapons, 302, 306–308, 312, 315, 316
Black Christmas, 174
Bon Sar Pa, 142, 143, 217
Bong Son camp, 66
Brimfrost, 243–250
Bronze Star, 158, 191, 192
Brooks, Edwin, 140–144
Bru tribe, 44, 55
Buon Brieng, camp, 140–142
Bush, George W., 255
C-rations, 45, 109, 131
C-team, 188

Cambodia, 97, 108, 141, 163, 165,
166, 167, 193, 195, 197,
210, 212, 216
Canada, 246
Canadian Airborne Commando,
248, 250
Canadian Paratroopers, 246, 250
Caviani, Jon, 222–241
Central Intelligence Agency
(CIA), 196, 197, 216,
304, 307, 313–315
Chandler, Billy G., 158, 159
Charlie Company, 258, 259, 293,
298
Chinese Nungs, 97, 98, 102, 107,
109, 110, 113, 114
Clinton, William, 312
Da Nang, 69, 116
Dak Seang camp, 146, 147
Dak To, 157, 158
De Opresso Liber, 99
Den Rawud, 260, 261, 269, 271
Department of Defense, 205, 301
Desert Storm, 315
Distinguished Flying Cross, 209
Distinguished Service Cross, 159
Dong Xoai, Ap, 107–109
Dulina III, Andy, 180–182
Feinstein, Diane, 312
Fonda, Jane, 171
Fort Benning, 146
Fort Bragg, 41, 118, 119, 121,
137, 138, 139, 146, 149,
206, 218
Smoke Bomb Hill, 118, 146
Fort Gordon, 72
Gillespie, Vernon, 140–144
Good Housekeeping Seal of
Approval, 153

Gorilla warfare, 271, 272
Green Beret magazine, 184
Grenada operation, 242
Gulf War, 8, 281, 301, 311, 312,
315, 316
Ha Tay camp, 73–75
Hanoi, 170, 171
Hanoi Hilton, 163, 166, 172–175
History, 118–120
Hmong tribe, 99, 154
Ho Chi Minh Trail, 13, 17, 23, 25,
27, 29, 34, 44, 164
Hussein, Saddam, 311
Individualism, 120, 121
Iraq, 255, 256, 277–283, 285, 286,
289, 292, 293, 295, 297,
299, 301, 304–306, 308,
309, 311, 316
Jacobson, Roy, 100–111
Jarai tribe, 67 68, 69, 99, 141, 147
John Wayne Memorial Shitter, 41
Kendenberg, John, 23–25, 35, 36
Kennedy, John F., 40, 118, 119,
121
Kennedy, Joseph Jr., 312
Khe Sanh camp, 44–48, 52–56,
61, 116, 232
Kincaid, Keith, 225–229
Kontum, 64, 65, 188
Korean War, 46, 72, 123, 202
Kubasik, Kenn, 81–98
Kurds, 255, 287, 290, 294, 295,
297
Kuwait, 305, 308
Laos, 14, 163, 164, 193, 195, 197,
212, 216–218
Leopold, Stephen, 163–175
Listening post, 54
Mack, Dennis, 13–39

Mann, Russell, 42–61
McPhail, Doy, 138, 139
Medal of Honor, 32, 35, 107, 158, 159, 162, 191, 232–240
Medics, 62–64, 66, 69, 70–72, 157, 181, 194, 247–249, 283
Military Advisory Team (MAT), 123, 127, 128, 176, 178
Montagnards "Yards," 14, 15, 21, 24, 42–44, 47, 48, 54, 55, 58, 65, 67, 68, 74, 80, 81, 86, 99, 113, 127, 128, 140–143, 147–151, 154, 156, 159, 160, 162, 164, 165, 167, 168, 178, 188,190, 203, 208, 210, 214, 218, 223, 225, 227, 229, 230, 233, 234, 236, 238
Morris, Jim, 184, 185
Navy SEALs, 242, 251, 256, 260
Nha Trang, 113, 129, 135, 141, 176, 177, 210, 218, 219
Nixon, Richard, 166, 193
North Vietnam, 48, 67, 129, 130, 141, 163, 206, 212, 222
Northern Alliance (NA), 252–254, 265
Office of Strategic Services (OSS), 118, 120
Operation Anaconda, 251–254
Operation Detachment Alpha 361, 261–263
Padgett, John, 64–79
Pakistan, 259, 265, 266, 268, 269
People's Defense Force, 127
People's Self-Defense Force (PSFD), 133–136

Pitzer, Dan, 186, 187
Polei Kleng camp, 188
Post-traumatic stress disorder (PTSD), 240, 241
Powell, Colin, 307
Prisoners of War (POWs), 167, 168, 172–175
Prisoner-snatch operations, 32, 34
Purple Heart, 209
Qui Nhon, 64, 67
Raye, Martha, 203, 204, 215, 218
Rhade tribe, 44, 48, 52, 99, 141, 147
Ruff-Puffs, 127–129, 131, 223, 224
Russia, 244, 259, 270, 273, 313, 314
Saigon, 82, 83, 141, 212, 219
Saudi Arabia, 302, 310
Schumacher, Gerry, 11, 123–137, 243–250, 301–316
Schwarzkopf, Norman, 306, 310
Scott, Clay, 188–192
Scrouning, 52
Scully, Bob, 116, 117
Sedang tribe, 147
Shit-can, 170, 171
Shumate, Walt, 138, 139, 217
Silver Star, 158, 159, 191, 209
Sincere, Clyde, 205–215
Son Tay prison, 163
South Vietnam, 58, 99, 124, 135, 141
Soviet Special Operations Forces, 245
Stringham, Joe, 87–92, 94–98, 100, 107, 108
Studies and Observation Group (SOG), 113, 193

319

Survival, Evasion, Resistance,
  Escape (SERE) program,
  186
T-rations, 256
Taliban, 251, 254, 258, 259, 261,
  263, 264–266, 268, 269,
  271, 273
Tet holiday, 84, 85, 130
Tet Offensive, 67
Thailand, 197, 216–218
Tieu Ea Da, 110, 111
Tremell, Mike, 30, 31
UN Peacekeeping Force, 248
U.S. Air Force, 132, 133, 151, 159,
  195, 199, 200, 211, 238,
  251, 292, 293
U.S. Army, 8, 40, 42, 50, 58,
  117–119, 121, 123, 127,
  133, 138, 139, 145, 149,
  186, 188, 201, 202, 205,
  207, 242, 251, 258, 260,
  266, 282, 292, 301, 302,
  304, 312
U.S. Army Rangers, 118,123, 146,
  147, 152, 252
U.S. Marines, 37, 44, 56, 69–71,
  114, 116, 297
U.S. Navy, 232, 251, 296, 300
Viet Cong, 67, 73, 82, 85, 129,
  141, 186, 187
Viet Minh, 130
Vietnamese LLDB, 58, 83, 96,
  101, 106, 214
Wedding massacre, 259–261
White Star Program, 93
Witcosky, Mike, 193–202
World War II, 41, 93, 116, 118,
  121, 146, 151, 175, 202,
  204, 241, 277